AF231261

FRANK ORDAZ

THE LAND ICONIC

Published by
THAXTON STUDIOS
1611 Williamswood Drive Raymond, Mississippi 39154

See more titles available at **thaxtonstudios.com**

Captions by Frank Ordaz
Book Design by Anthony Thaxton

ISBN: 978-0-692-97062-1 Paperback

Printed in the United States of America

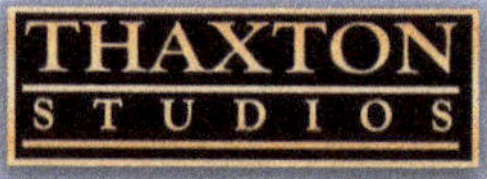

FRANK ORDAZ

THE LAND ICONIC

FOREWORD BY LORRIE KEMPF

ACKNOWLEDGEMENTS

I'd like to express my great appreciation to Frank Ordaz for his willingness to make this book happen. I am proud of his work and am excited to bring it to a wider audience. Frank is a fun guy, and his talent is both God-given and wonderful! Thanks to Betty Shoopman for first introducing us and starting this friendship. Tremendous gratitude also goes to David R. Darrow, Debra Rheinlander and Amy Thaxton for their efforts, time and support in helping us proofread and in helping make this book even better. Thank you, Lorrie Kempf, for the *Introduction*. Thanks to Frank's fantastic boys – Isaac and Big Dave Ordaz. Thanks to my wonderful kids – Bryant and Sydney Beth Thaxton. And thank you, reader, for supporting this project. Enjoy.

ANTHONY THAXTON
Publisher

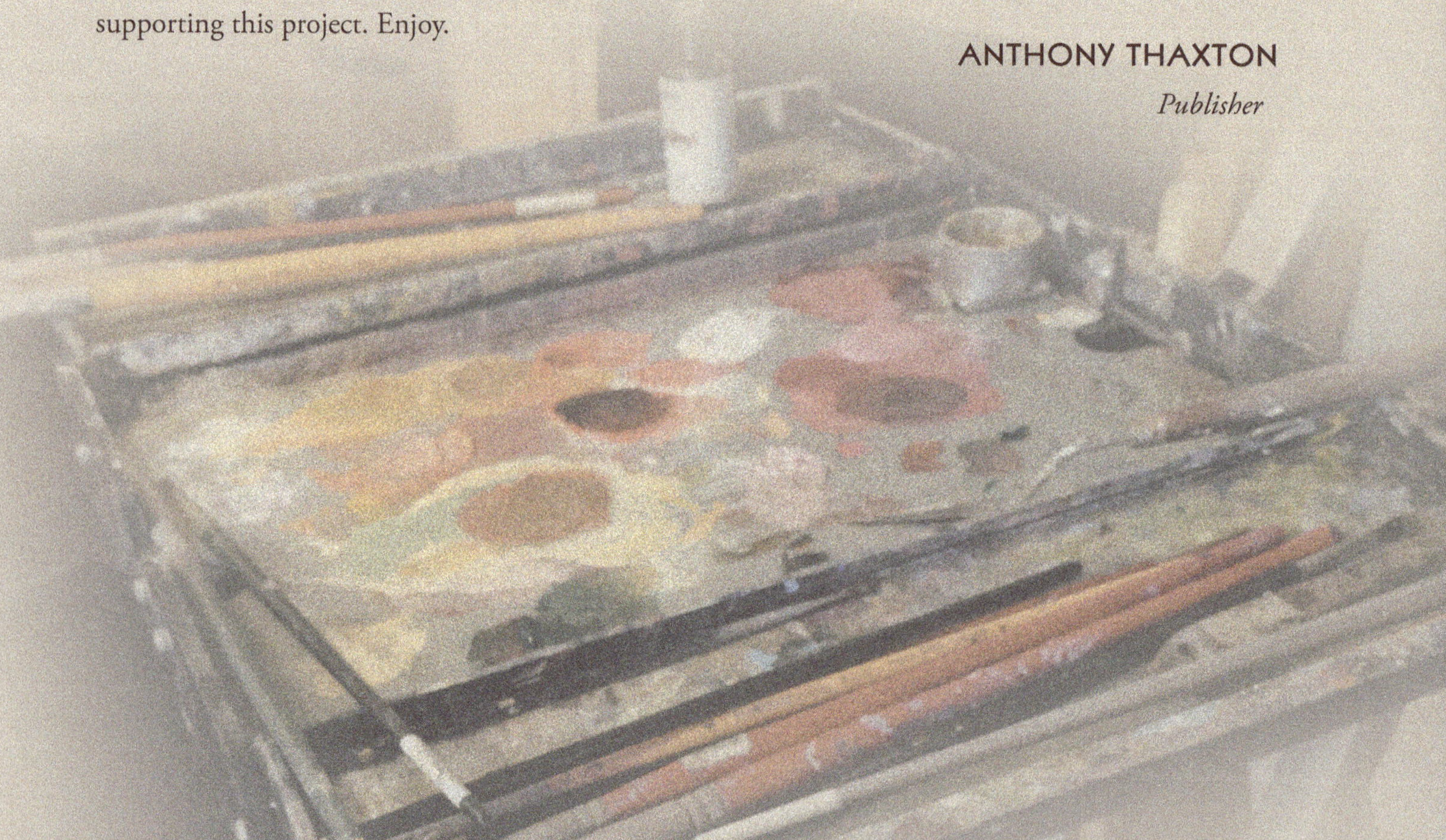

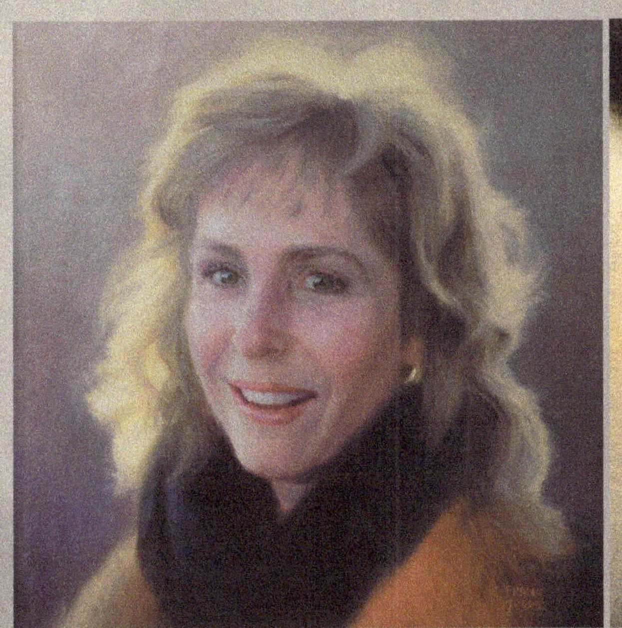 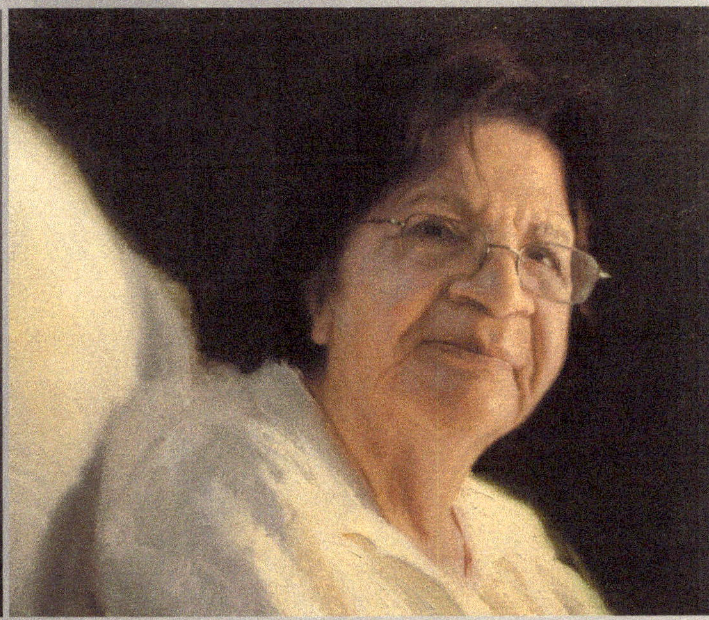

Dedicated to my beautiful wife and friend, Jana, and to Momma Lupe who would take me on the bus across town to art lessons.

Behind every successful man there are two women.

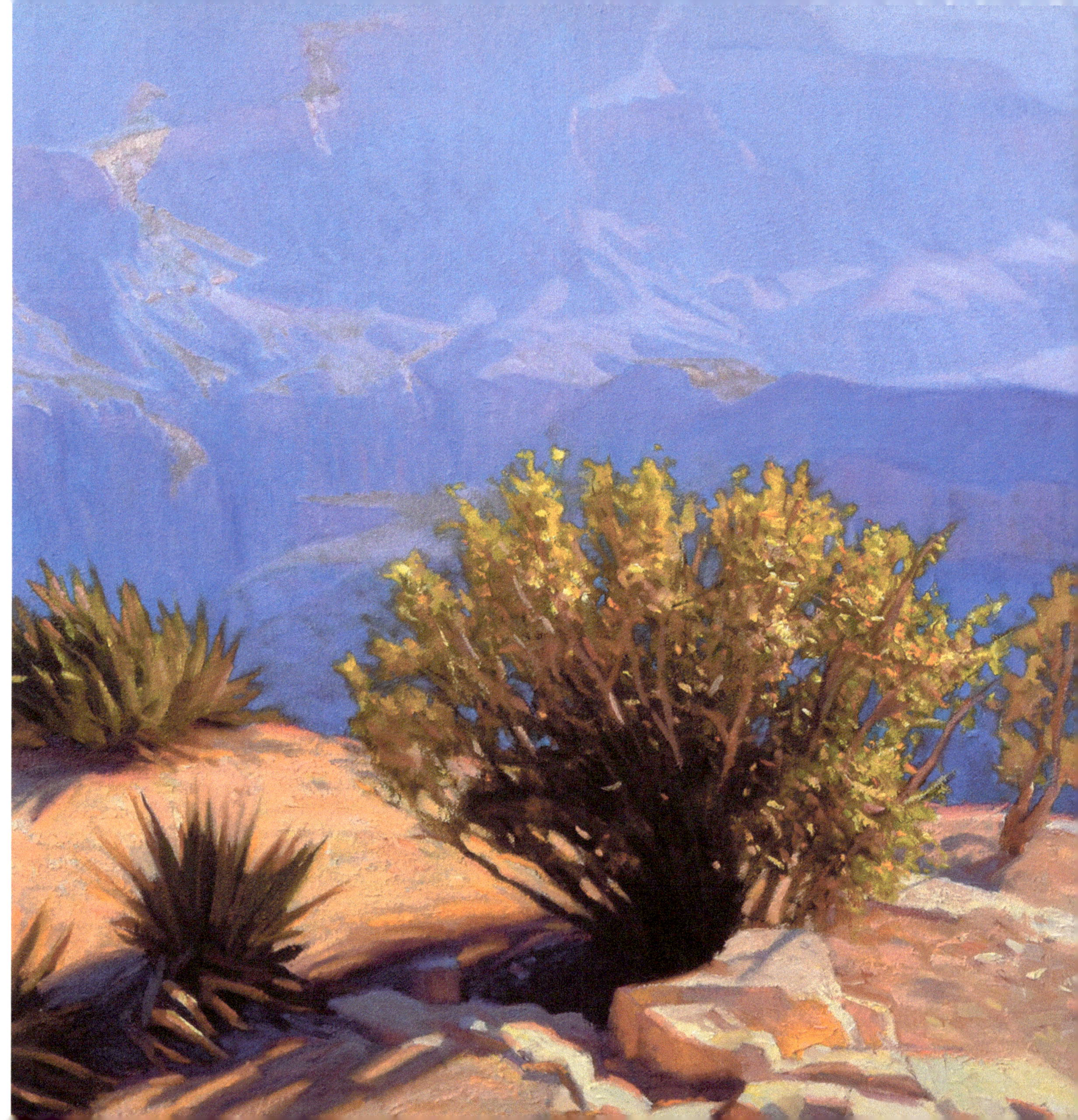

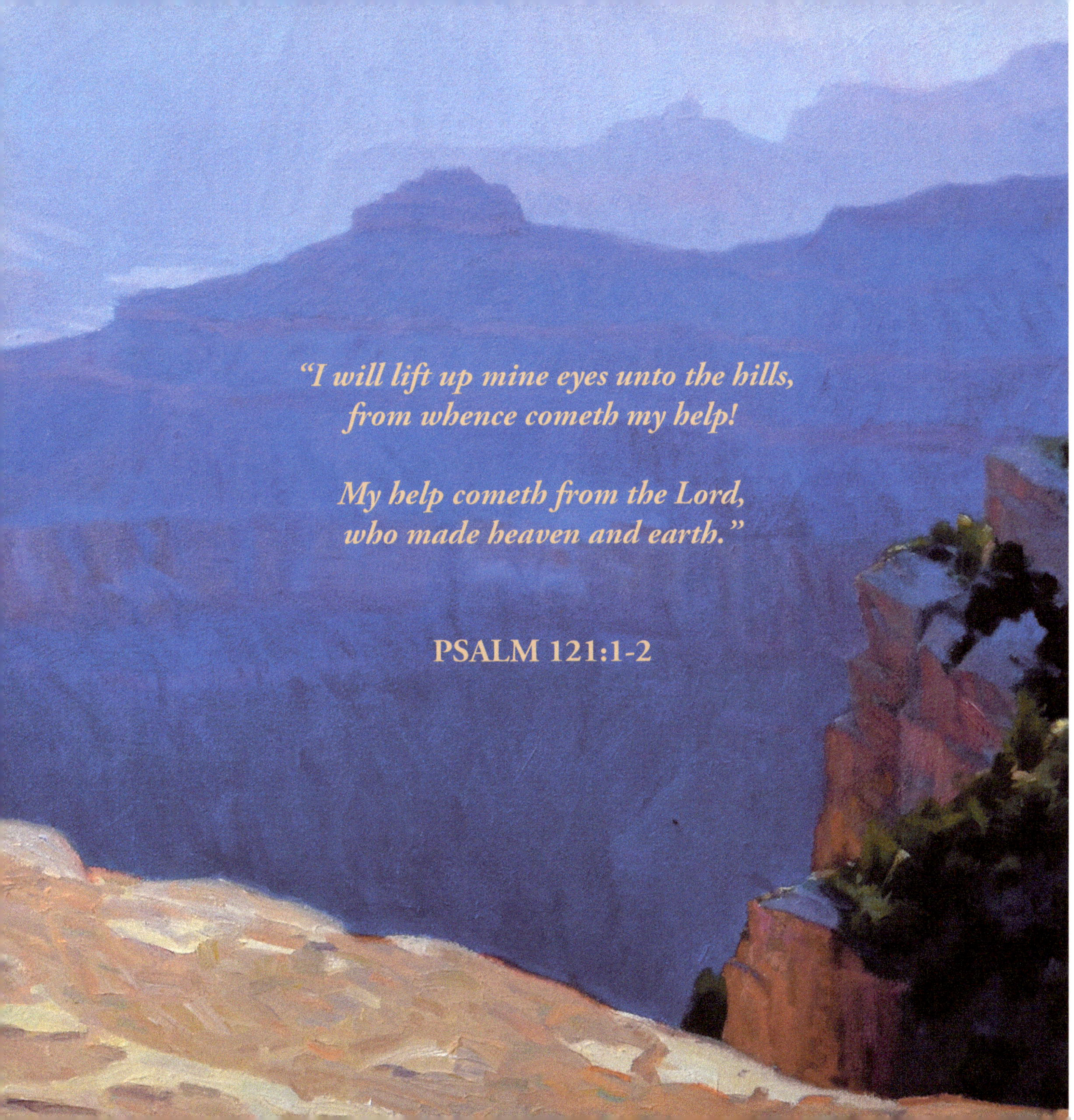
"I will lift up mine eyes unto the hills,
from whence cometh my help!

My help cometh from the Lord,
who made heaven and earth."

PSALM 121:1-2

FOREWORD

BY LORRIE KEMPF

THE WAY IN WHICH Frank Ordaz captures the color, light, drama and spiritual characteristics of the Big Sur coastline is a source of delight and awe for his audience — the spiritual qualities being perhaps the most elusive, yet by far the most important.

I believe, having watched Frank work *en plein air*, his ability to capture this oft-elusive quality is due to his long-held spiritual faith. His approach is immediate and confident but always sensitive as he studies the terrain and looks for the most elegant composition within the vast scenery. No doubt his decades-long, celebrated practice as a painter, then illustrator, then painter again, informs this approach. His fertile landscapes are at once eagle-eye observations and keen attention for the story the land confides in him. It's this quality of observation that allows Frank to participate with the viewer in a way that allows the viewer to not only see the formal visual characteristics of the subject, but to smell the wild sage, to feel the cool temperature of the air, to hear the water or the trees — to be transported.

While growing up in East Los Angeles, Frank dreamed of faraway places across America — romantic, natural environments in contrast to the urban environment he hoped to someday escape. This intention set the trajectory of his life-long passion. From age ten, Frank studied with renowned California master painter Theodore Lukits. By 1980, after studying

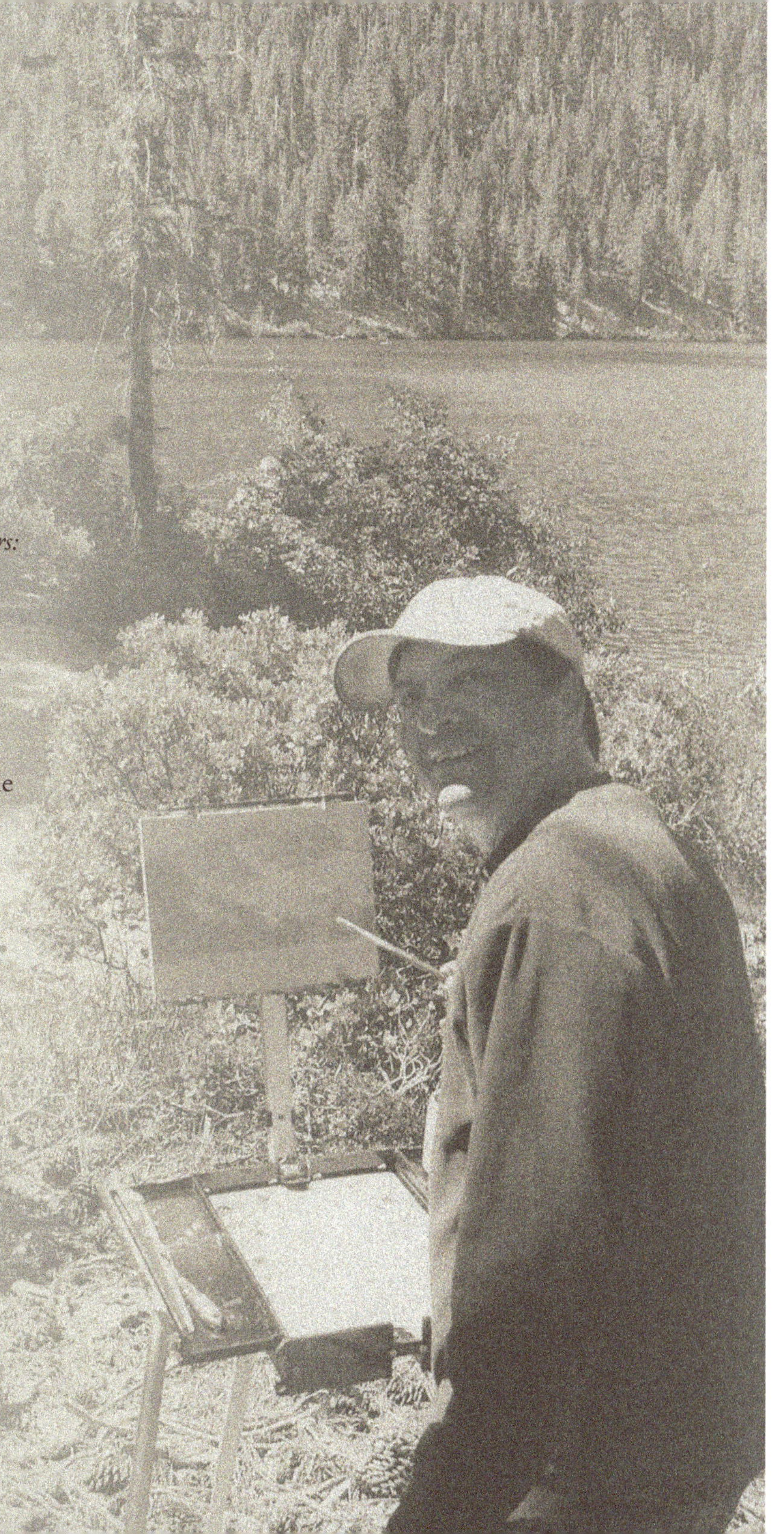

Painting at the University of Southern California
and majoring in Illustration at Art Center College of
Design in Pasadena, Frank began working at Lucasfilm
painting background matte paintings for specialized
movie production effects on films such as *E. T. the
Extra-Terrestrial, Star Trek: The Wrath of Khan, Star Wars:
Return of the Jedi* and *Indiana Jones and the Temple of
Doom*. This experience shaped his vision in capturing a
larger-than-life, cinematic moment in a landscape — a
vision that continues to inform his approach and enable
him to capture familiar vistas, seen by so many, in
such a unique and personal way.

LORRIE KEMPF

Big Sur, California

September 2016

---

*LORRIE KEMPF is the Artist and Curator of
Sacramento Metropolitan Arts Commission
Art in Public Places Program.*

INTRODUCTION
BY FRANK ORDAZ

BACK IN THE DAY of hand-painted movie set backgrounds, I worked for George Lucas' Industrial Light and Magic. One of my first assignments was painting an "establishing" shot for the opening of the movie *ET.* The idea was to establish a mood and environment the characters in the story would inhabit and to also capture the imagination in the minds of the audience. In many ways that carries over to *The Iconic Land* paintings I now produce.

The Land is the context that affects how we will dress, what we will eat, how we will build and how we will play. The Land's climate informs our movements and identifies how we will create Culture.

I live in the foothills of the Sierra in California. Nearby is the American River Canyon where we play and also where we get our water that fills our reservoirs. I love film and having worked in the film industry, I am drawn to an iconic, cinematic effect in my painting. It's as if I am painting a postcard that declares that this is the Land I live on and this is the Land I love.

It is with that respect that I paint the Pacific Coast, The Southwest where my ancestral family is from, and my home of Auburn, California. The idea is to have these paintings be a point of contact where you might say, "Gosh. . . I want to go there and be able to experience that!"

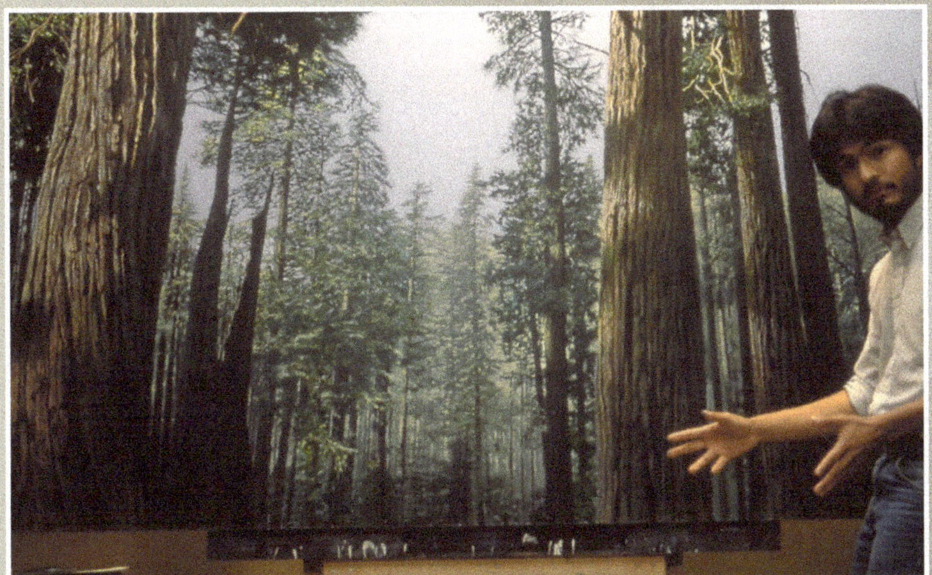

Frank Ordaz in 1982 working on Return of the Jedi *at Industrial Light and Magic.*

The layout of this book is roughly chronological from around 2008 to the present. It represents the time I started to paint Land images again and also when I opened the Ordaz Gallery in downtown Auburn.

Blessings.

FRANK ORDAZ

Auburn, California

September 2016

THE LAND ICONIC

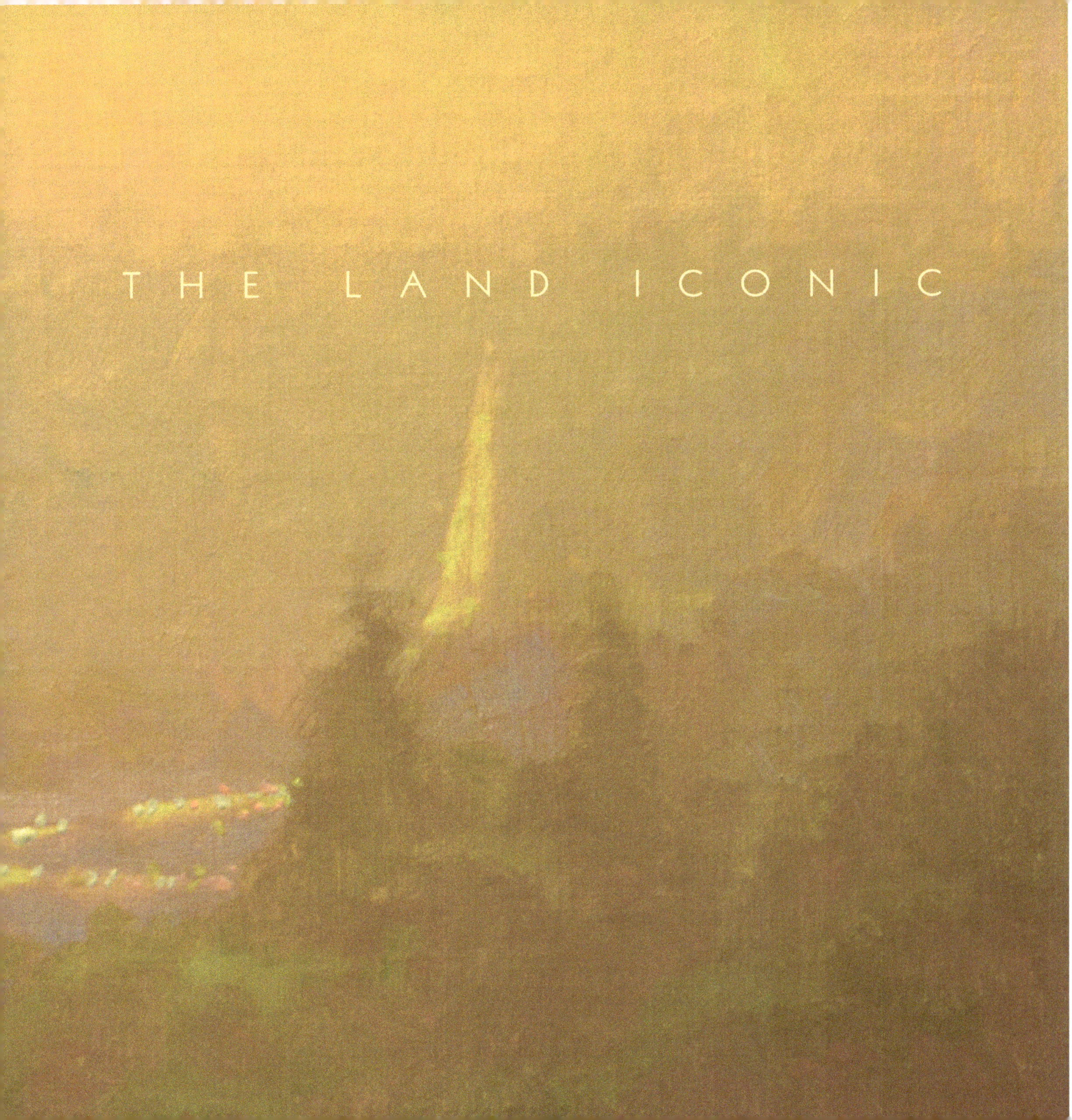

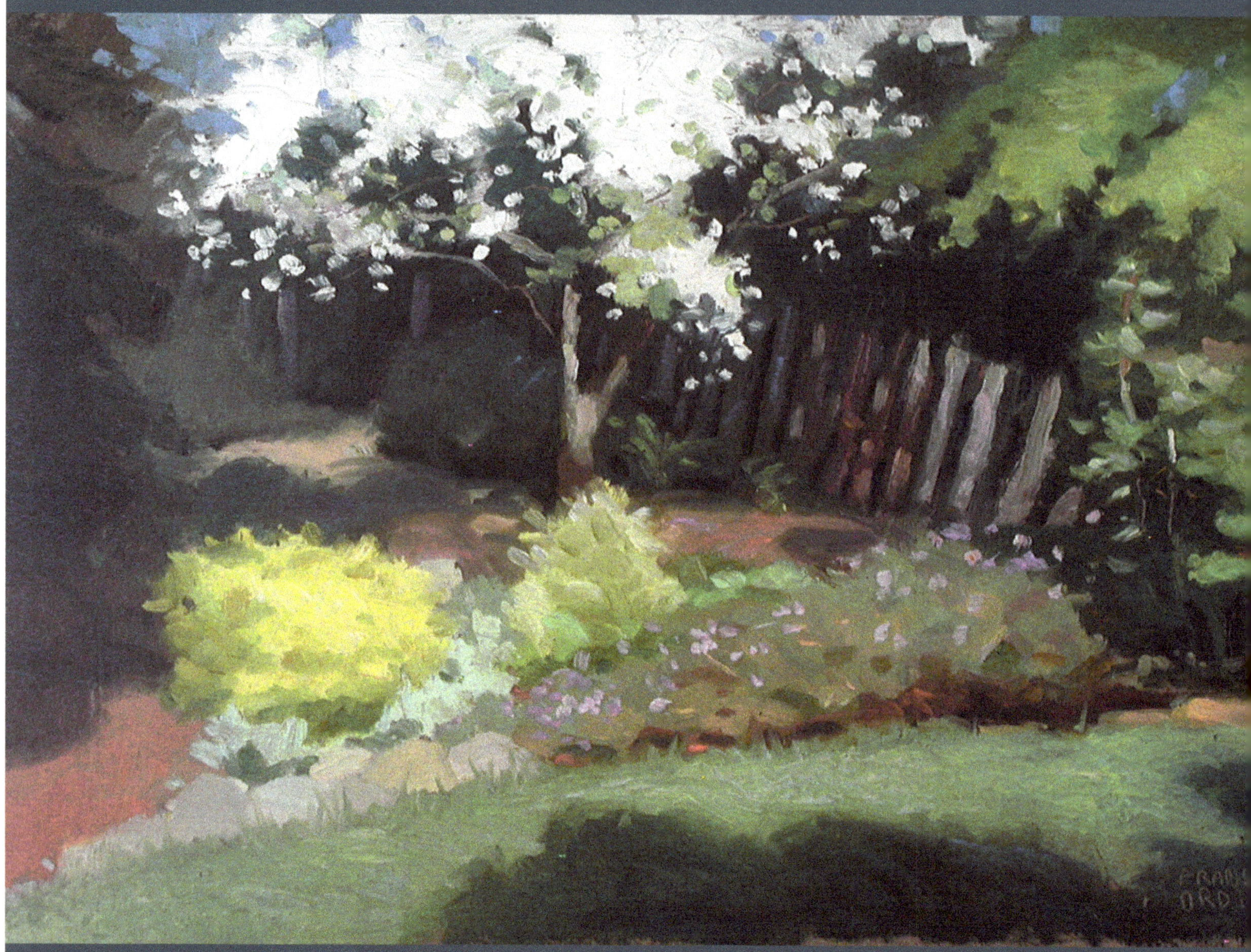

BACK YARD DOGWOOD | Auburn, California | 2007 | 11 x 14" | Oil on Panel

Painted on location in my backyard. I was inspired by my flowering Dogwood
that easily steals the show from the other spring bushes and flowers.

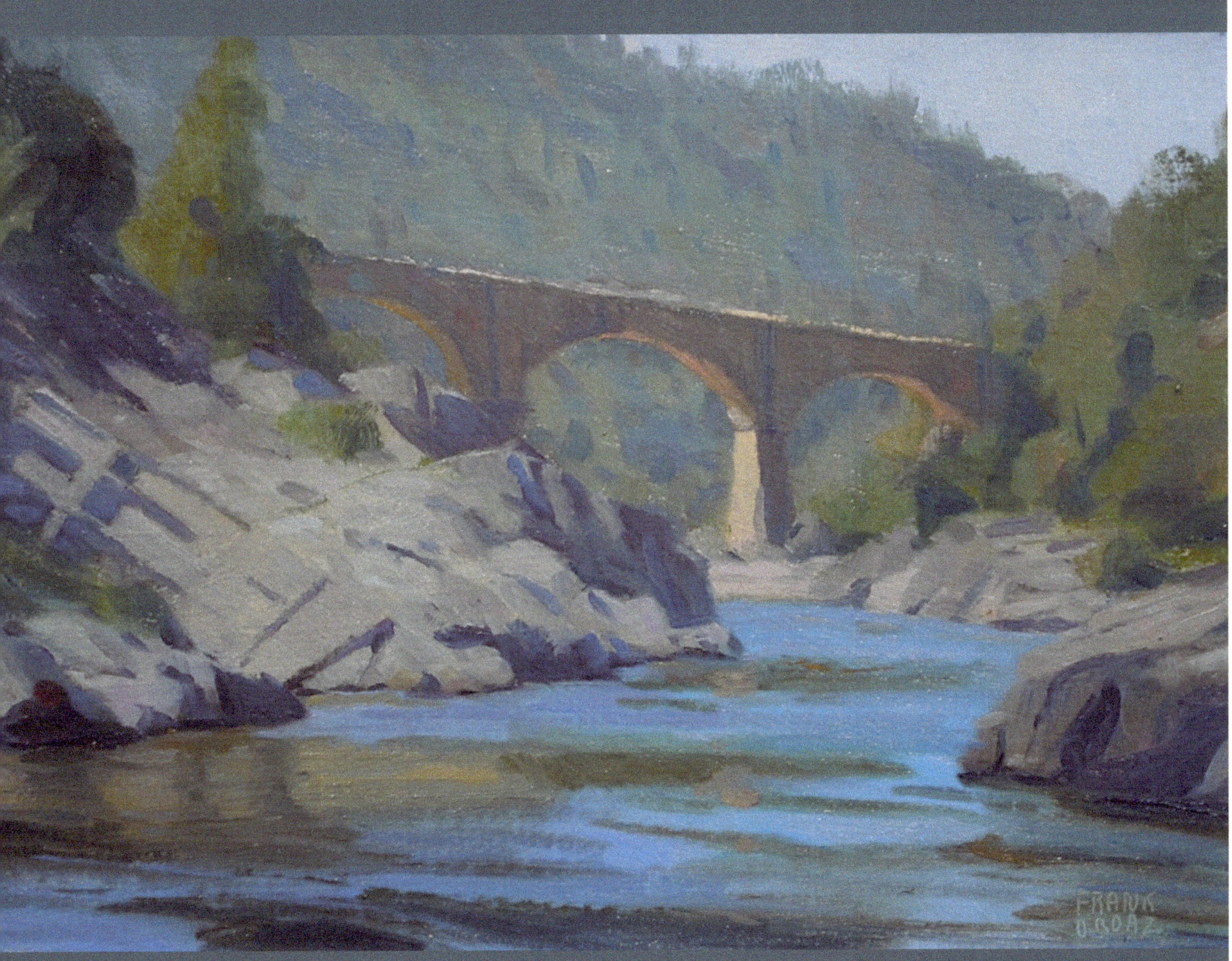

NO HANDS BRIDGE #1 | Auburn, California | 2009 | 9 x 12" | Oil on Panel

This was a wonderful spring day on the American River. Our beloved No Hands Bridge is a concrete bridge that was used during mining days around the American River Canyon. In 2008, I started to paint outdoors in earnest, developing a mindset to get an Iconic statement of the Land.

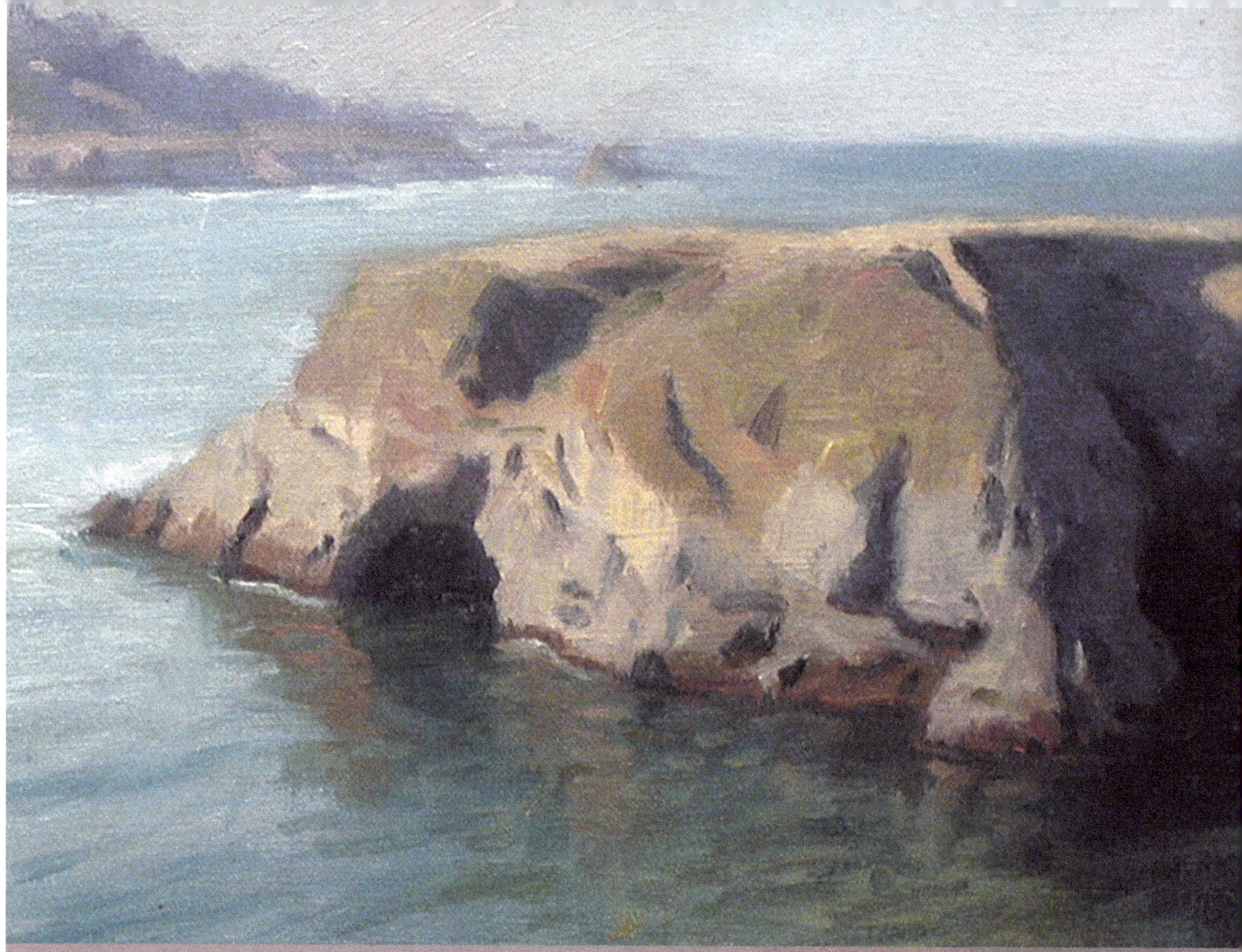

THE POINT AT MENDOCINO | Mendocino, California | 2008 | 9 x 11" | Oil on Panel

Painted on location in Mendocino, I was reacquainting myself with plein air painting. Although I painted outdoors in my early twenties and on and off during my time as an illustrator through the years, I was now intentionally painting outdoors to capture the light and accept the challenge of capturing the Land firsthand. My style was starting to develop and capturing the light and feel of that moment in time was exhilarating.

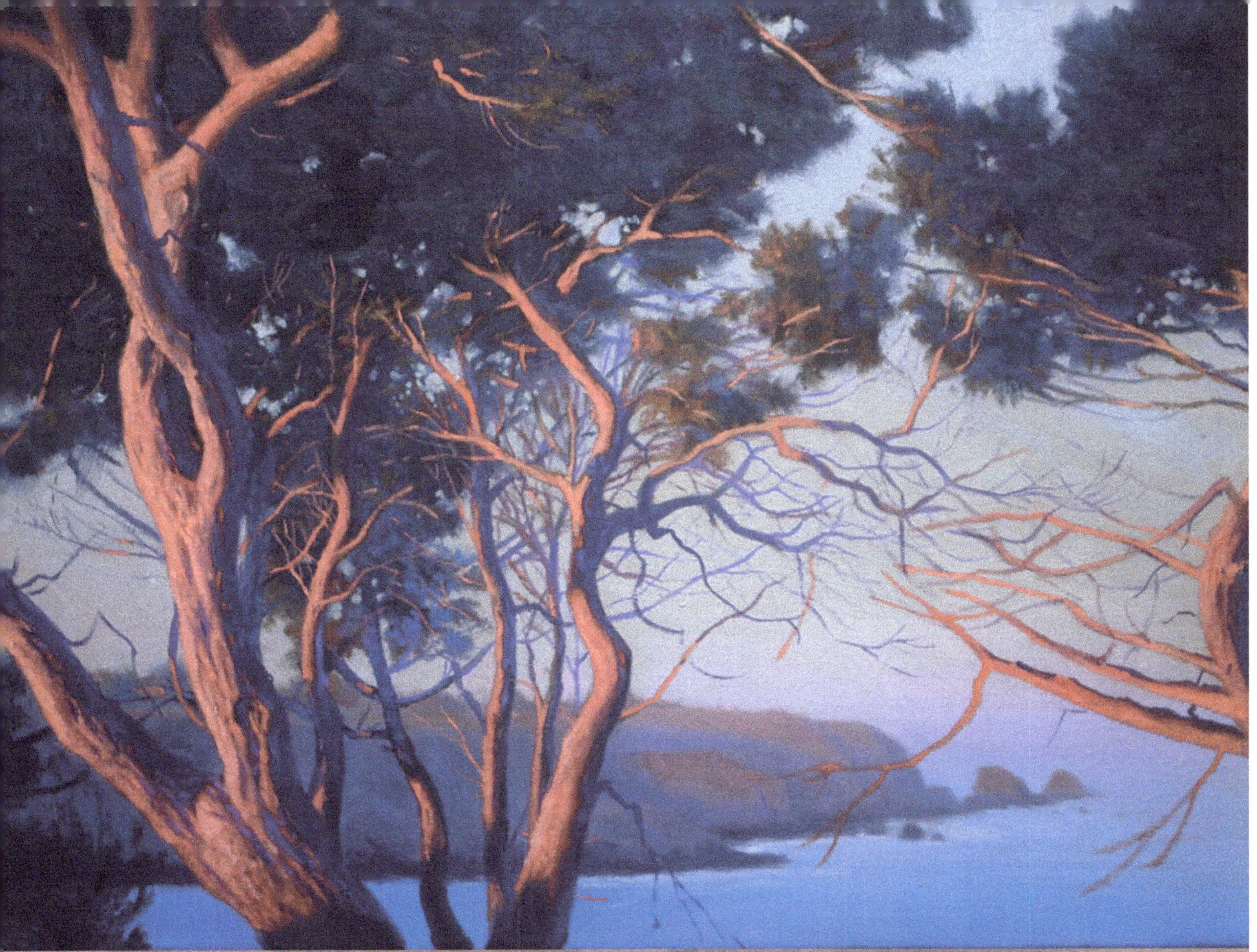

MENDO MORN | Mendocino, California | 2009 | 14 x 11" | Oil on Panel

*I painted this in my studio after I experienced that reddish morning glow that
radiates off of the cedar's bark in Mendocino. My iconic approach was starting to
appear, and I was soon to discover texture in my painting style.*

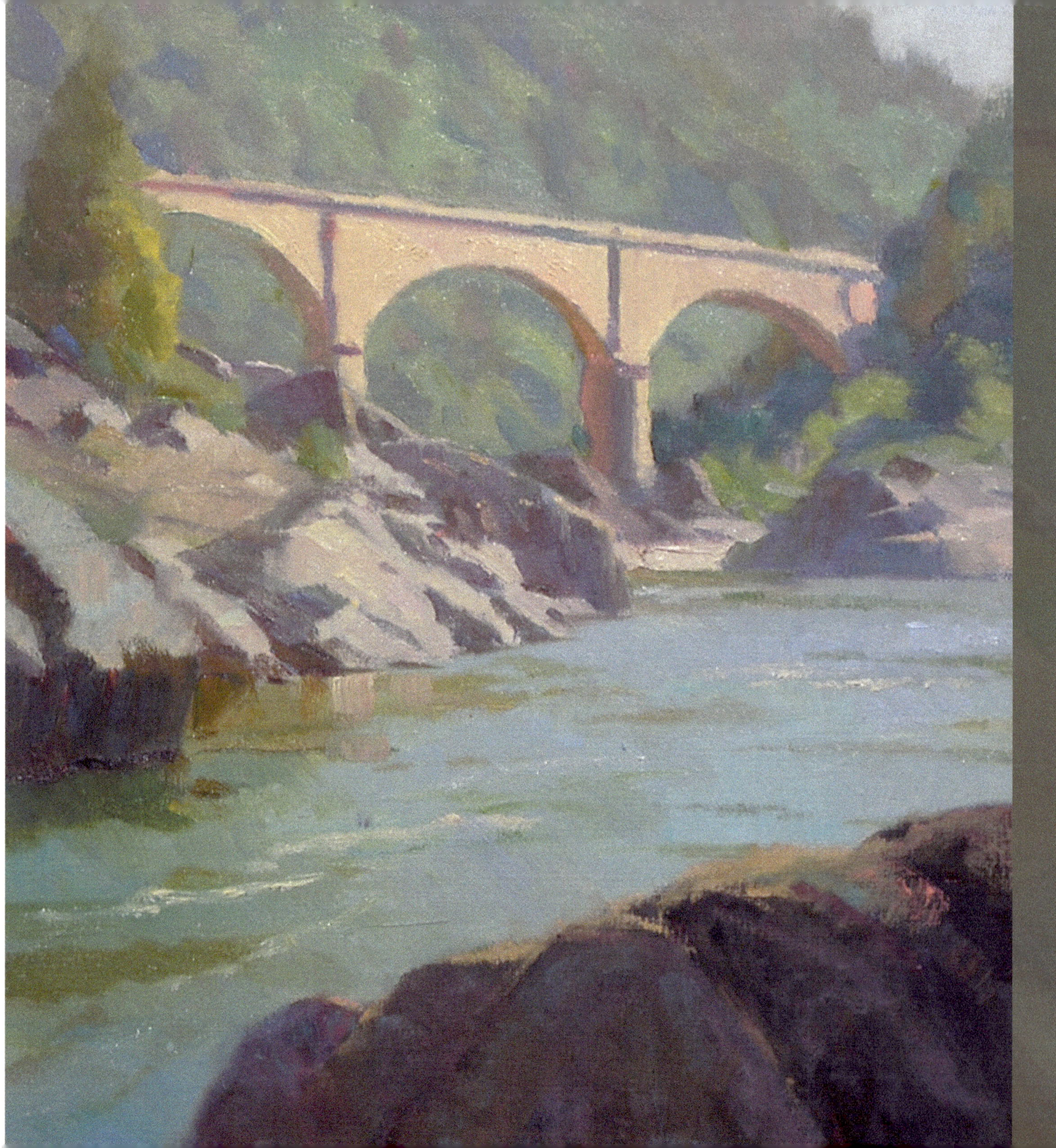

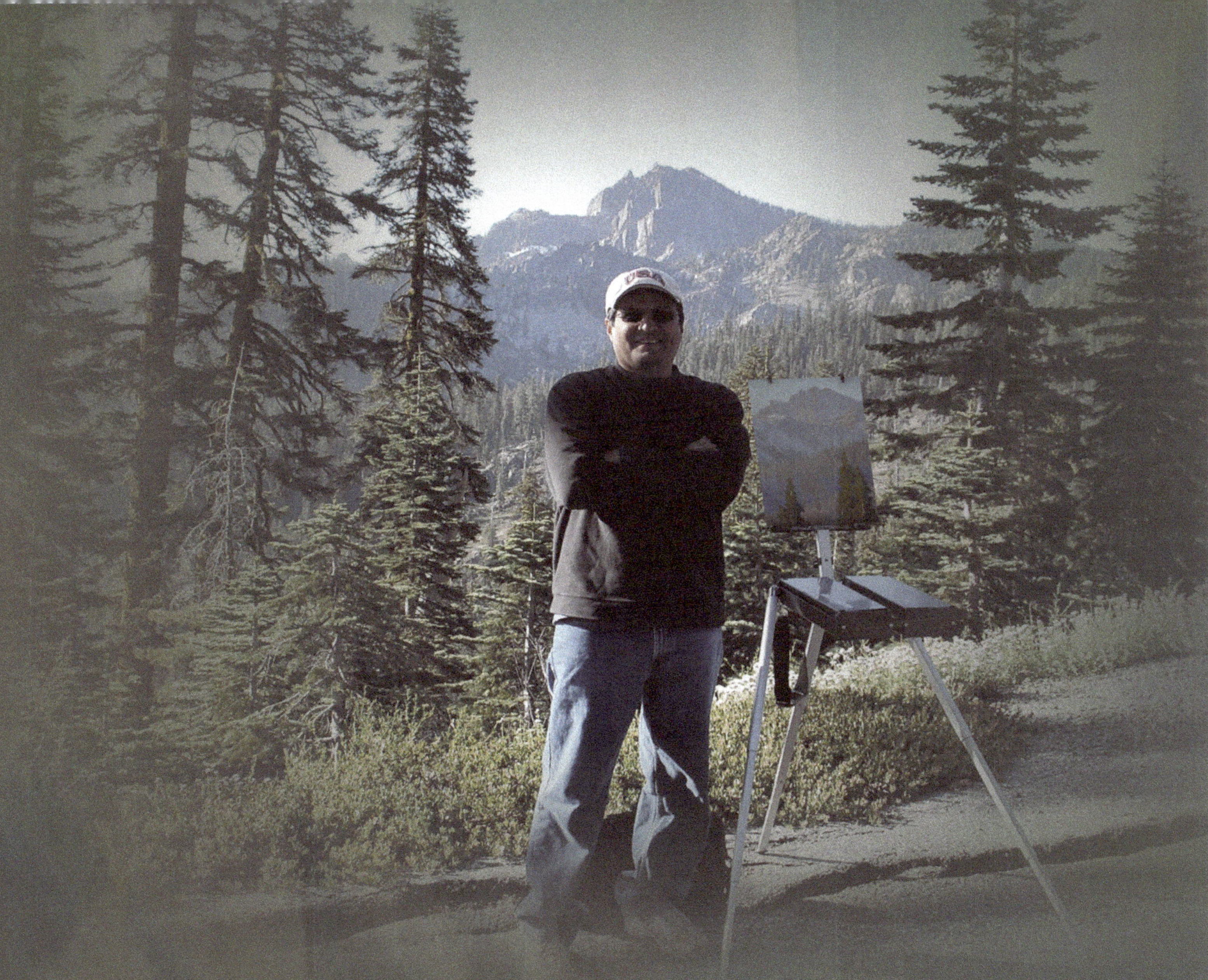

NO HANDS BRIDGE AT 3 | Auburn California | 2009 | 14 x 11" | Oil on Panel

I painted this as a record of the light and colors of the bridge and surrounding trees and brush. I was thinking of painters like Edgar Payne who used outdoor sketches not so much as finished pieces but as visual records of the light. Then the larger paintings were done using these small sketches as color references. This was painted plein air during a two-hour session.

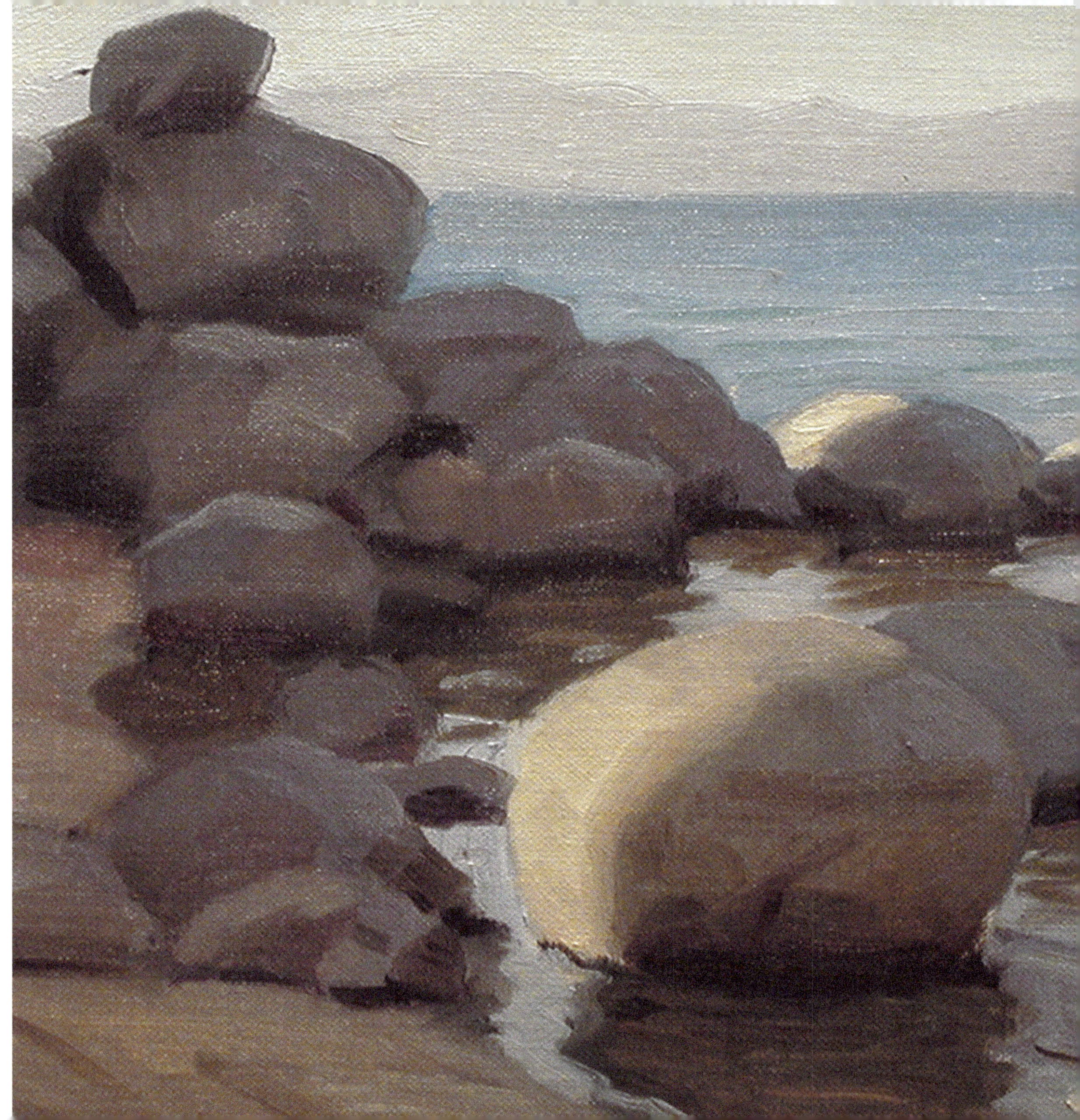

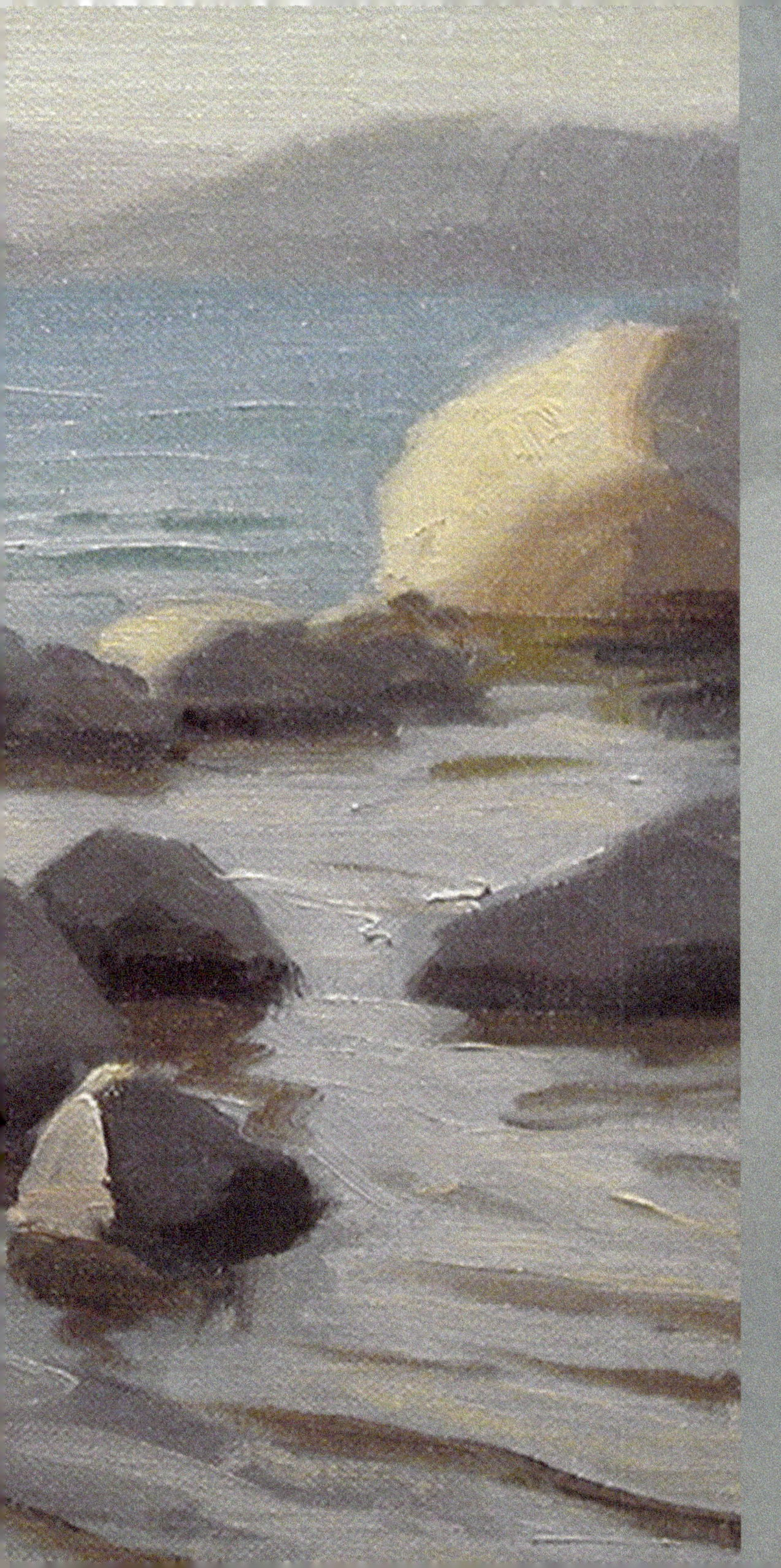

SAND HARBOR

Lake Tahoe, Nevada | 2007 | 9 x 12" | Oil on Panel

I came back to Sand Harbor and painted the sunset light on the rocks by the shore. It was a learning process as to what I should include and leave out. Around this time I was starting to embrace the painting philosophy of moving elements here and there in order to create a stronger composition. I was moving to the mindset of painting the impression of the land as opposed to an accurate recording of all the elements in front of me. I was starting to get excited about this new freedom. Painted on location on the Nevada side of Lake Tahoe.

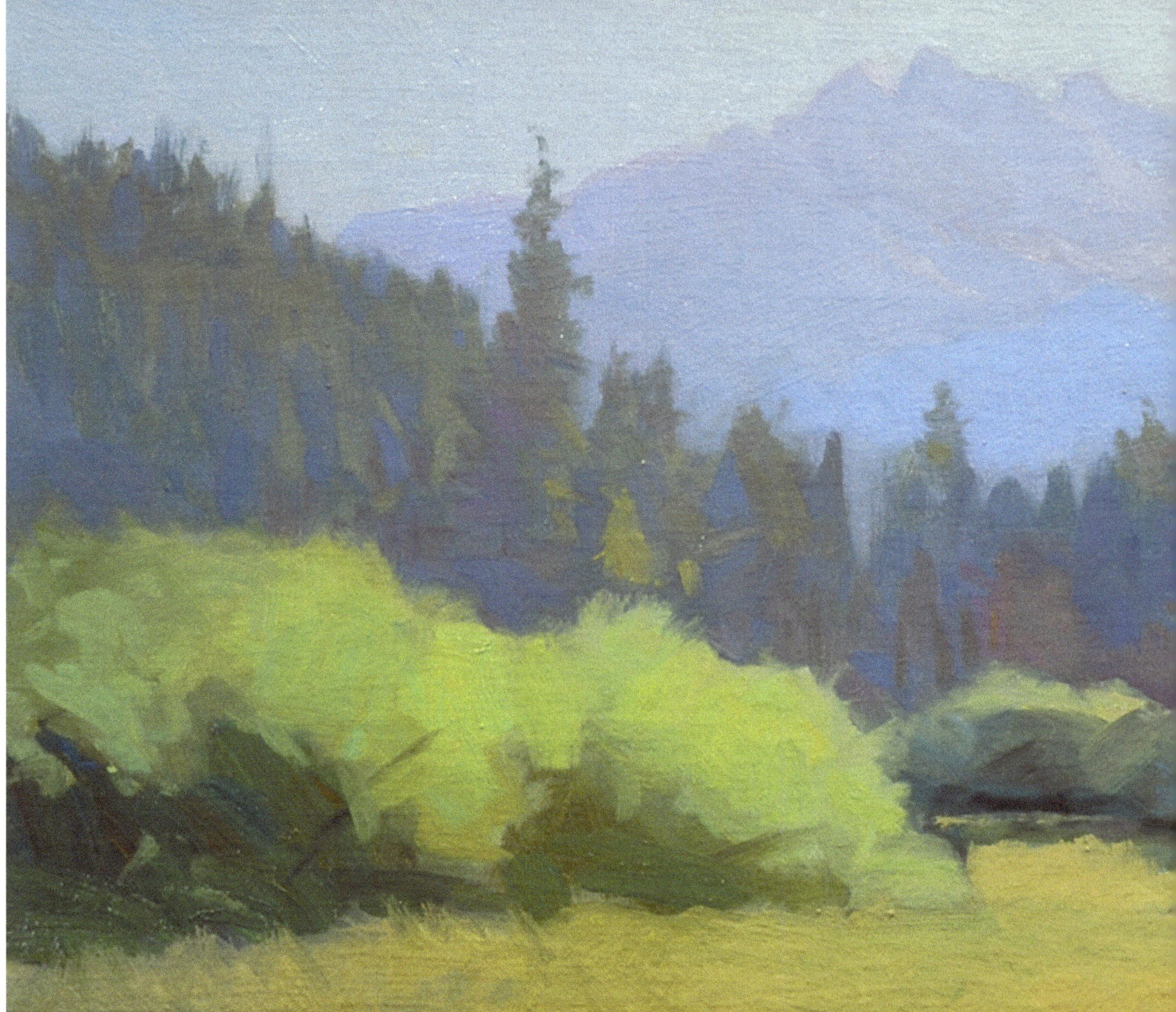

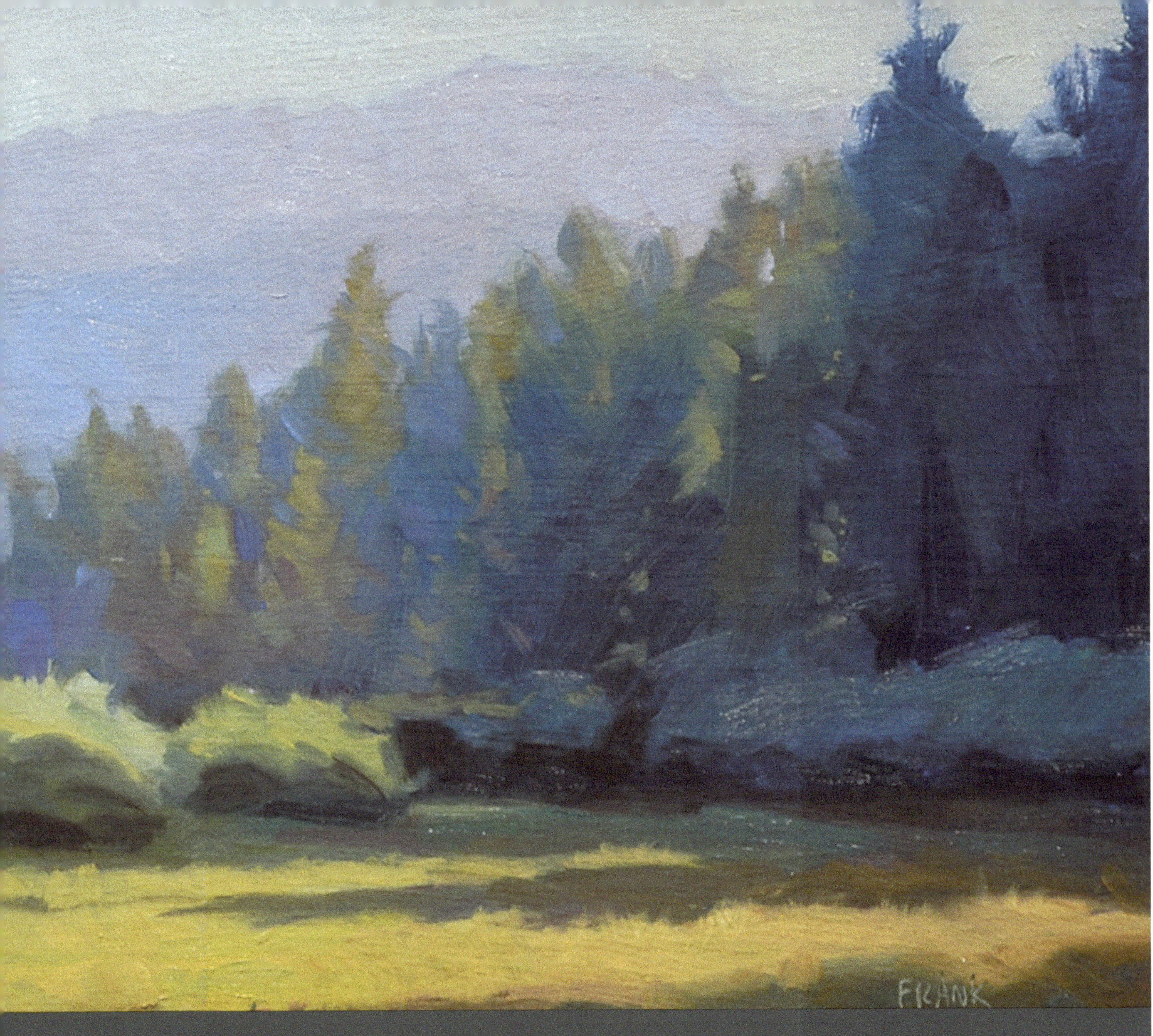

I was pleased with this effort and focused on the light effect more than the details of the trees and mountain. This was painted on location outside Sardine Lake, California.

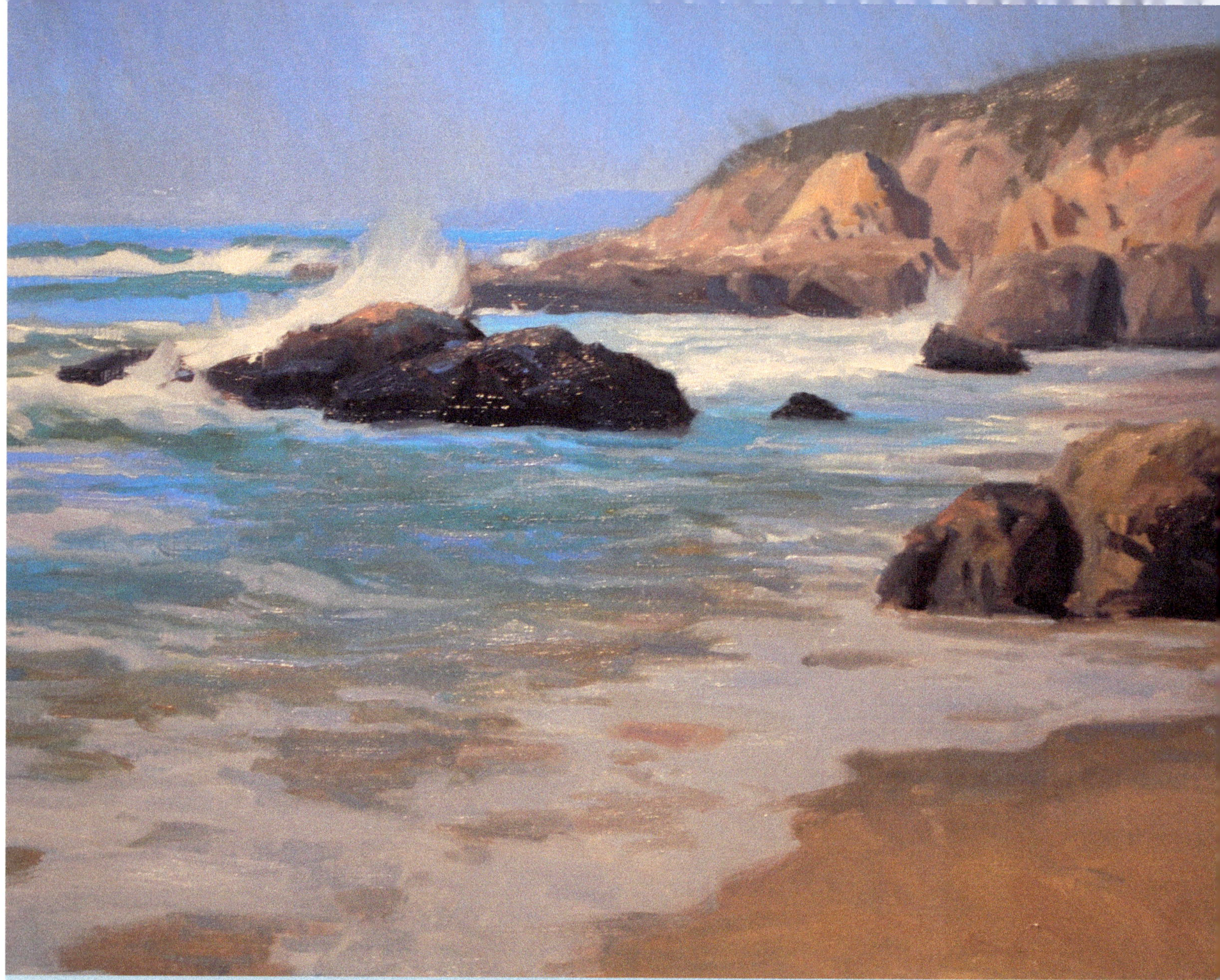

BODEGA HEAD BAY | Bodega Beach, California | 2010 | 11 x 14" | Oil on Panel

I was teaching a lot in 2010 and this small painting was done as a demo. It was during this time that I was starting to formulate my artist's statement. What kind of landscapes did I want to paint? What drew me to these locations? I was subconsciously starting to discover the mythic qualities of landscape. The people buying these paintings were telling me how they connected to this place and the memories that were forged there that made a significant marker for their lives and identity.

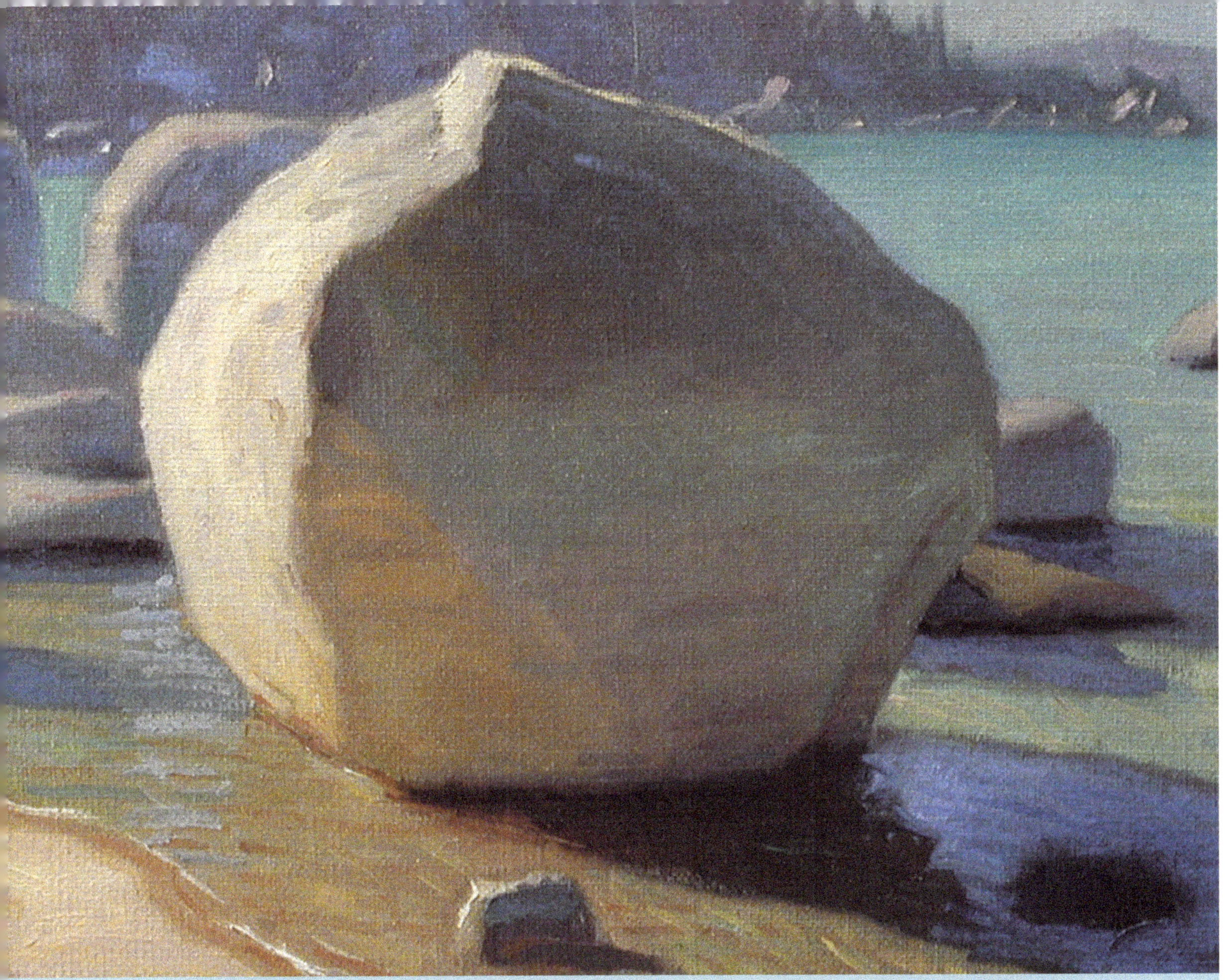

BIG ROCK IN SAND HARBOR | Sand Harbor, Nevada | 2007 | 11 x 14" | Oil on Canvas

This small painting is still one of my favorites. In the photo I took, I really saw the limitations of digital photography. So I painted this rock to remember the amazing colors that I saw. Oils could help me communicate what I saw with my eyes and heart.

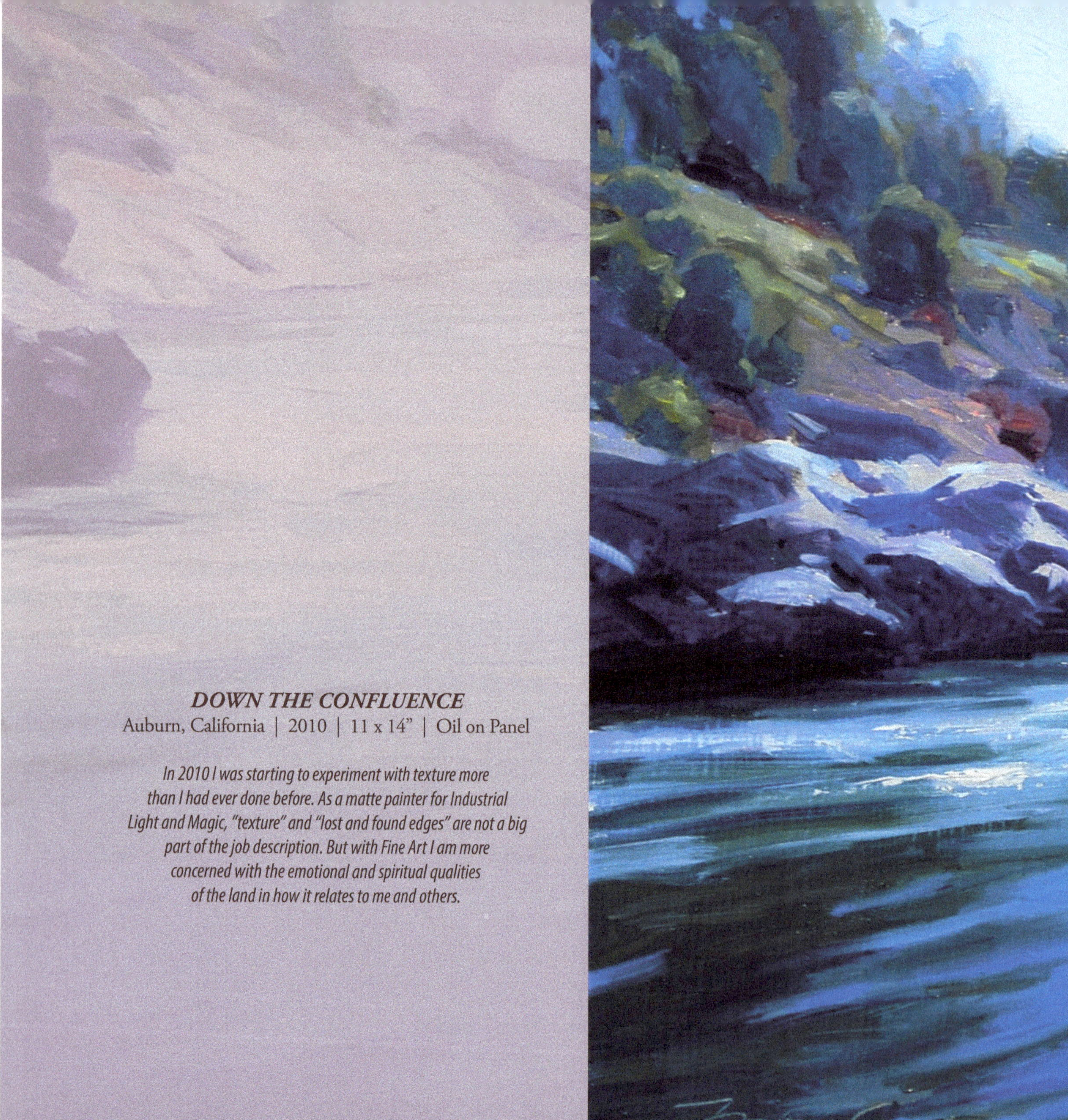

DOWN THE CONFLUENCE
Auburn, California | 2010 | 11 x 14" | Oil on Panel

*In 2010 I was starting to experiment with texture more
than I had ever done before. As a matte painter for Industrial
Light and Magic, "texture" and "lost and found edges" are not a big
part of the job description. But with Fine Art I am more
concerned with the emotional and spiritual qualities
of the land in how it relates to me and others.*

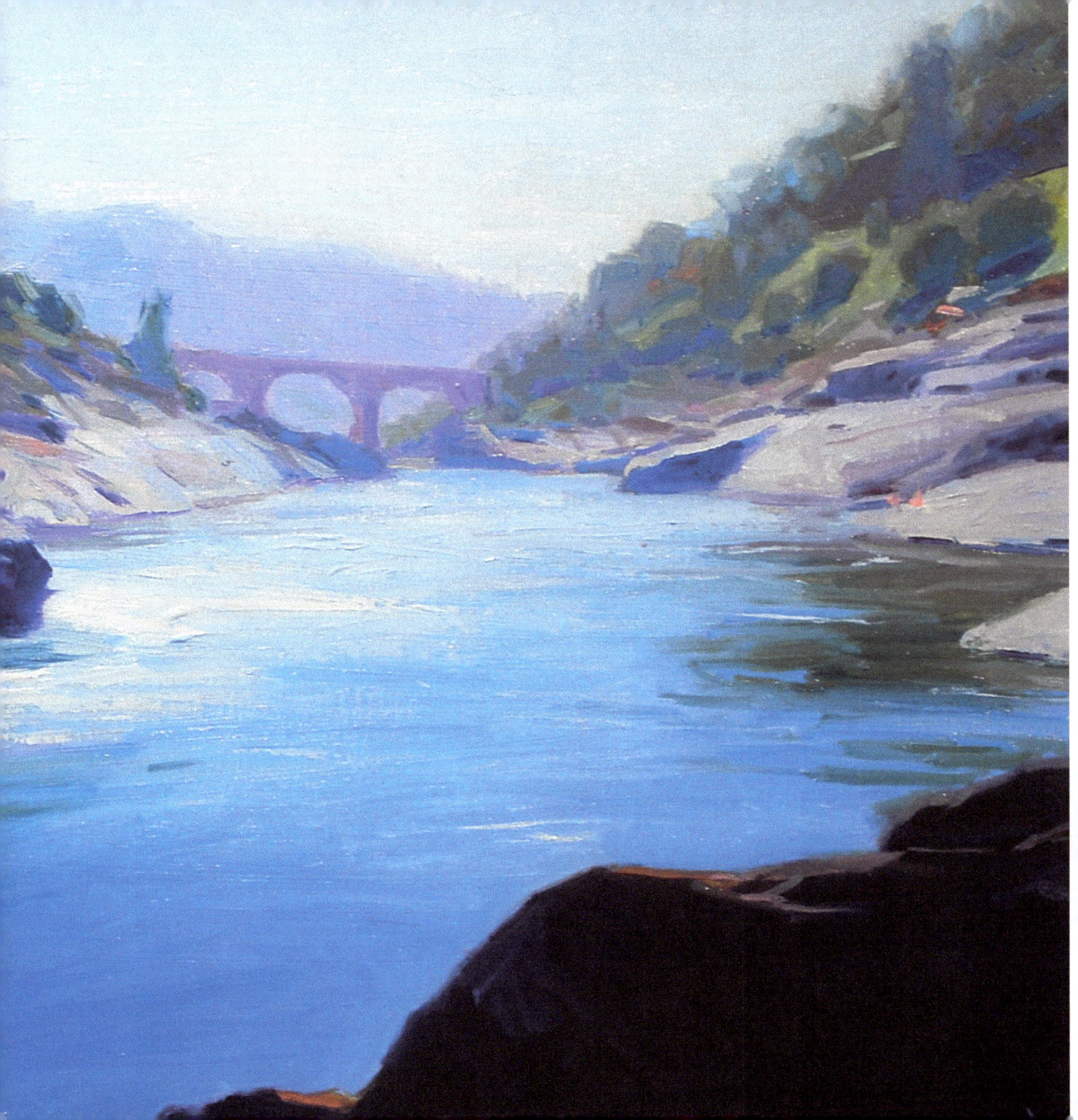

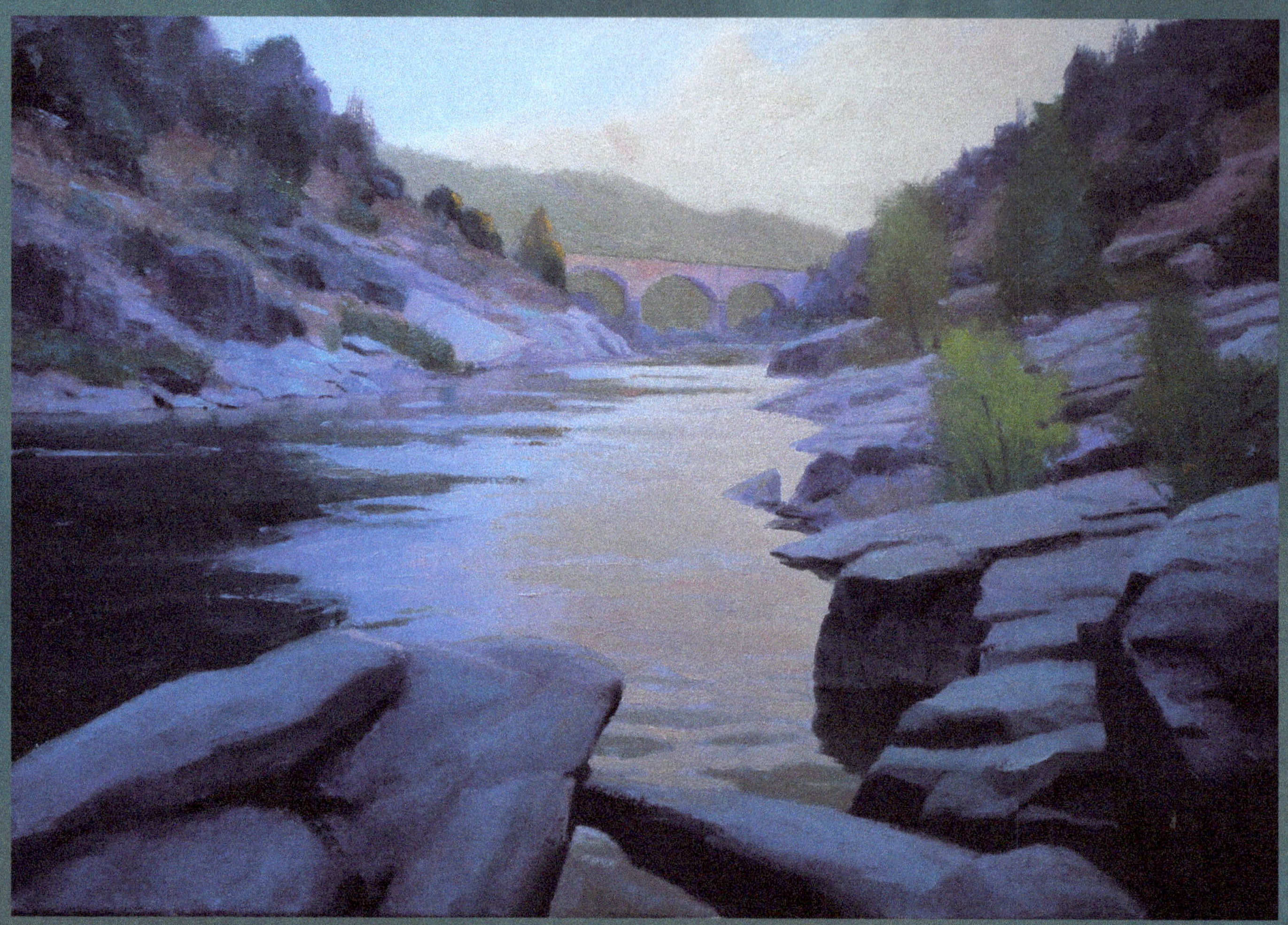

I was developing an iconic translation of Mountain Quarries Bridge when I started this painting in 2011. It was a breakthrough year as I was starting to use light to emphasize the transcendent feeling of place and being. How one exists is directly related to the land. The land and its environment dictates an emotional and rational response in survival. Land affects food, clothing, music and religion. In essence: Culture.

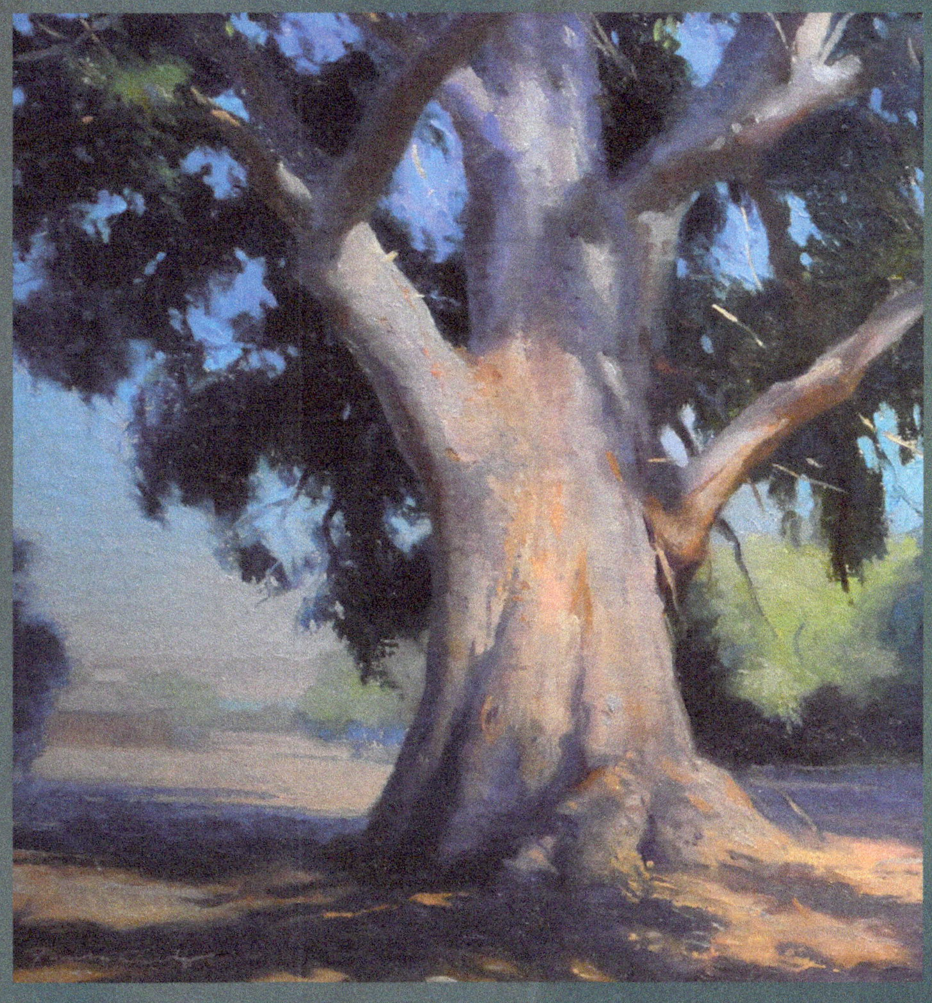

OLOMPALI EUC | Novato, California | 2011 | 14 x 11" | Oil on Canvas

*California is blessed with these massive sentinels from Down Under. There are over
one hundred varieties of eucalyptus, and with age, they tower over any landscape. The trees can
make a wonderful windbreak when planted in rows. This specimen stood alone.*

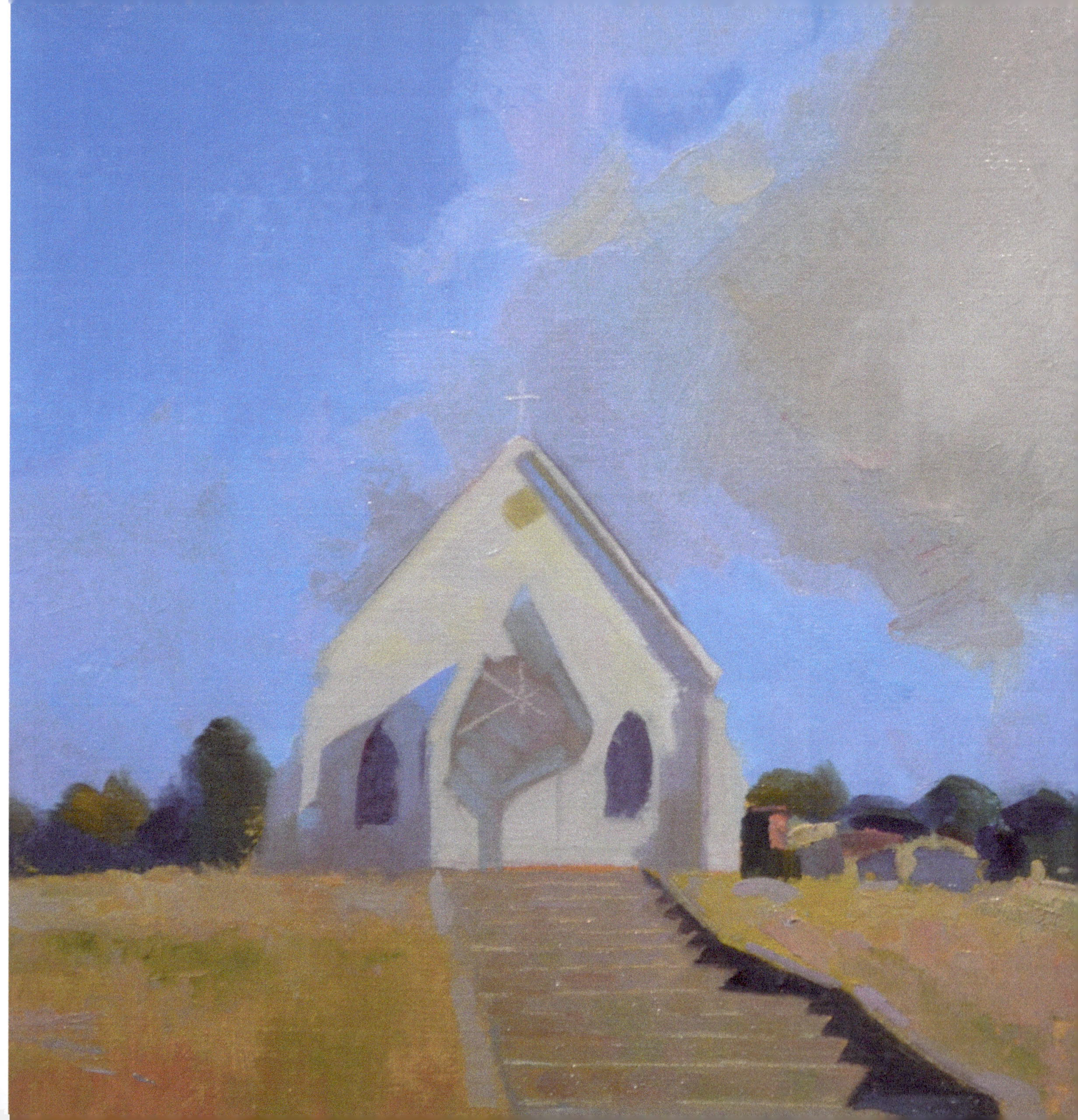

OLD ST. HILARY'S CHURCH
Tiburon, California | 2011 | 9 x 12" | Oil on Panel

*One of the most iconic prairie churches in Marin County rests
on the hills of Tiburon. This historic landmark is now used mostly for
weddings but was, at one time, an active Catholic church.*

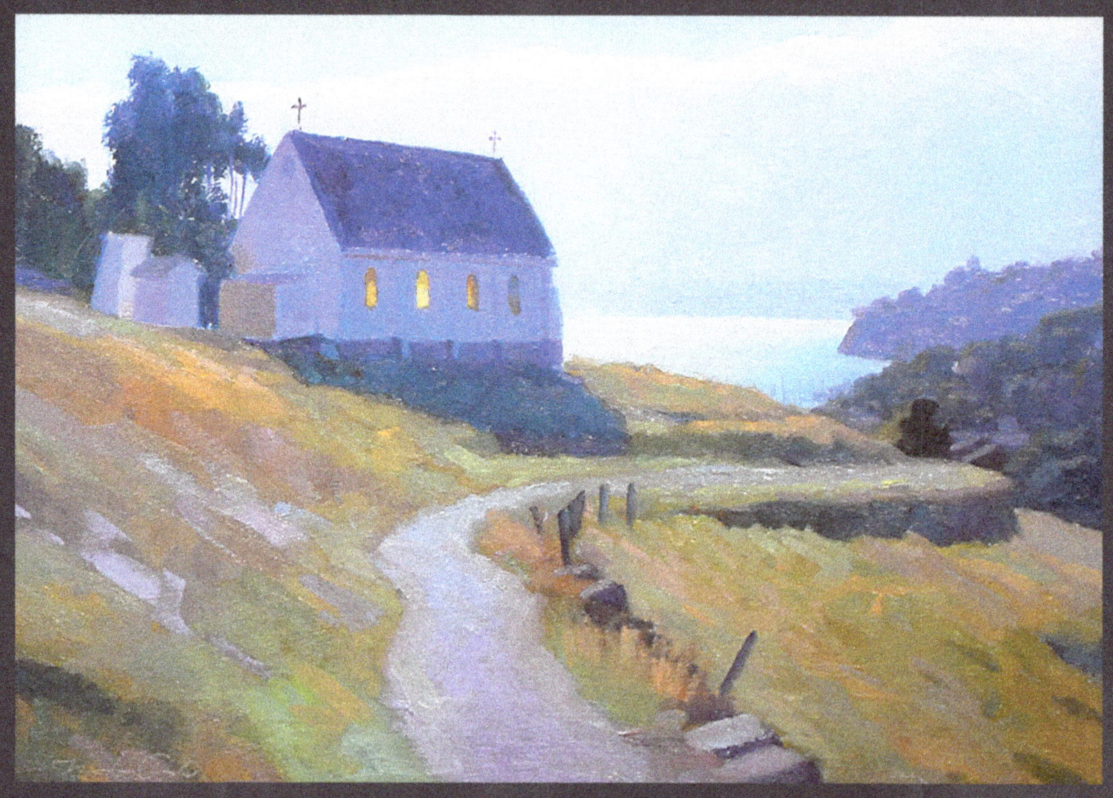

OLD ST. HILARY CHURCH #2 | Tiburon, California | 2011 | 12 x 9" | Oil on Panel

This is an important painting for me as my style was beginning to change in 2011.
I loved the colors, and I was developing a stylistic translation of the land. I was beginning to see the image
as making a mythic statement. St. Hilary's Church in Tiburon was the start of this mindset.

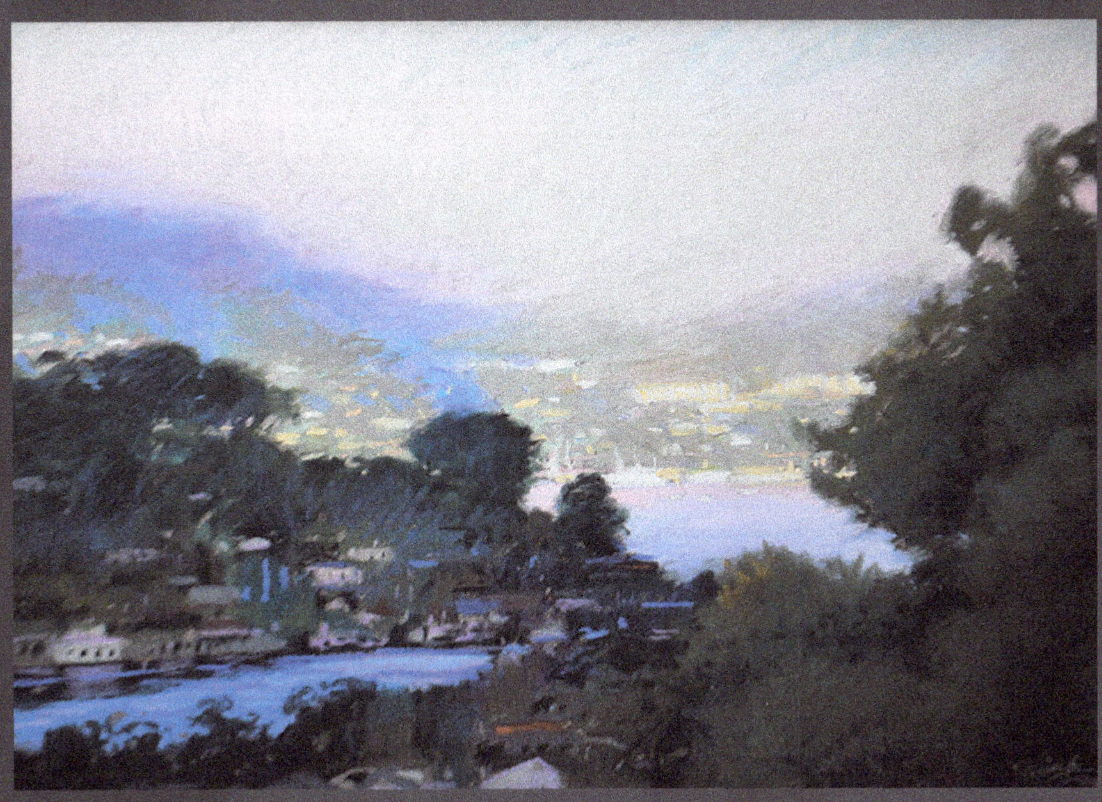

FOG BLANKETS TIBURON | Tiburon, California | 2012 | 11 x 14" | Pastel on Paper

Fog rolling over the Tiburon hills is a constant occurrence for
the inhabitants of this town. Pastel captured that mood.

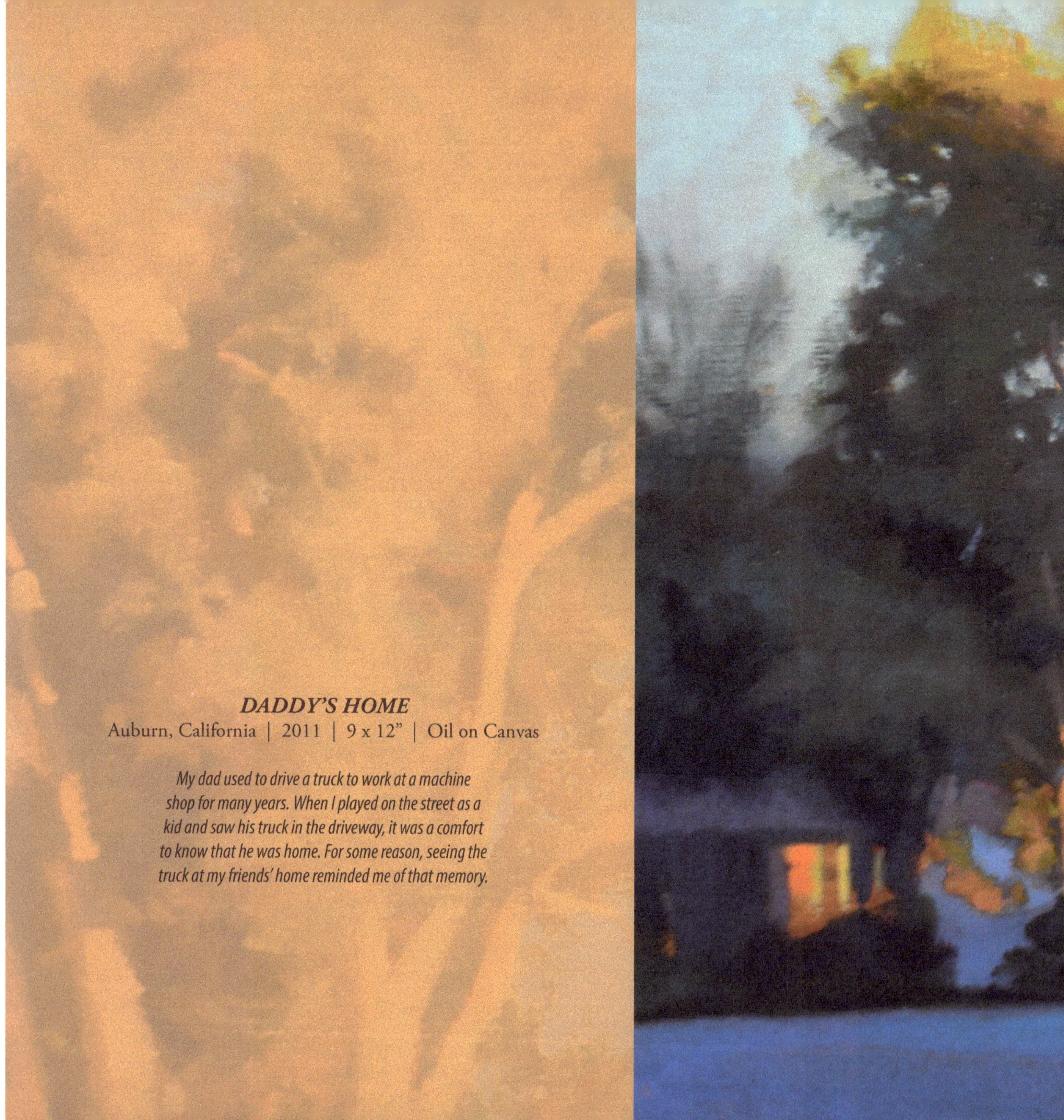

DADDY'S HOME
Auburn, California | 2011 | 9 x 12" | Oil on Canvas

My dad used to drive a truck to work at a machine
shop for many years. When I played on the street as a
kid and saw his truck in the driveway, it was a comfort
to know that he was home. For some reason, seeing the
truck at my friends' home reminded me of that memory.

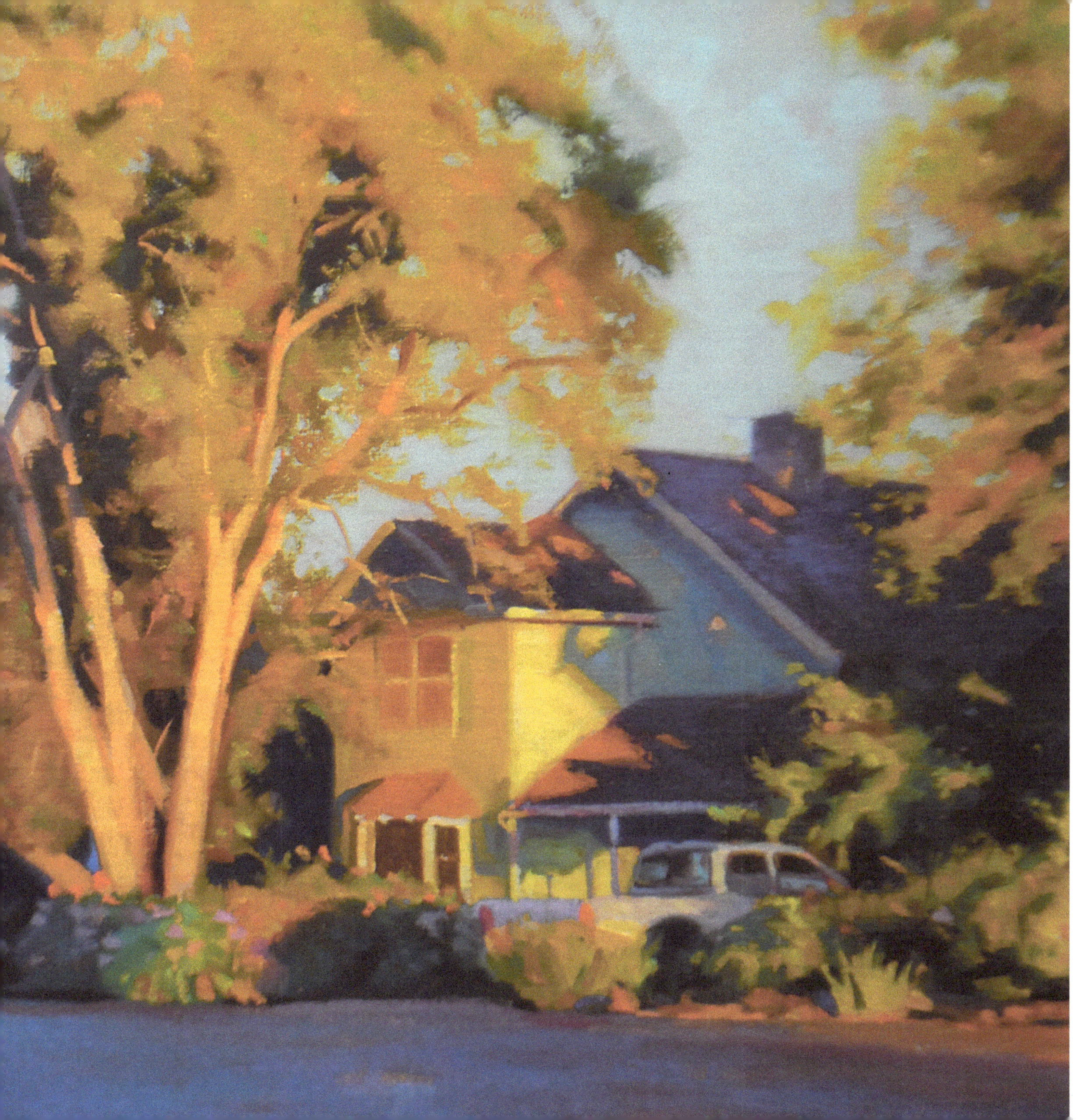

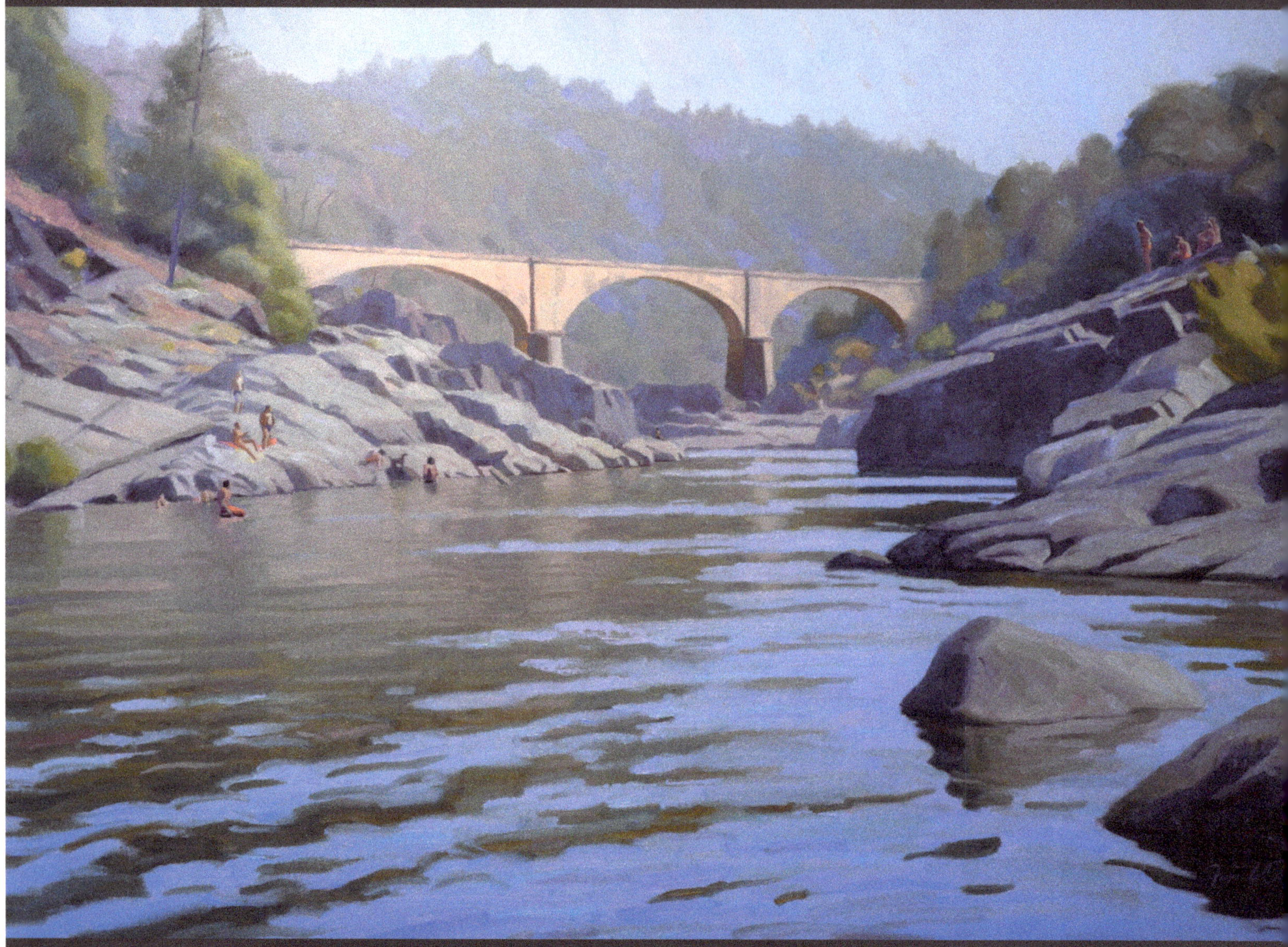

RIVER FUN | Auburn, California | 2012 | 24 x 30" | Oil on Canvas

The temperature gets higher than 100 degrees during the summer months in Auburn.
It's a dry heat and many locals make their way to the American River. They wade in
the water which, by then, is just a mellow flow. Teenagers hang out and jump
from the protruding rocks a good 20 feet to the cool water.

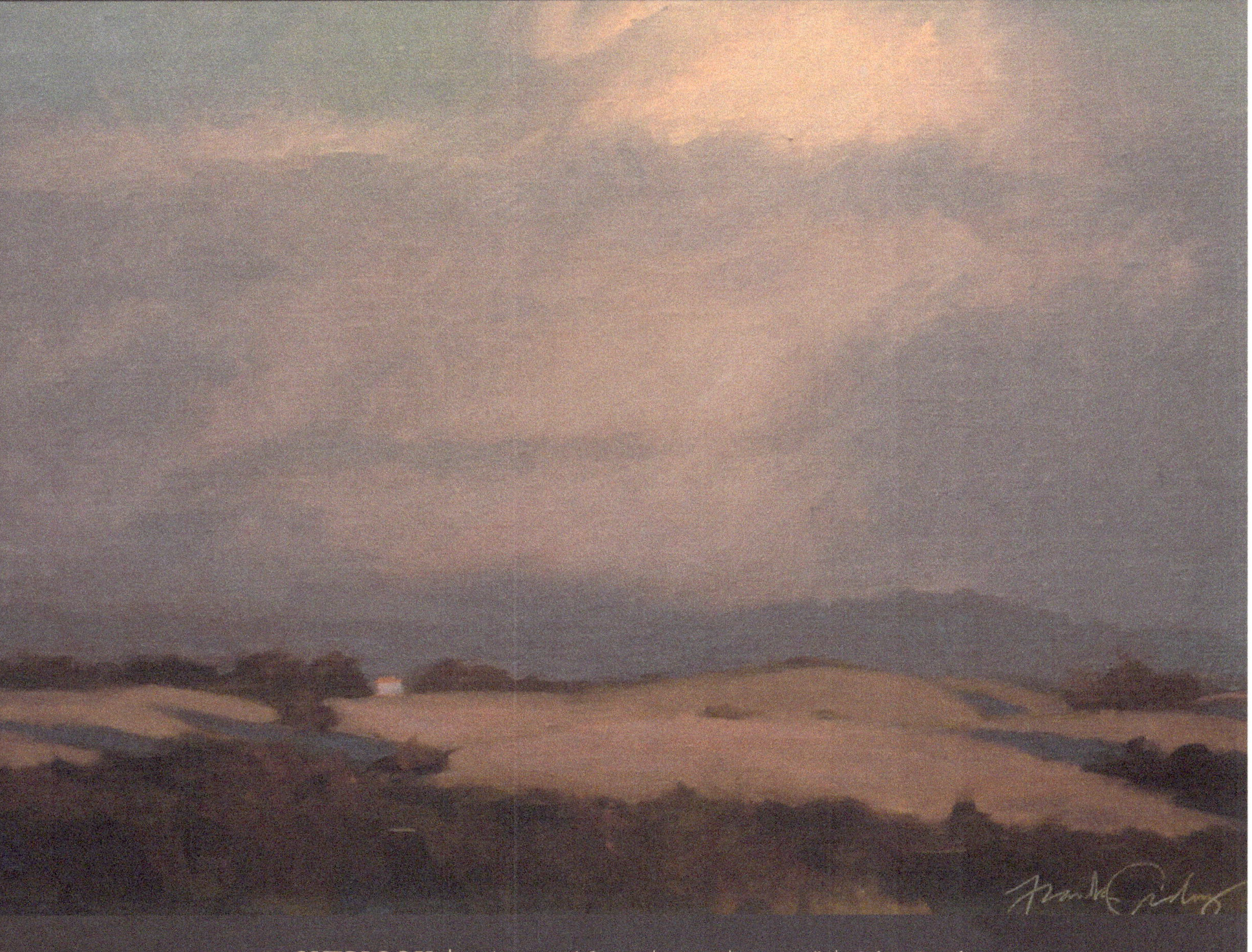

OVERLOOK | Auburn, California | 2013 | 11 x 13" | Oil on Panel

In Auburn there is a overlook where you can see across the canyon of the American River and view the river as well as El Dorado County.
Many times, after a day of painting, I go there to see the sunset light against those hills. This small painting was just one of those many evenings.

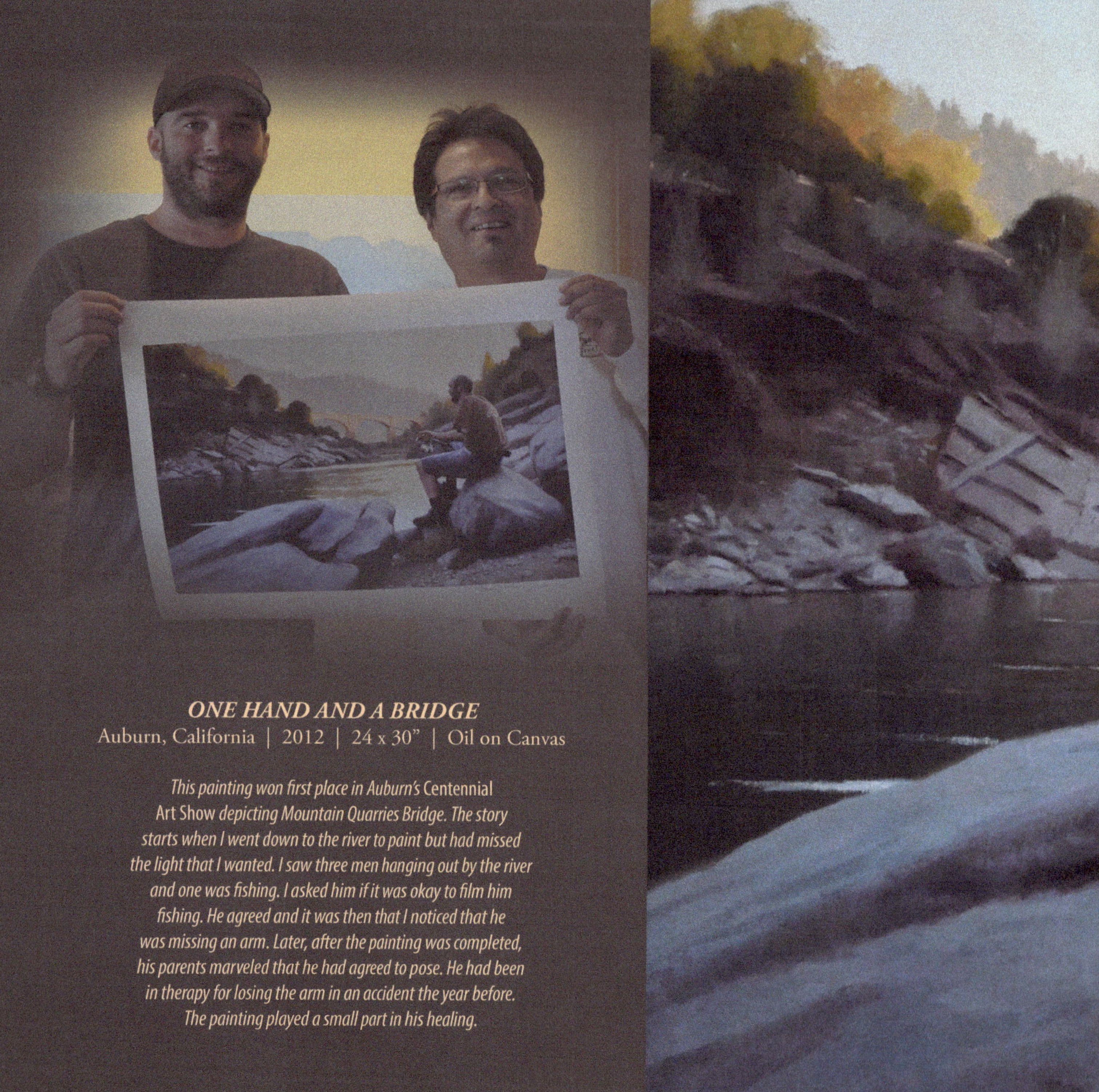

ONE HAND AND A BRIDGE
Auburn, California │ 2012 │ 24 x 30" │ Oil on Canvas

This painting won first place in Auburn's Centennial
Art Show depicting Mountain Quarries Bridge. The story
starts when I went down to the river to paint but had missed
the light that I wanted. I saw three men hanging out by the river
and one was fishing. I asked him if it was okay to film him
fishing. He agreed and it was then that I noticed that he
was missing an arm. Later, after the painting was completed,
his parents marveled that he had agreed to pose. He had been
in therapy for losing the arm in an accident the year before.
The painting played a small part in his healing.

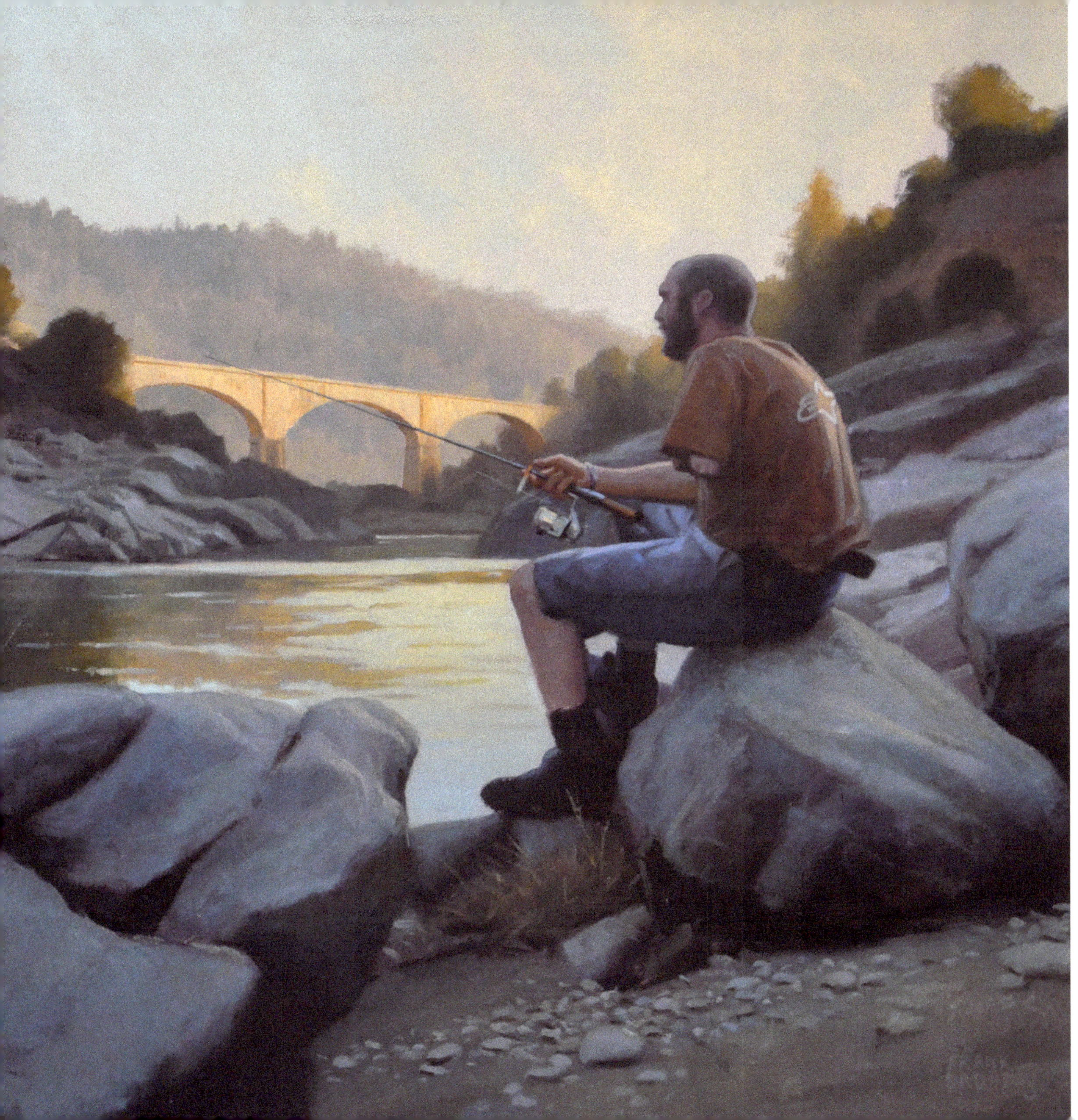

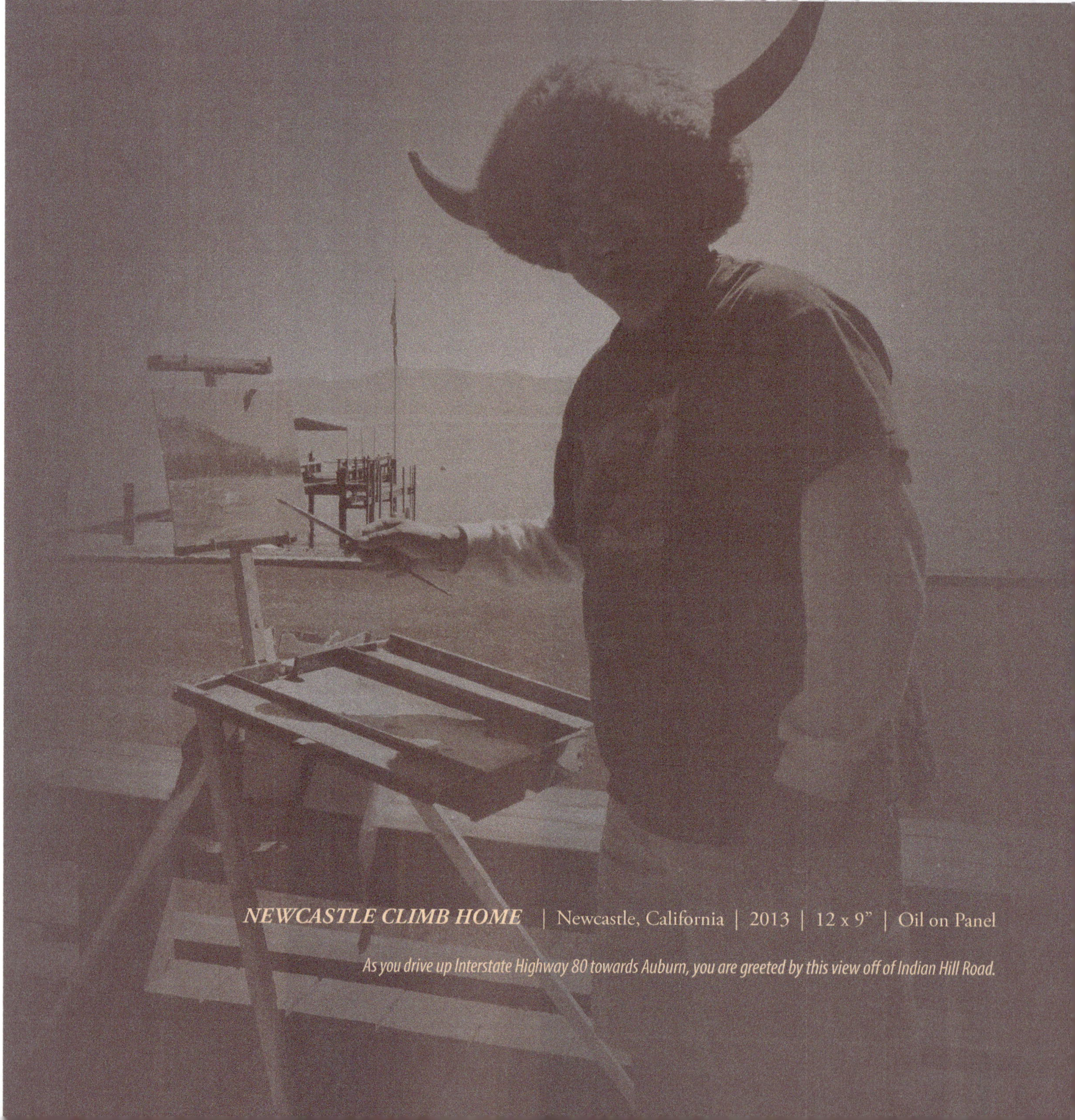

NEWCASTLE CLIMB HOME | Newcastle, California | 2013 | 12 x 9" | Oil on Panel

As you drive up Interstate Highway 80 towards Auburn, you are greeted by this view off of Indian Hill Road.

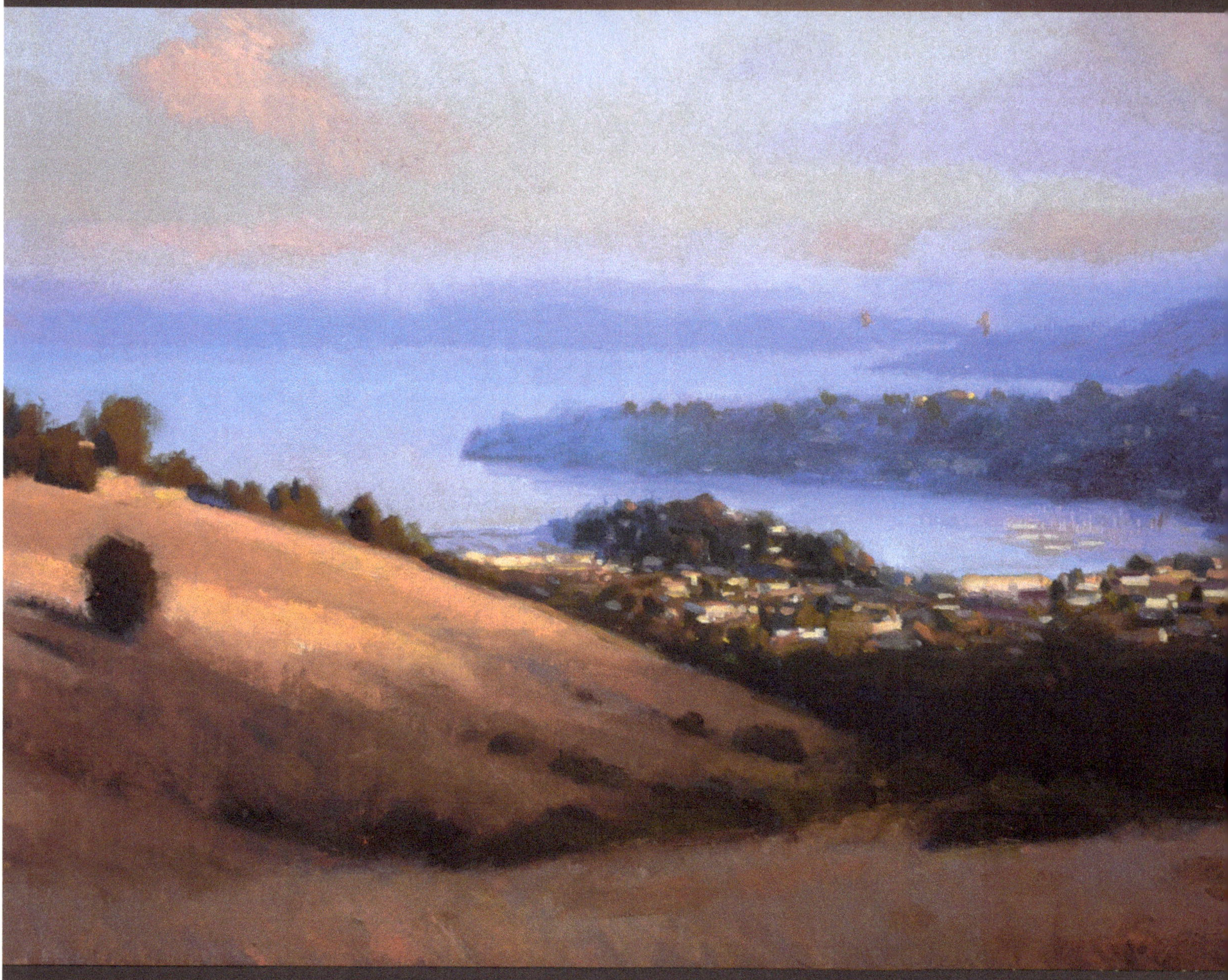

TOWARDS THE GATE IN TIBURON | San Francisco, California | 2012 | 11 x 14" | Oil on Panel

At the top of Round Hill in Tiburon the views of The Bay and Marin are just spectacular.
As I made the hike one stormy day, I was drawn to the distant, passing clouds moving over
San Francisco while Tiburon was in light. I love this effect in nature.

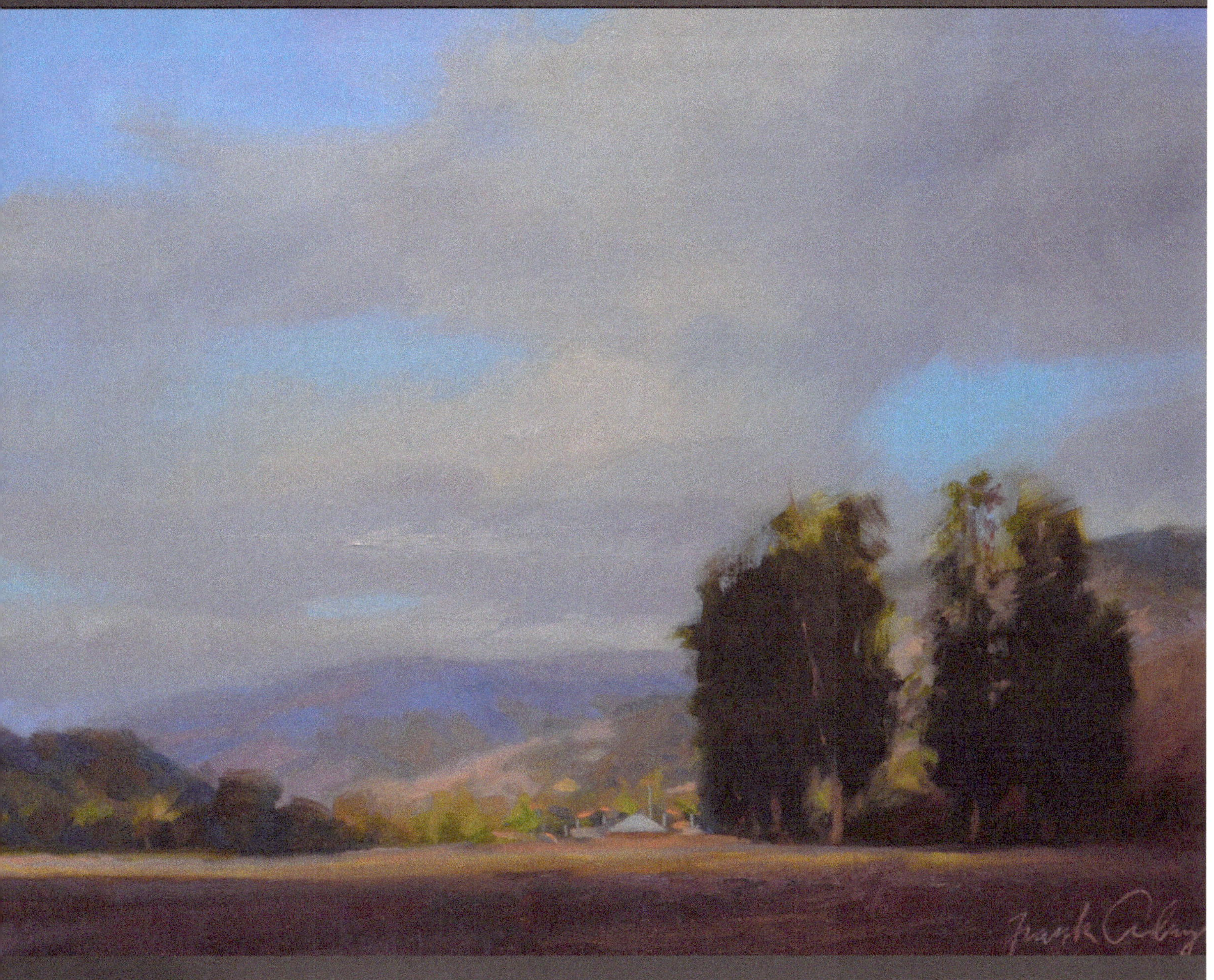

SKYWALKER VALLEY | San Rafael, California | 2013 | 11 x 14" | Oil on Panel

Looking down Lucas Valley Road you will see these verdant hills that cradle the narrow valley below.
Nestled along the way off the road lies Skywalker Ranch which was built by filmmaker George Lucas.

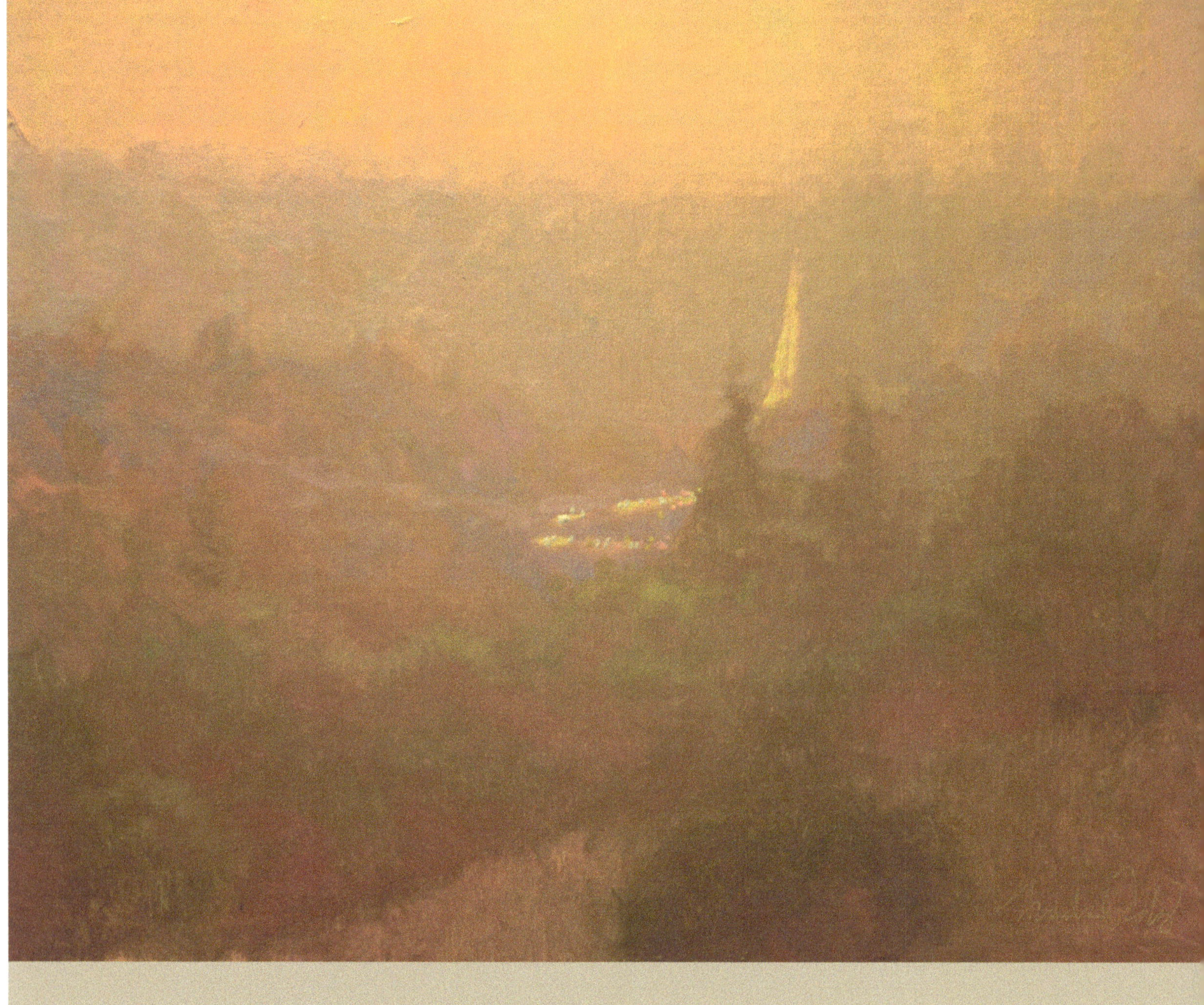

DOIN' MILES FROM AUBURN TO DAVIS | Newcastle, California | 2013 | 9 x 12" | Oil on Panel

A little pun can sometimes work when you are in the mood.

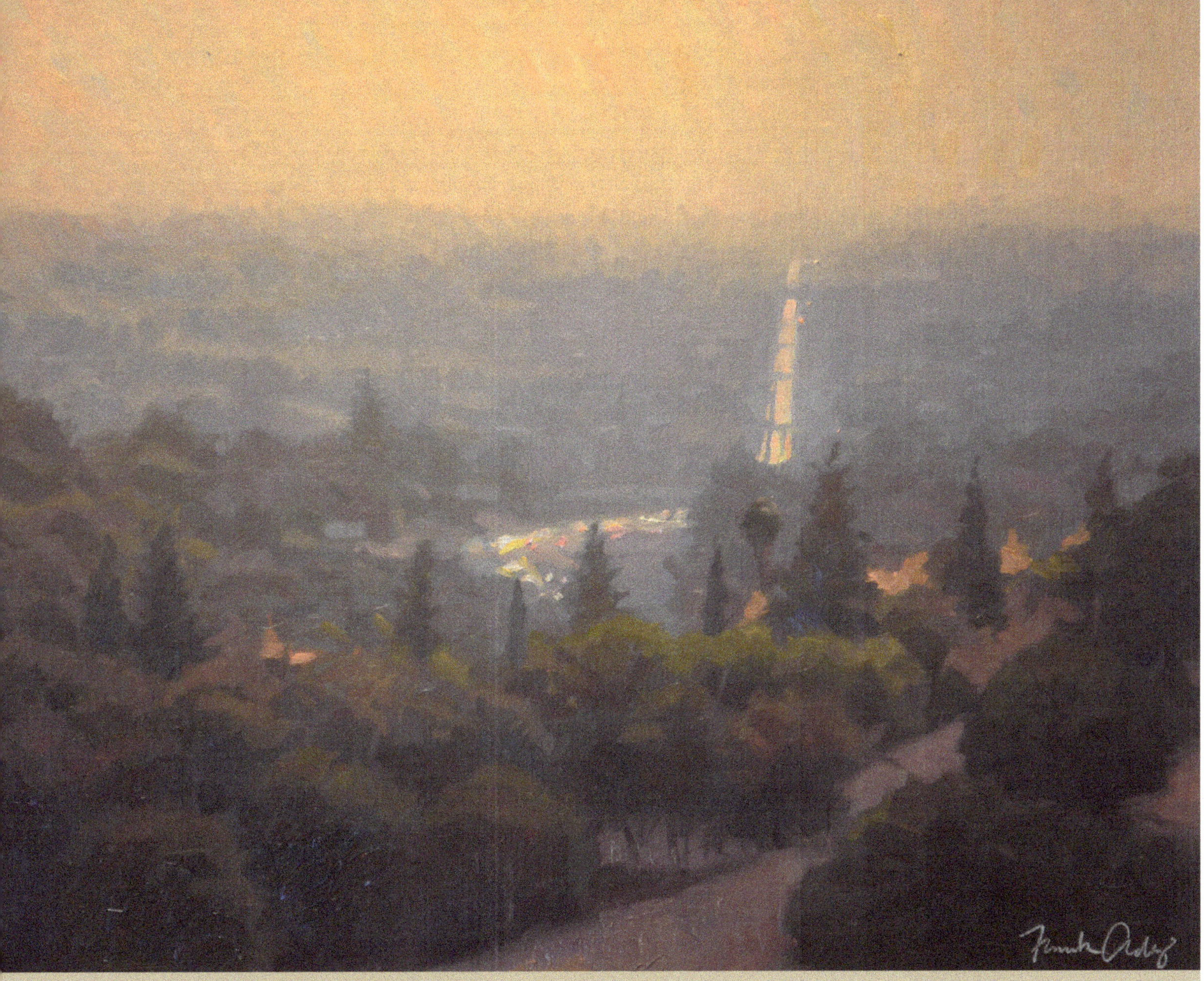

DOIN' MILES FROM AUBURN TO DAVIS 2 | Newcastle, California | 2013 | 9 x 12" | Oil on Panel

This is my groove state of mind when I venture to the John Natsoulas Gallery in Davis. I just put on Miles Davis' Kind of Blue and driving takes on another dimension. This painting was juried into the 2015 California Art Club Gold Medal Show.

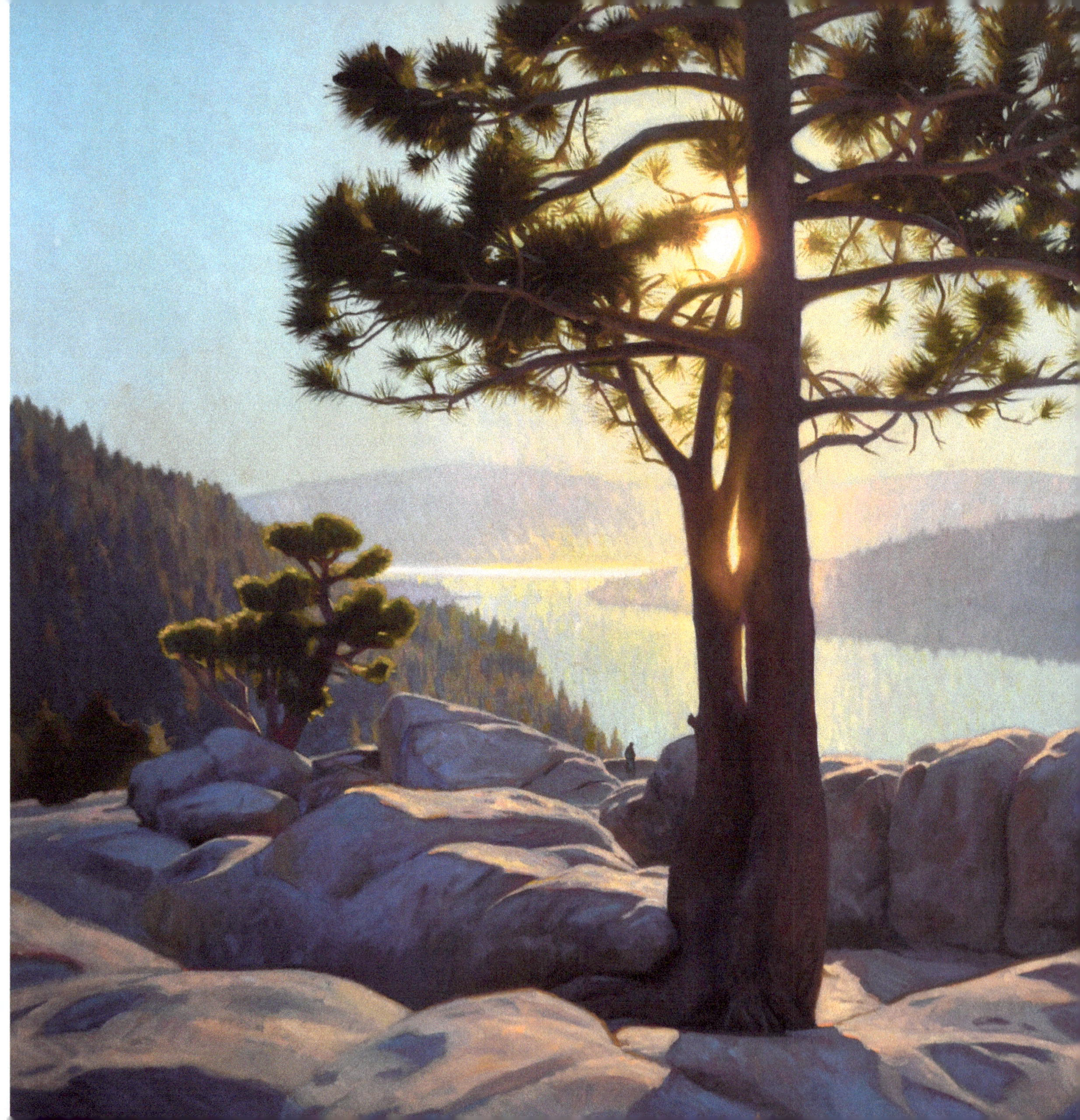

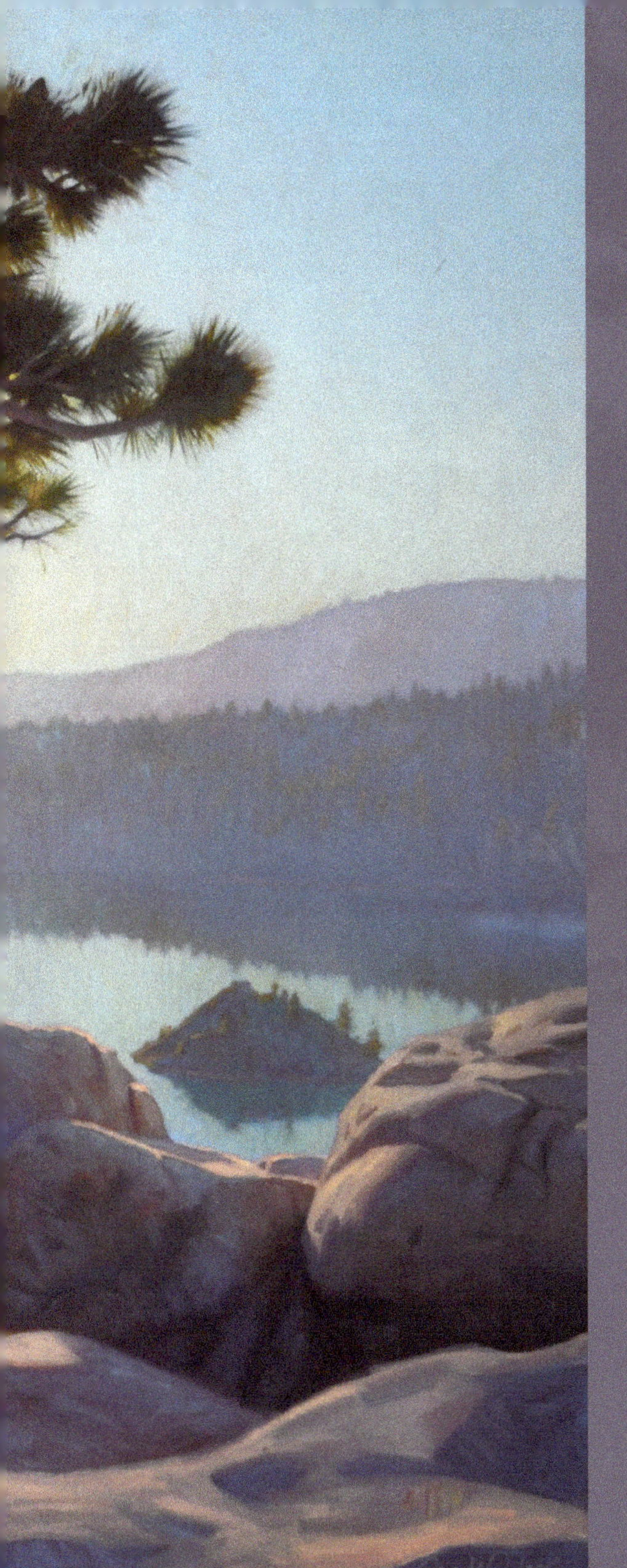

WHEN A SEED PIERCED THE EMERALD ROCK
Lake Tahoe, California | 2014 | 48 x 60" | Oil on Canvas

With God nothing is impossible. Consider a seed that
finds water amidst granite rock and grows and grows and is
finally a testament to possibility and promise. Yes and Amen.

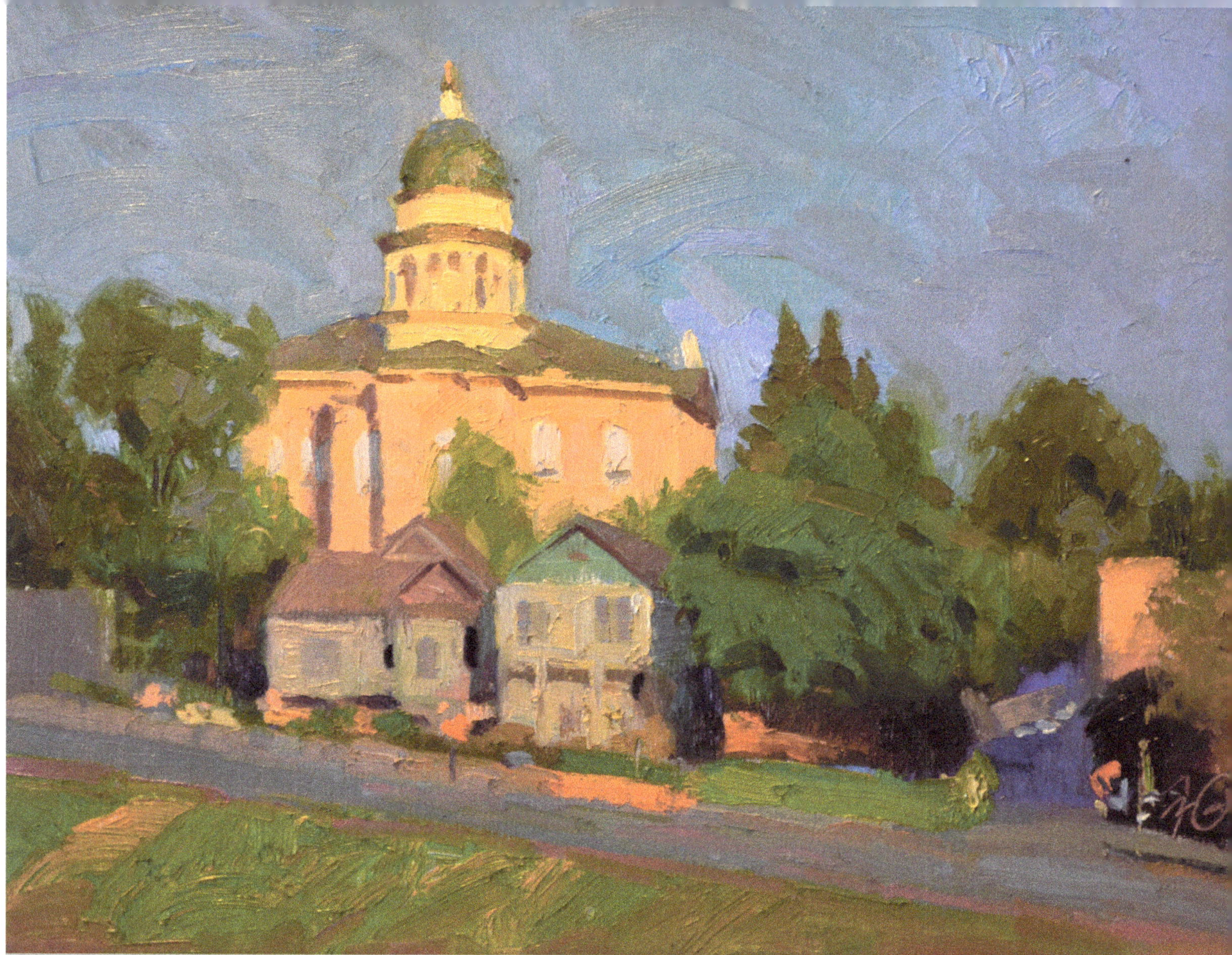

DAYS END OVER AUBURN | Auburn, California | 2014 | 9 x 12" | Oil on Panel

This painting was donated to aid the campaign of a friend running for City Council in Auburn, California.
It was painted on location on the other side of Highway 80 at the old gas station that now sells camper shells.

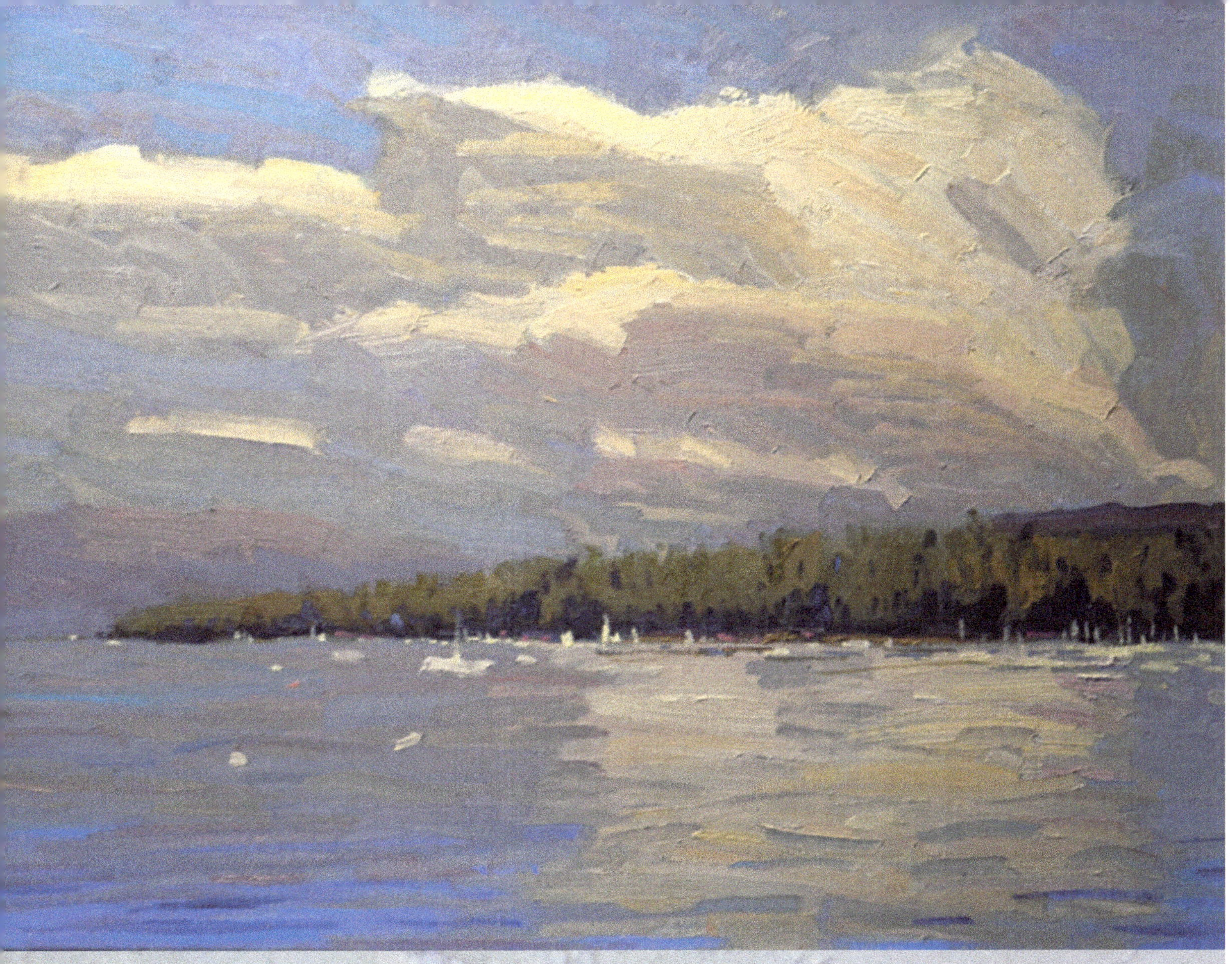

TITANS OVER TAHOE | Lake Tahoe, California | 2014 | 9 x 12" | Oil on Panel

On location, this storm cloud was like a giant spacecraft over the distant landscape. These cloud formations are always fun to paint and challenge me to think in "planes" and "color values."

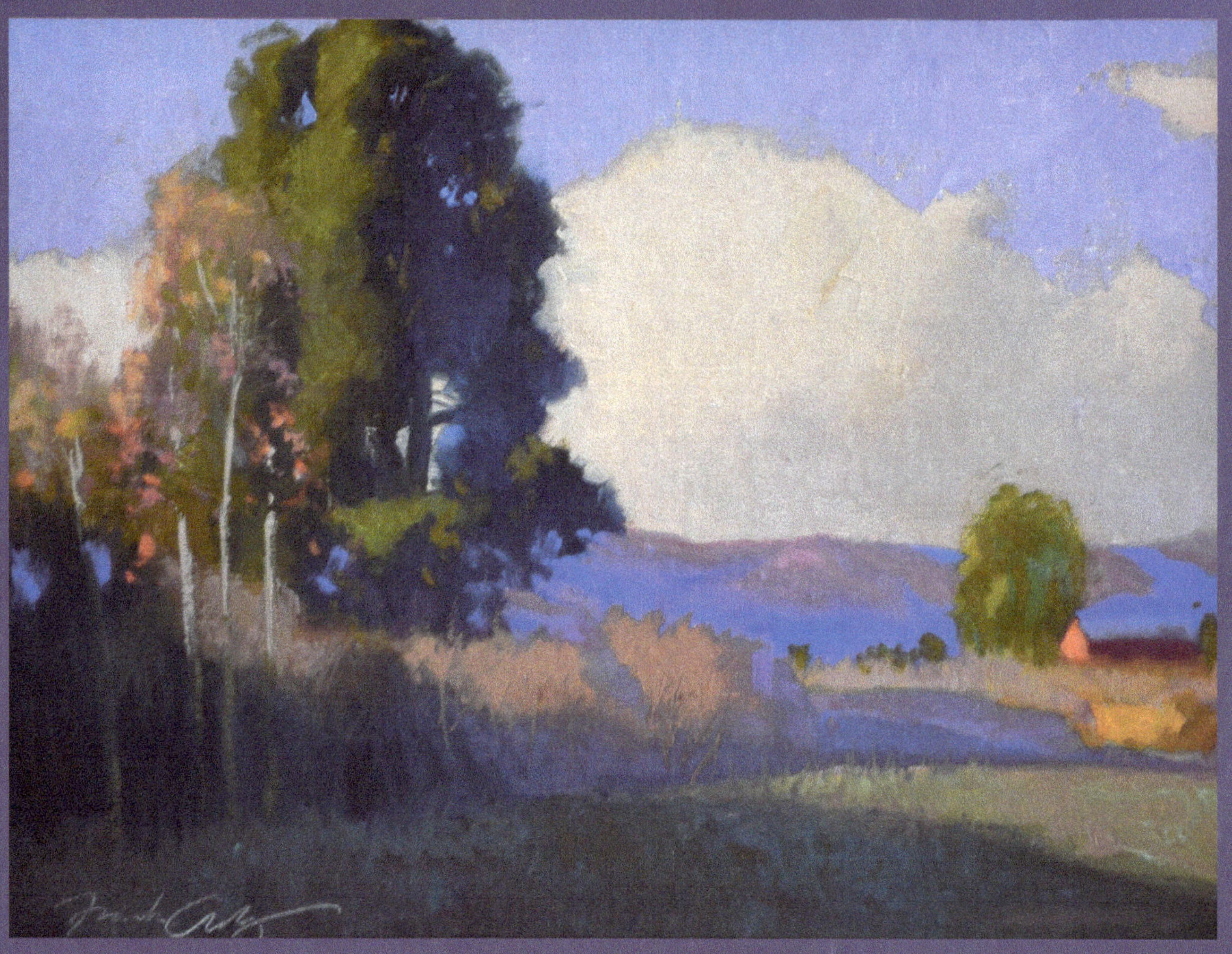

A FIELD IN SONOMA | Sonoma, California | 2014 | 9 x 12" | Oil on Panel

*Inspired while driving home through the winding roads of Sonoma, this painting is a composite
of elements that I find characteristic of the backroads around Kenwood and Glen Ellen.*

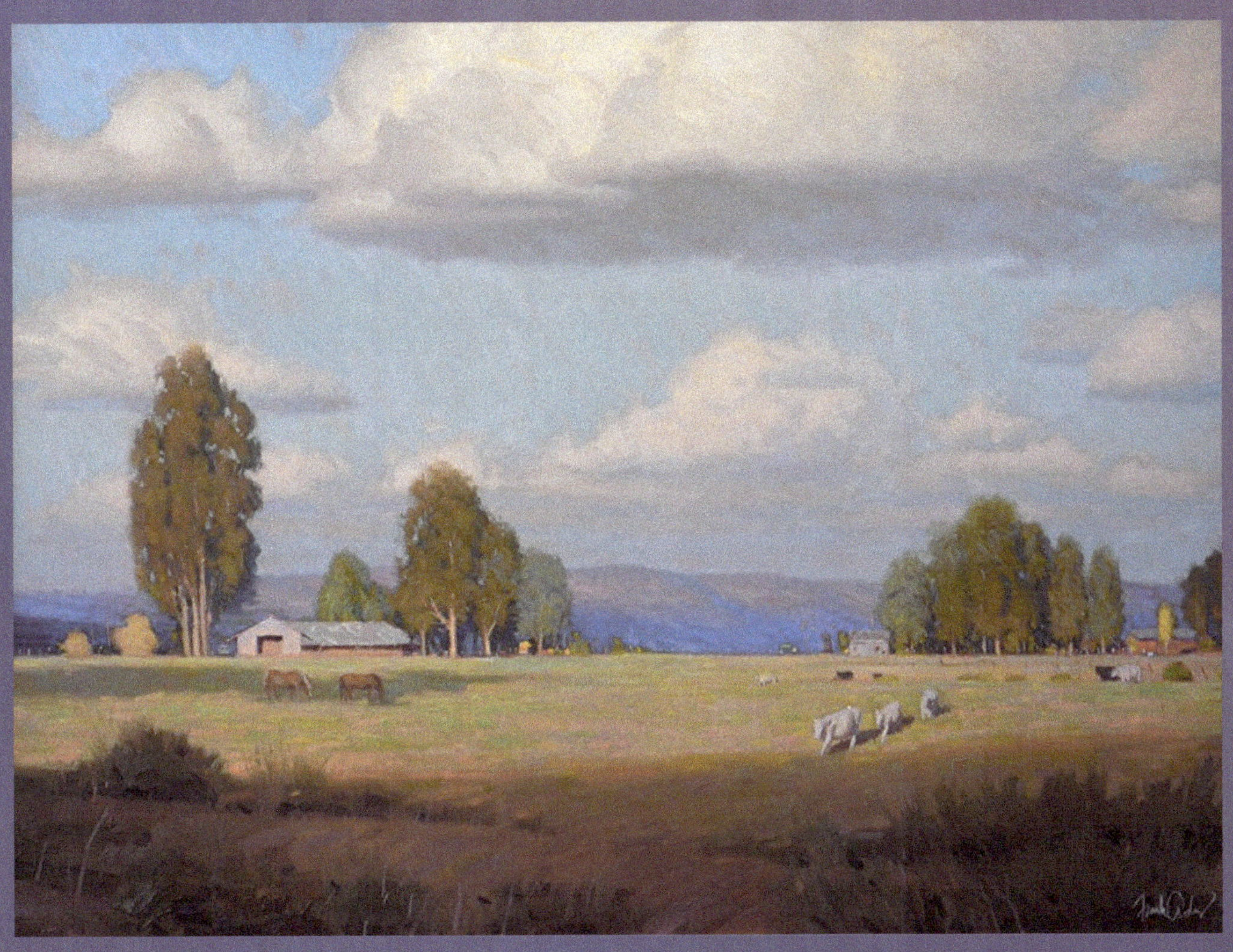

THE LAND OF PLENTY | Woodland, California | 2014 | 30 x 40" | Oil on Canvas

This painting was created for a show about art and agriculture in the greater Sacramento Valley at the Sutter County Memorial Museum in Yuba City. There is a great stretch of farmland as you drive from Lincoln to Marysville, and it reminds me of slower days when America was an agrarian country.

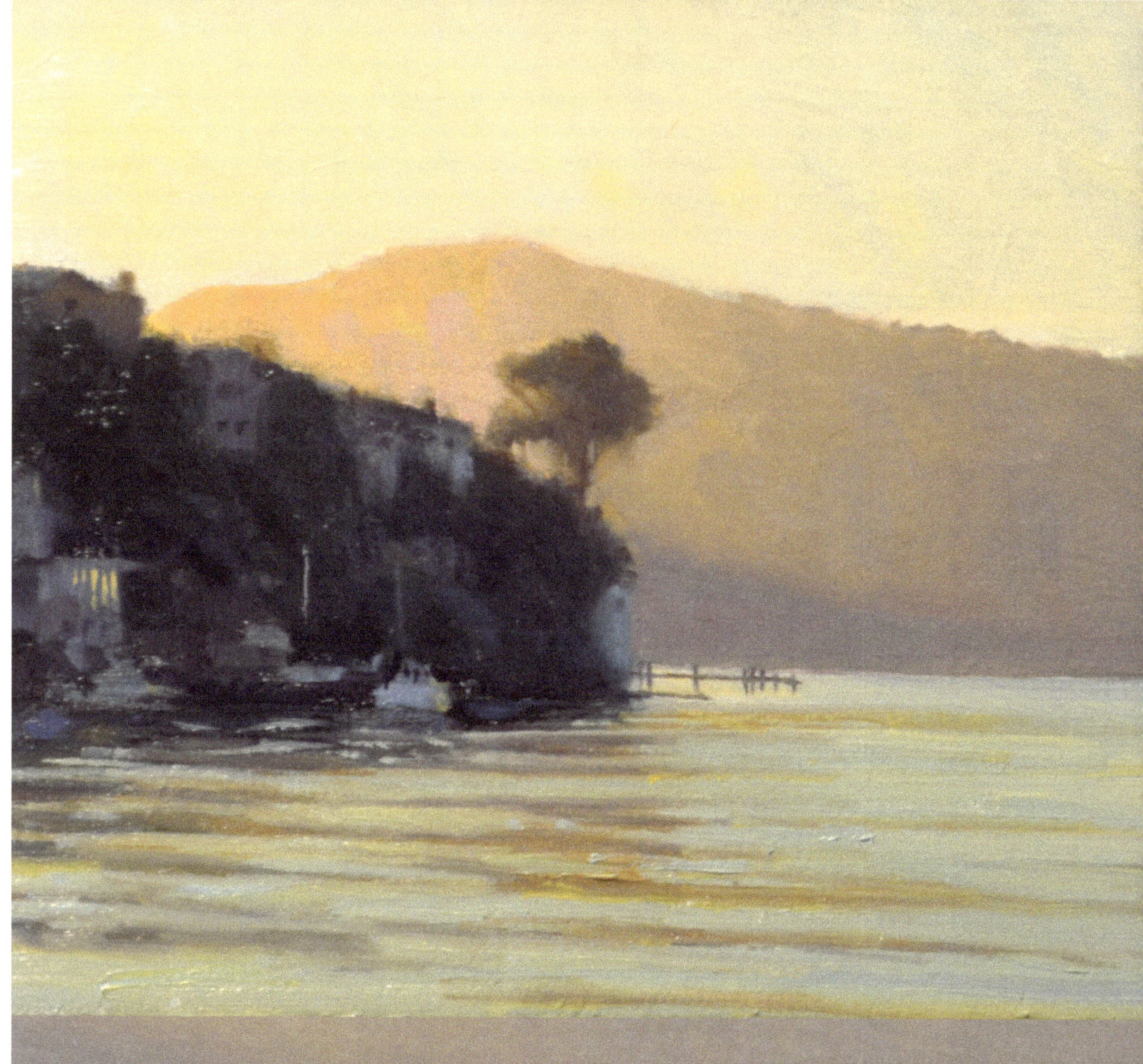

THE ANGEL AWAKES | Tiburon, California | 2014 | 7 x 14" | Oil on Panel

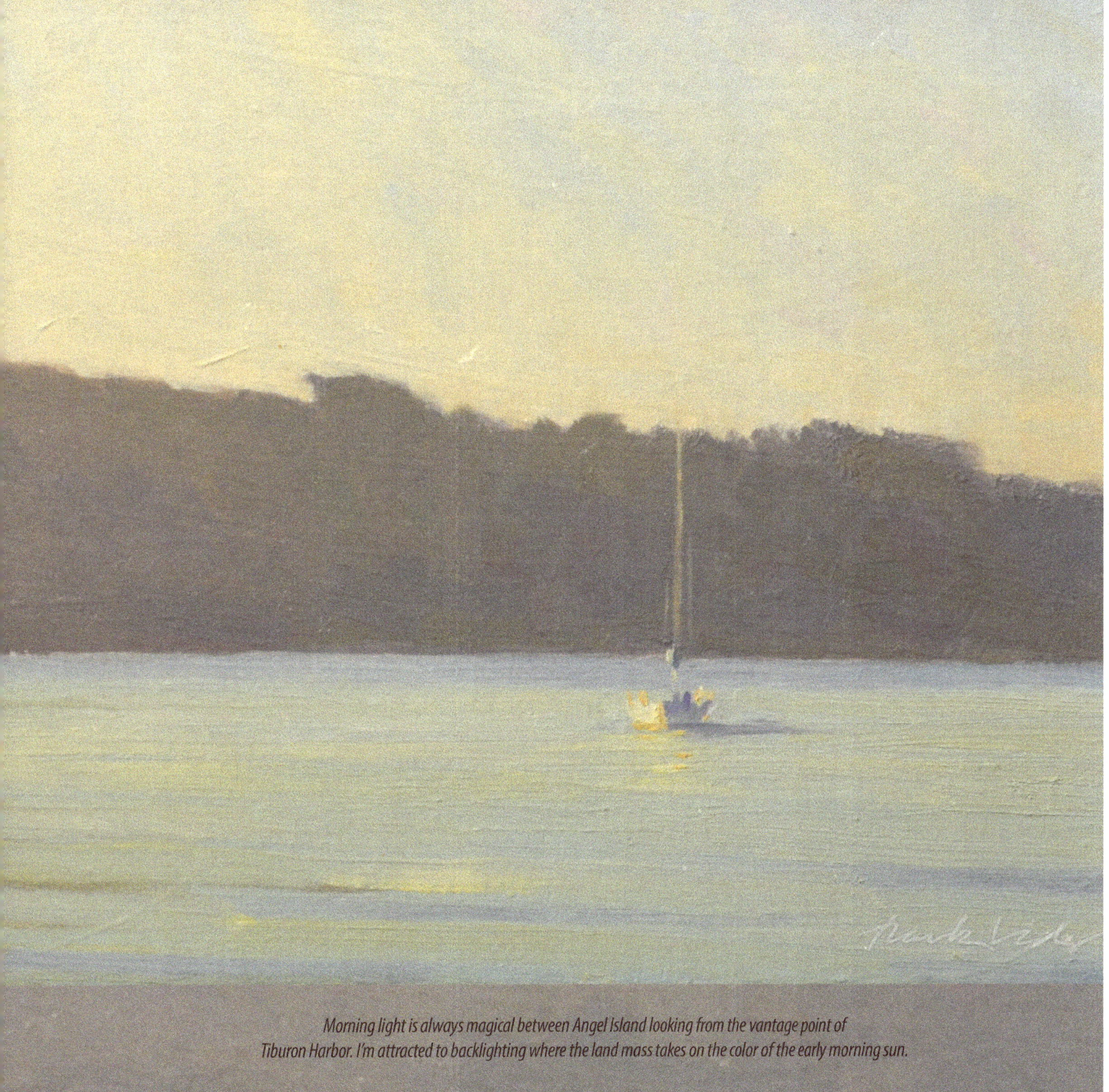

*Morning light is always magical between Angel Island looking from the vantage point of
Tiburon Harbor. I'm attracted to backlighting where the land mass takes on the color of the early morning sun.*

ON THE GOLDEN RIM
Grand Canyon, Arizona | 2014 | 16 x 20" | Oil on Canvas

Some days you can go to the Grand Canyon and it is clear and bright.
Other times the storm clouds gather and the canyon changes continually as
shadows dance across the rock temples. It is at sunset where the dark values of
the clouds create a dramatic background for the golden light
upon the surface of the canyon.

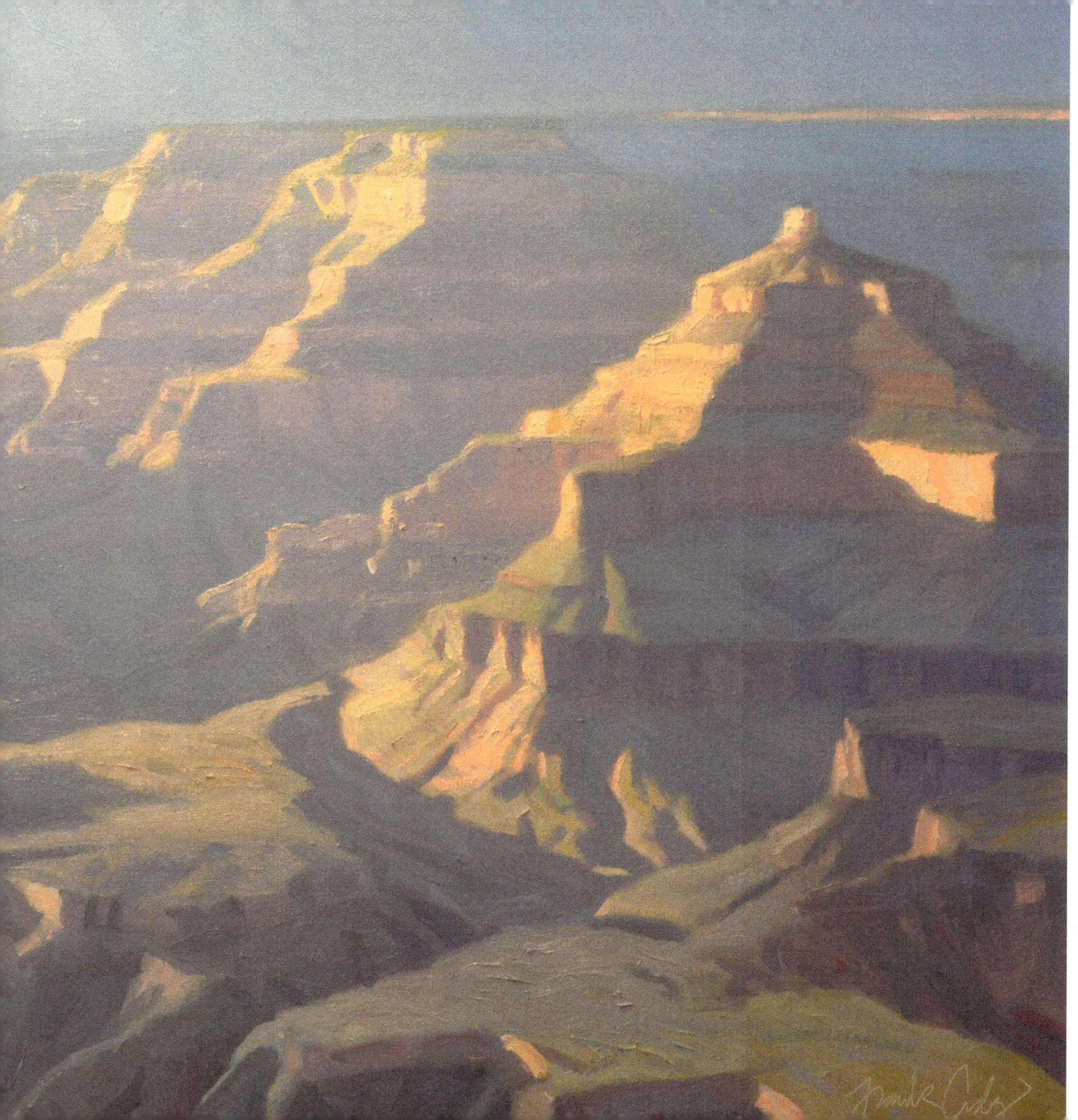

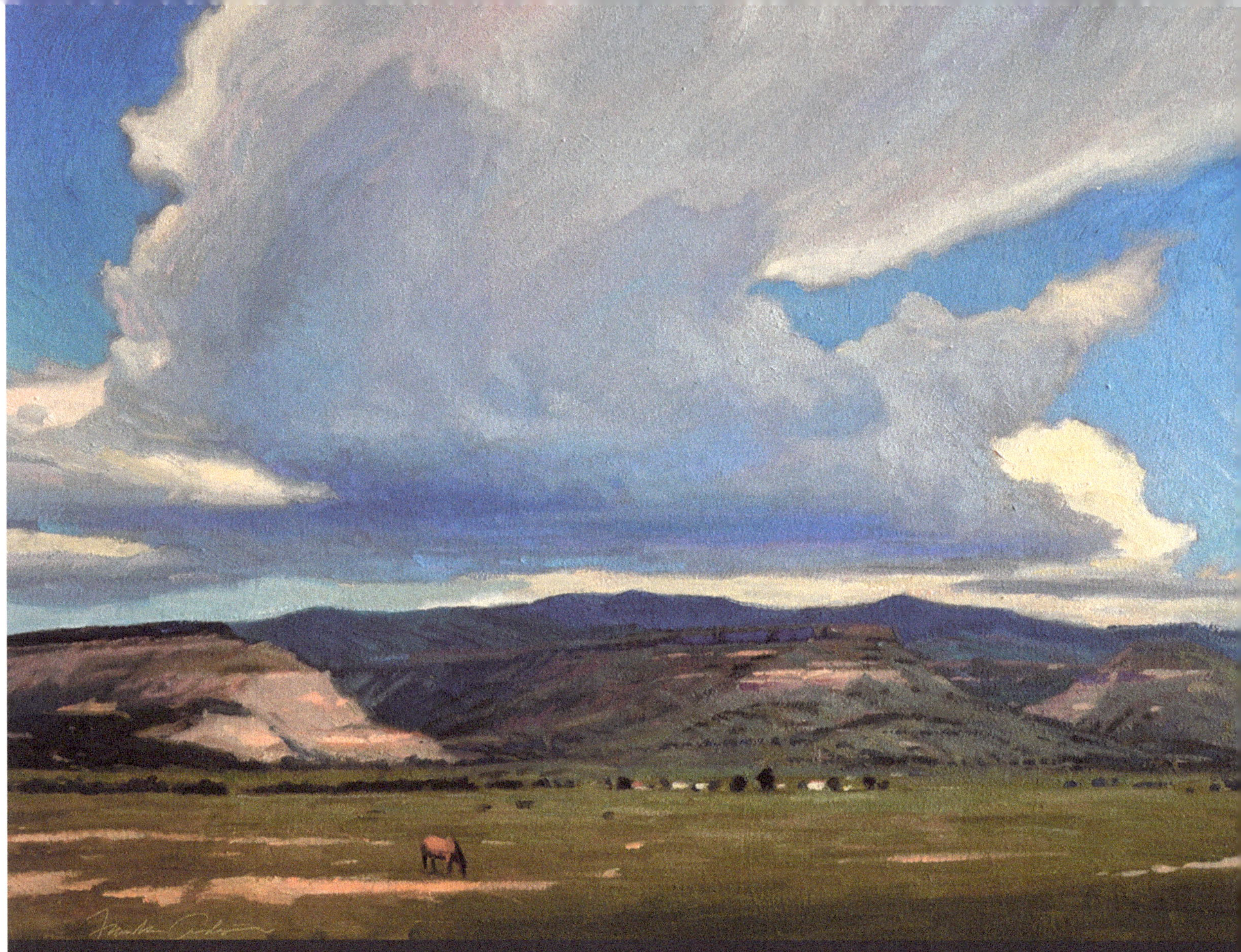

SHADOWS AND LAND | Navajo Nation, New Mexico | 2014 | 24 x 30" | Oil on Canvas

My family on my mother's side are from New Mexico. We have traveled there many times from California, in the early days by rail on the El Capitan passenger train, and now either by plane or automobile. I love driving there because the land is so different than California or Arizona. Once you drive into Gallup, the mesas greet you with their reddish hues and the landscape is punctuated with massive cloud formations during the monsoon season. It's all about the land and sky. They enchant me and create in me a strong passion to paint it.

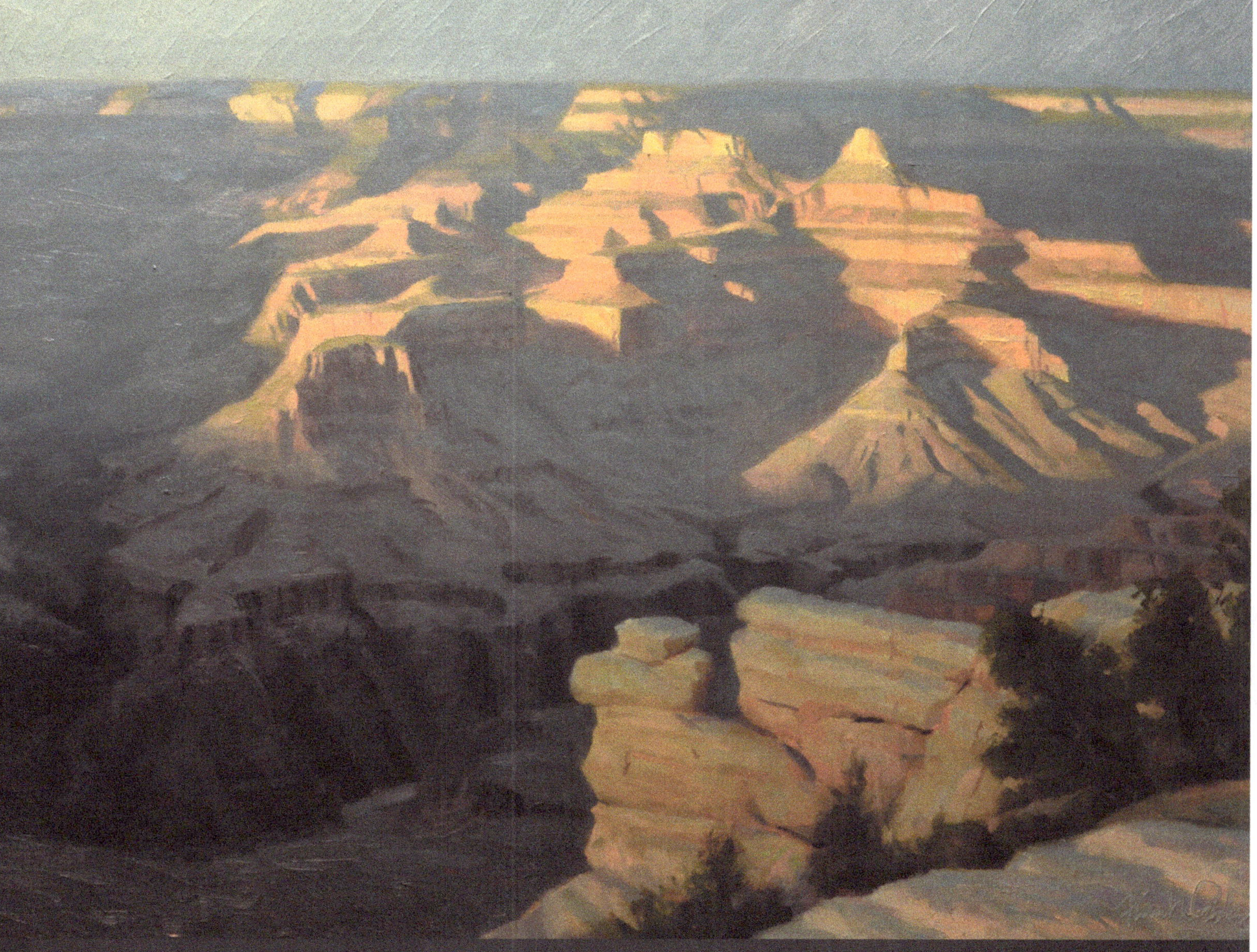

TEMPLES UPON TEMPLES | Grand Canyon, Arizona | 2014 | 16 x 20" | Oil on Canvas

I was fortunate to be able to capture the light at sunset at the Grand Canyon this day. The Rangers told us earlier it was fogged over and that you could barely see anything. Sure enough when I got there it was pretty hard to see anything. I went back to my car and fell asleep as it began to thunder and rain. I woke up about an hour later and blue sky greeted me. I ran to the rim and this is what I saw as the sun went down. It pays to rest and sleep.

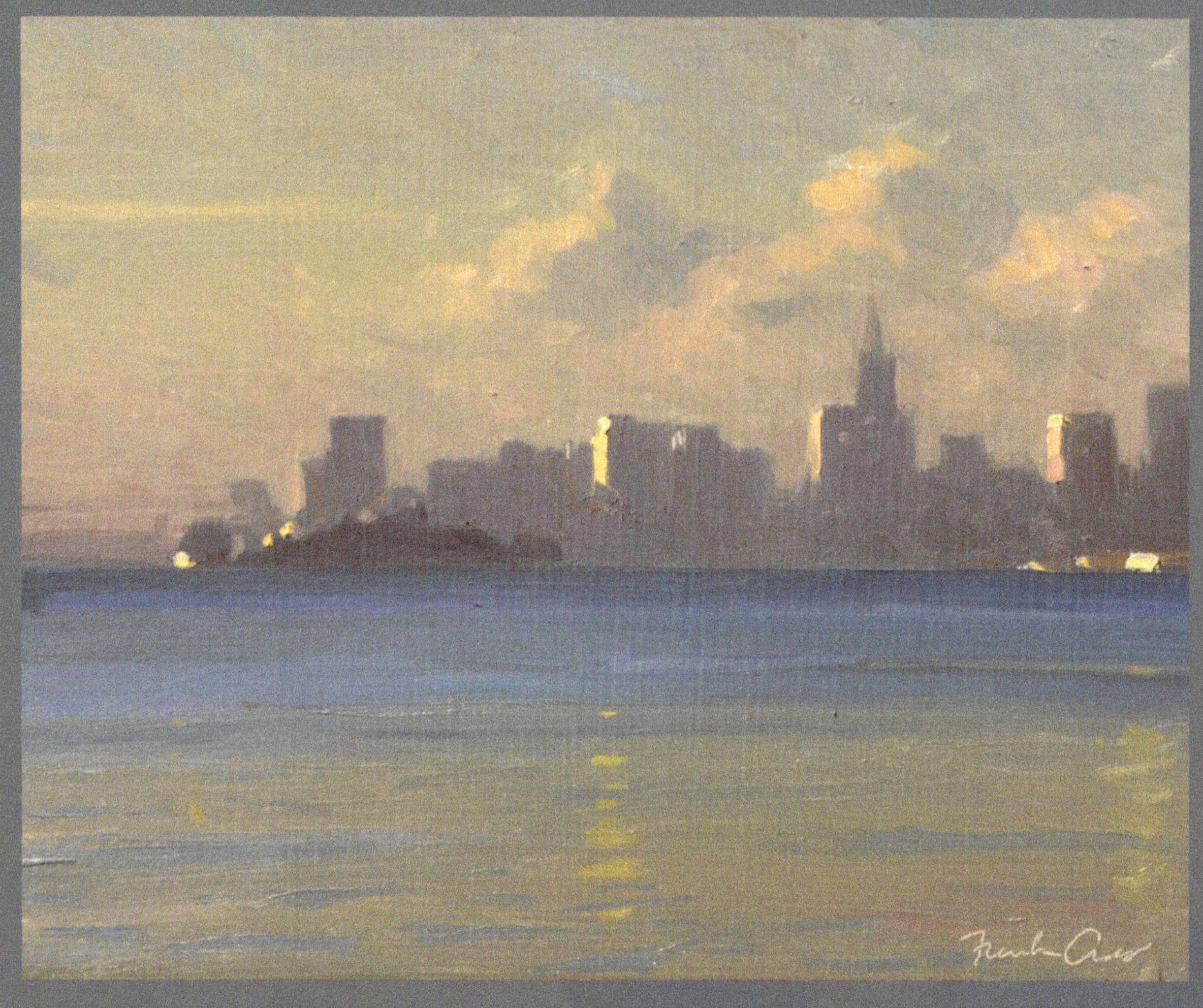

BAGHDAD BY THE BAY IN AMBER | San Francisco, California | 2014 | 6 x 6" | Oil on Panel

A nice moody piece of The City from the vantage point of Tiburon, California.

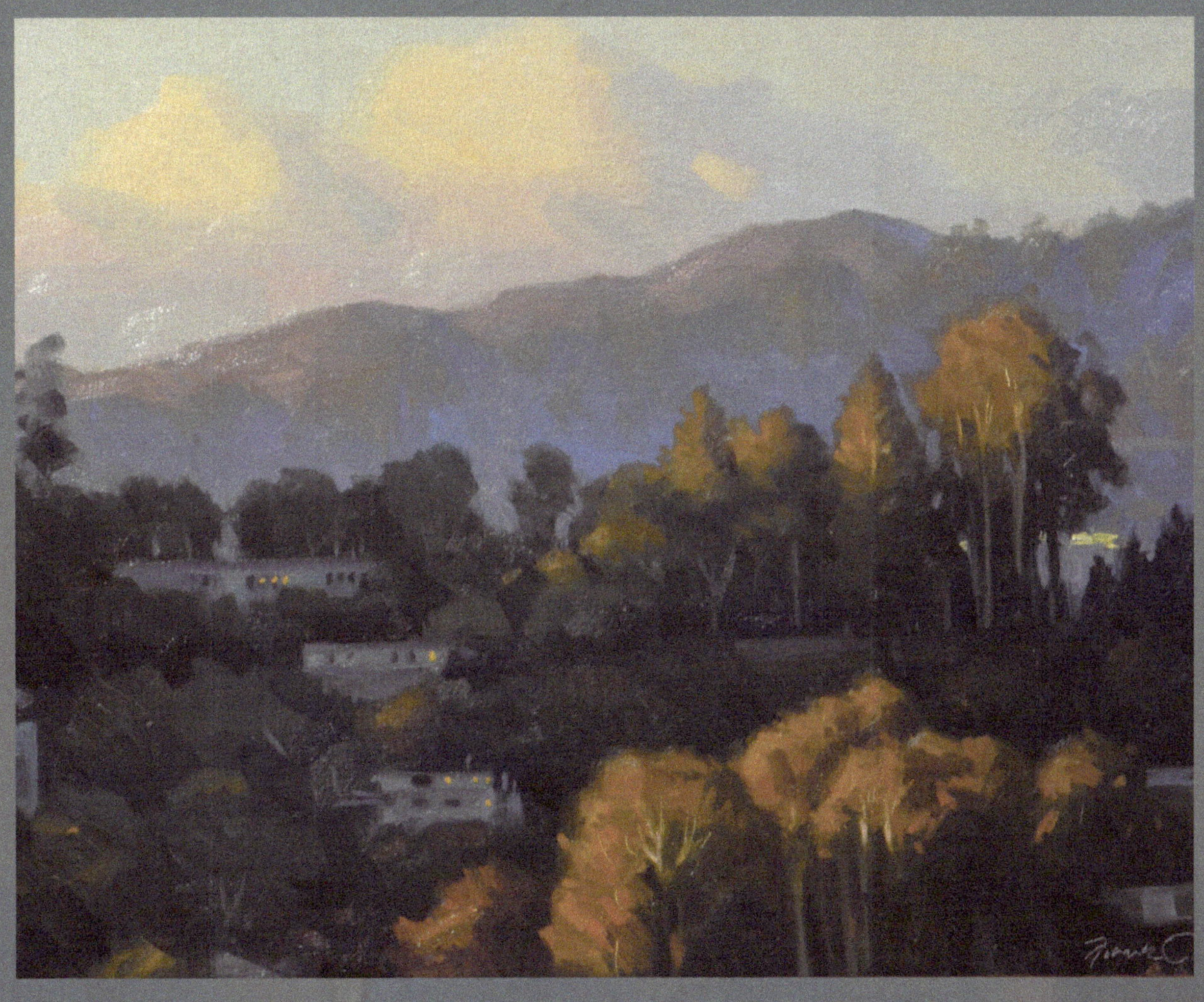

A BALMY SATURDAY IN MARIN | Tiburon, California | 2014 | 11 x 14" | Oil on Panel

My friend Frank has a great view from one of the hills above Tiburon. This is what it feels like at dusk and why people pay a steep price to live there.

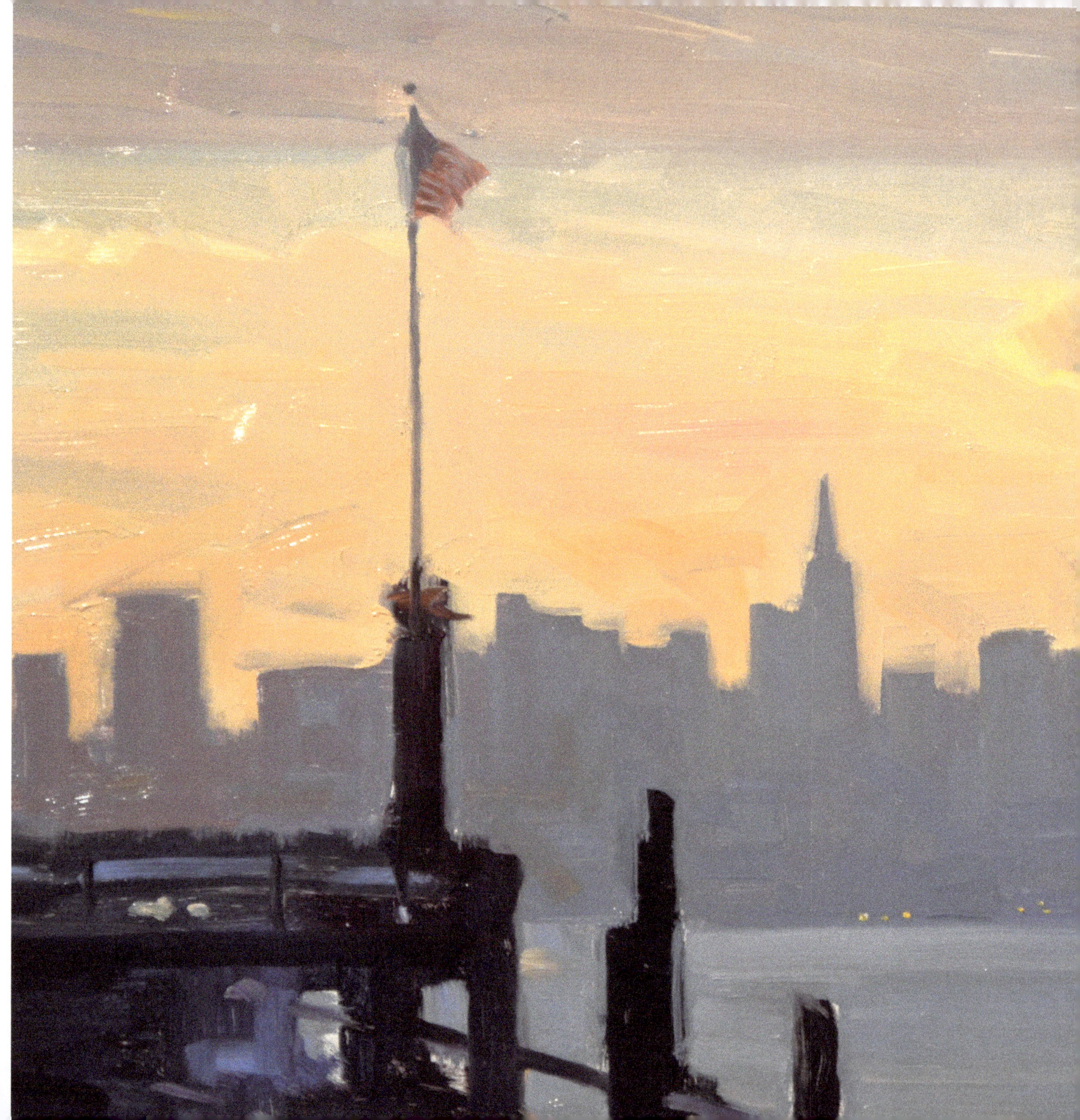

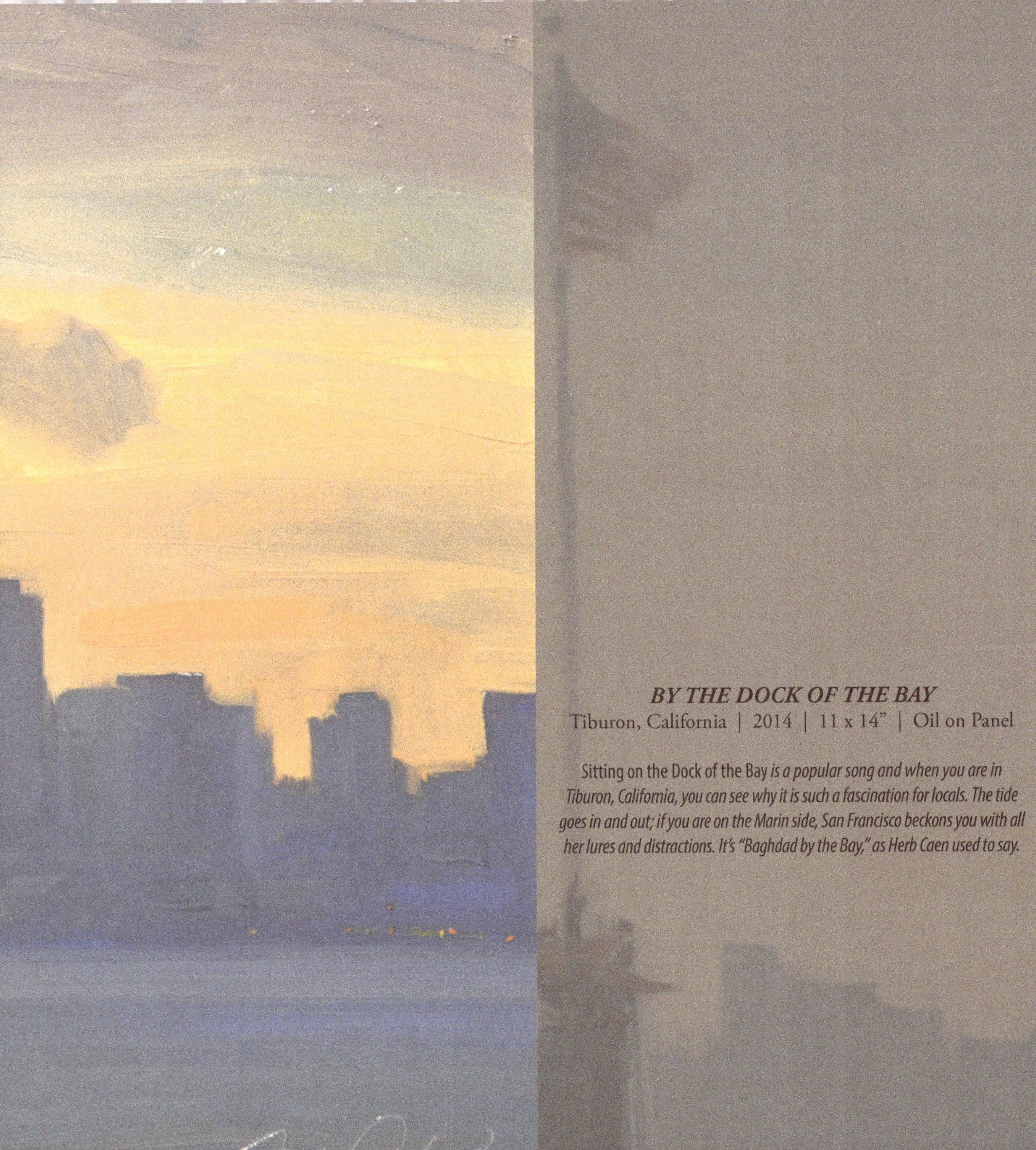

BY THE DOCK OF THE BAY
Tiburon, California | 2014 | 11 x 14" | Oil on Panel

Sitting on the Dock of the Bay *is a popular song and when you are in Tiburon, California, you can see why it is such a fascination for locals. The tide goes in and out; if you are on the Marin side, San Francisco beckons you with all her lures and distractions. It's "Baghdad by the Bay," as Herb Caen used to say.*

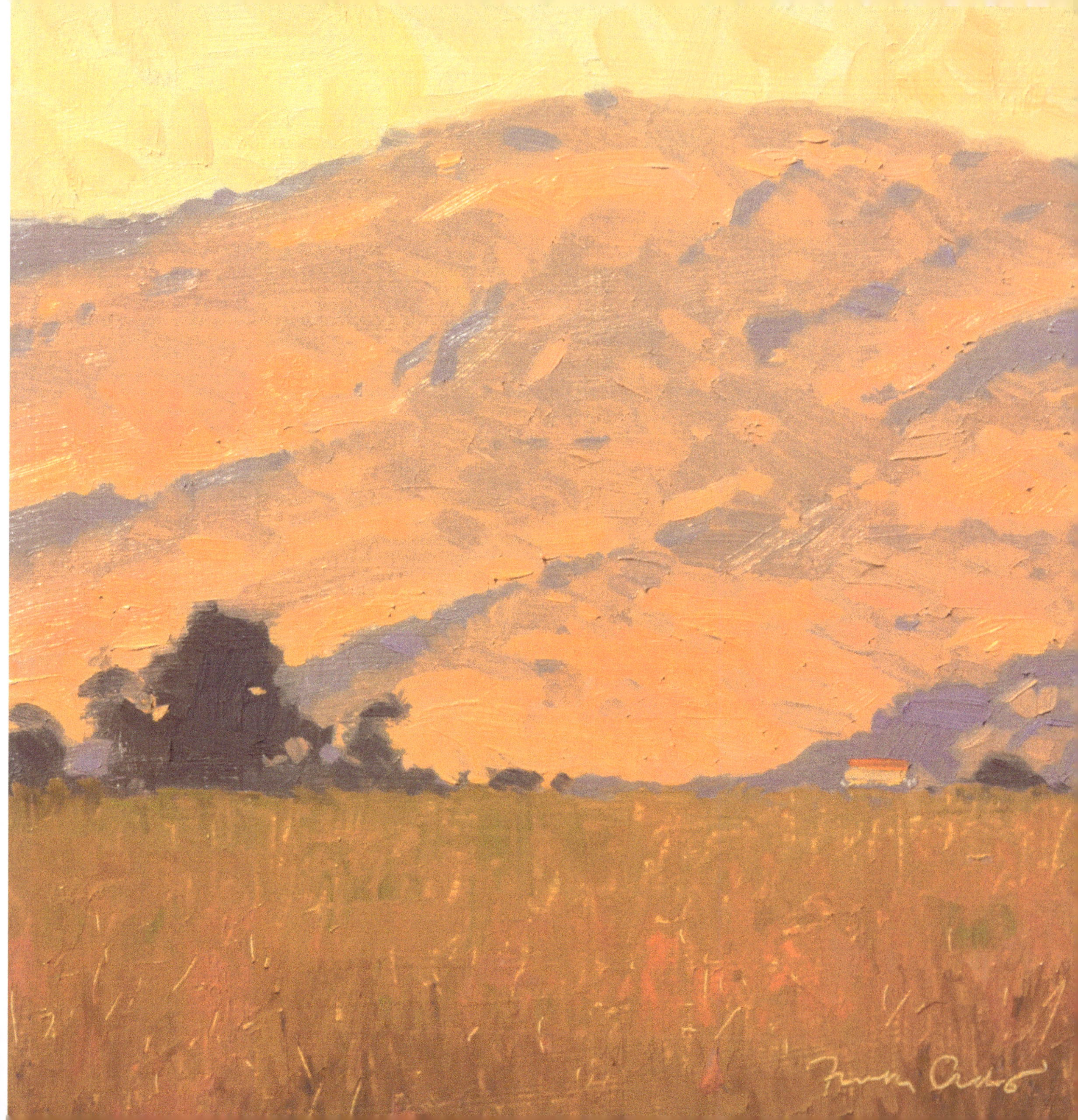

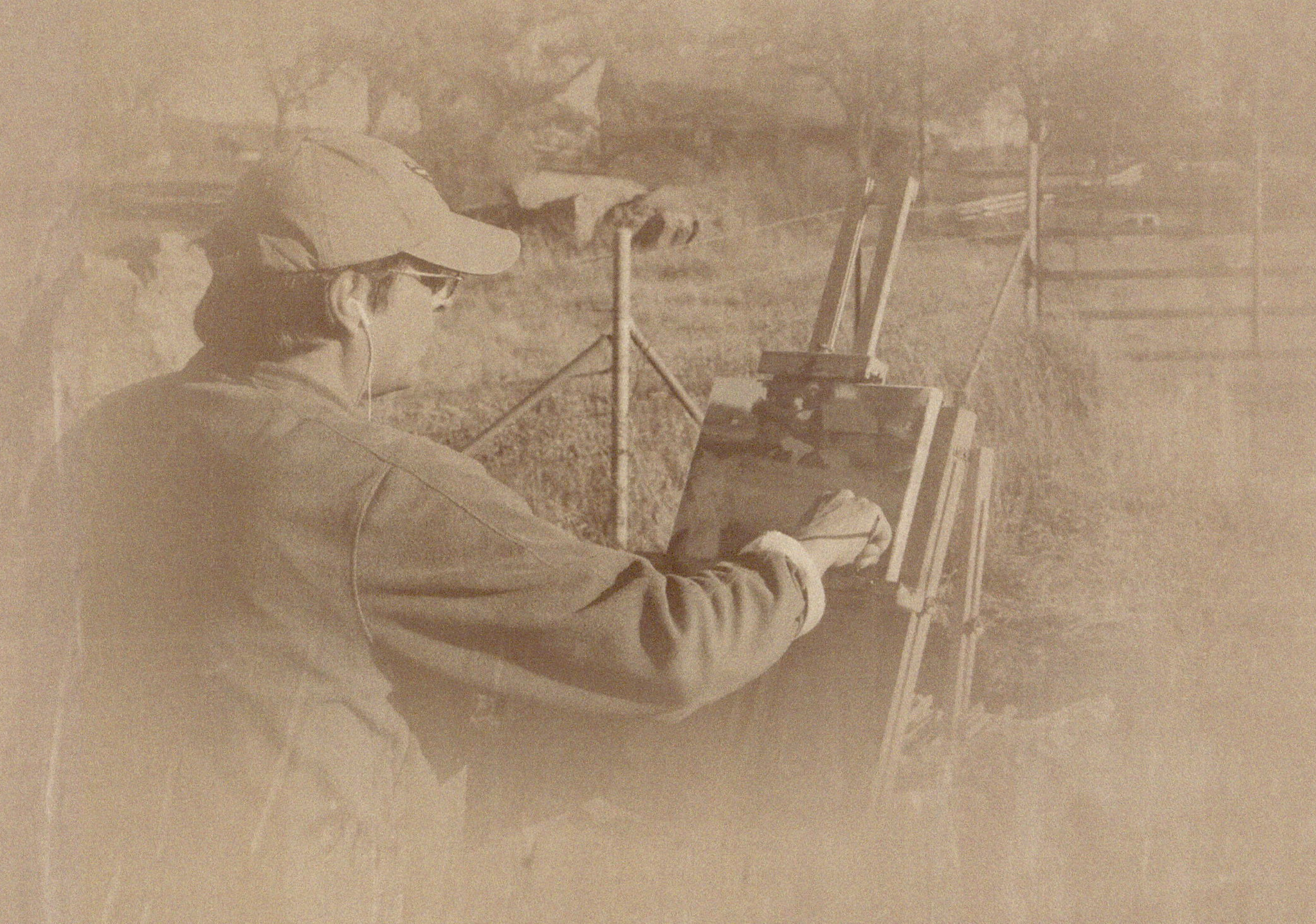

GOLDEN NAPA | Napa, California | 2014 | 6 x 6" | Oil on Panel

This is a tiny painting. One fall evening I was stuck in traffic on State Route 12 when I saw this light effect on the far hills of the Silverado Trail. This is just one of the outstanding attractions that greet visitors to California's premier wine country.

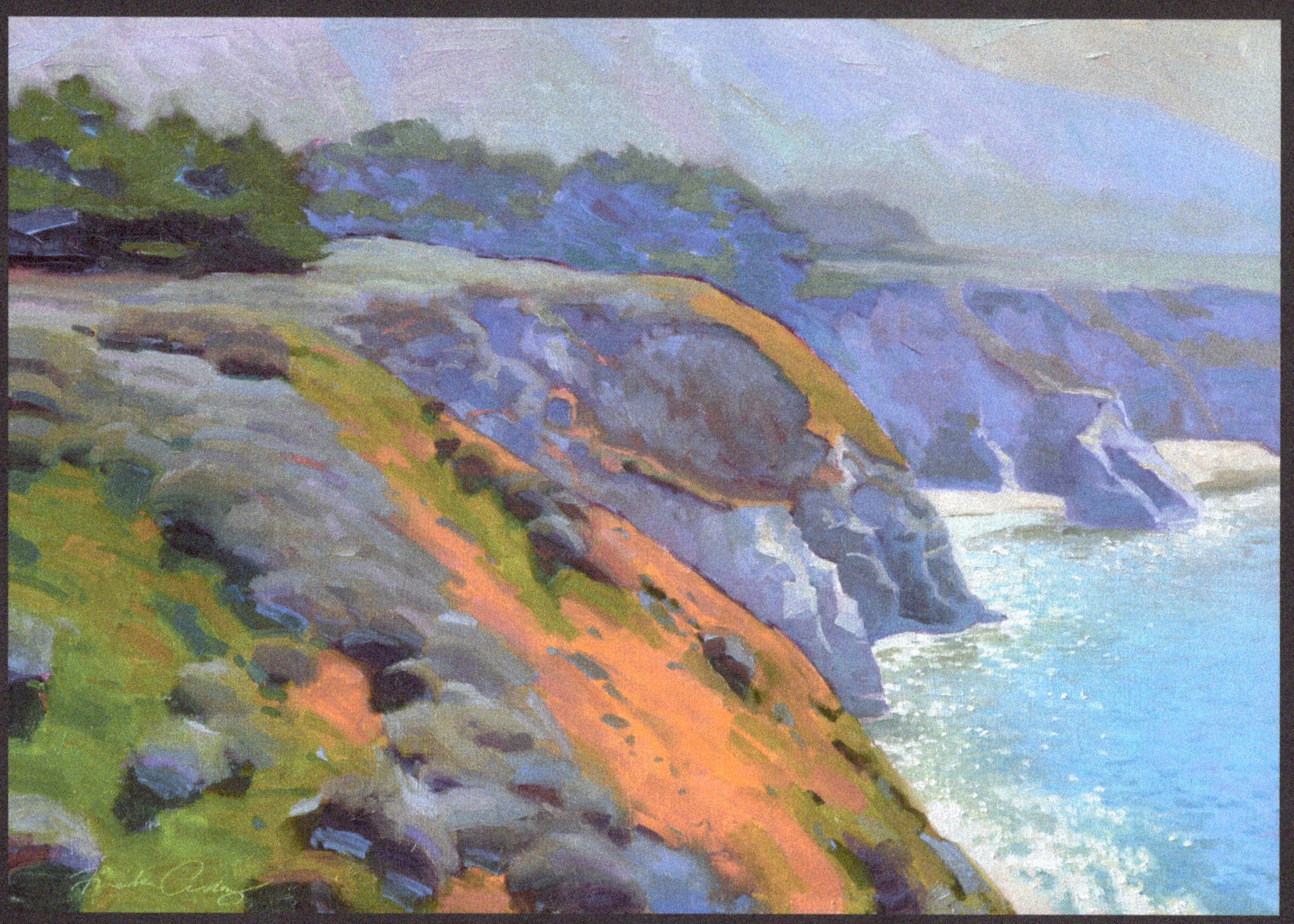

BURNING LIKE A FABULOUS ROMAN CANDLE | Big Sur, California | 2015 | 16 x 20" | Oil on Panel

Taken from a line by Jack Kerouac, the ice plant on the cliffs of Garrapata Beach seem
to be on fire as they turn to orange and red during summer. You really have to see it first-hand to
believe the brightness of those succulents as they shield the sandy cliffs like native robes.
They are incredible complements to the azure blue of the ocean.

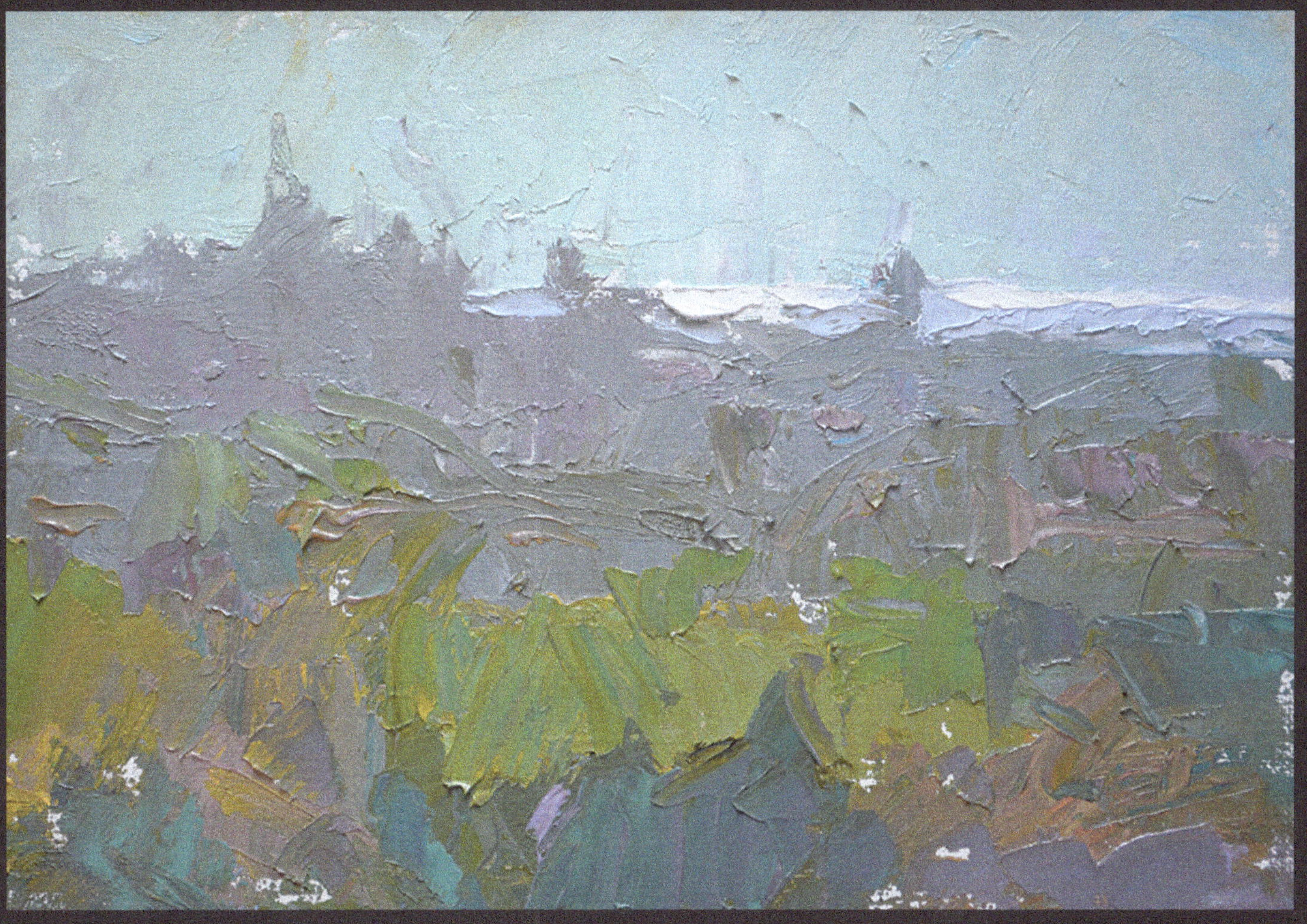

RAILHEAD 1 | Auburn, California | 2014 | 5 x 7" | Oil on Panel

*In early 2014, I did a series of experimental outdoor sketches overlooking Railhead Park
looking north across Auburn toward the snow-capped Sierra. I love the loose feel
and spontaneity that this tiny piece embodies.*

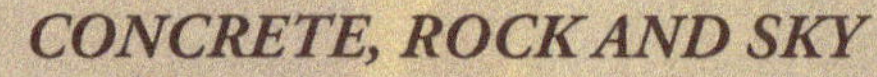

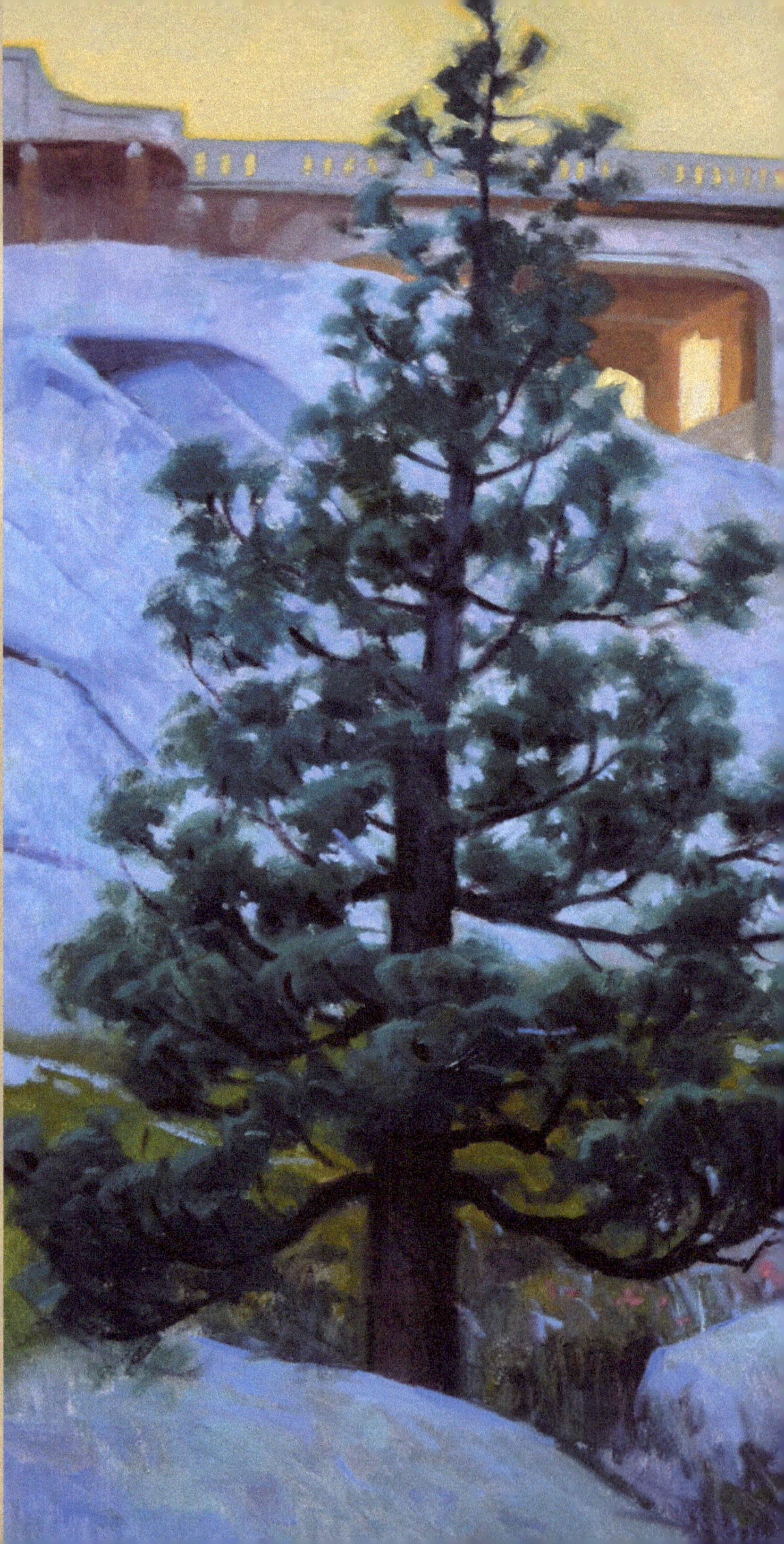

CONCRETE, ROCK AND SKY
Donner Lake, California | 2015 | 48 x 60" | Oil

*This was one of the featured paintings at my One Man Show
at the John Natsoulas Gallery in 2015. The bridge spans a section
along a highway above Donner Lake. Many concrete bridges
in this style can also be seen along the Pacific Coast Highway in
California. The Donner Lake area is famous among locals for rock
climbing, hiking and cycling adventures. It's an honor that
my local councilman owns this painting.*

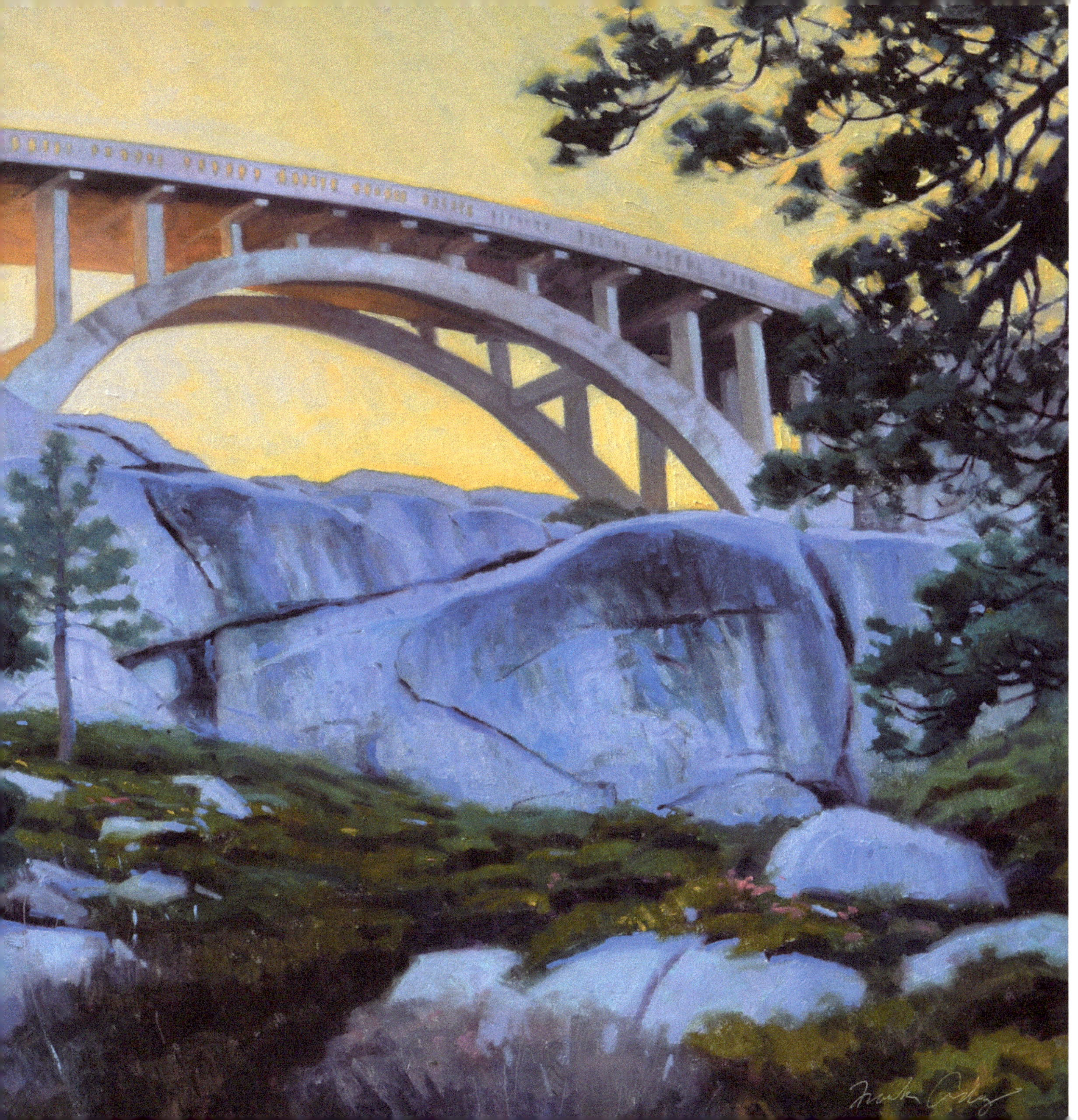

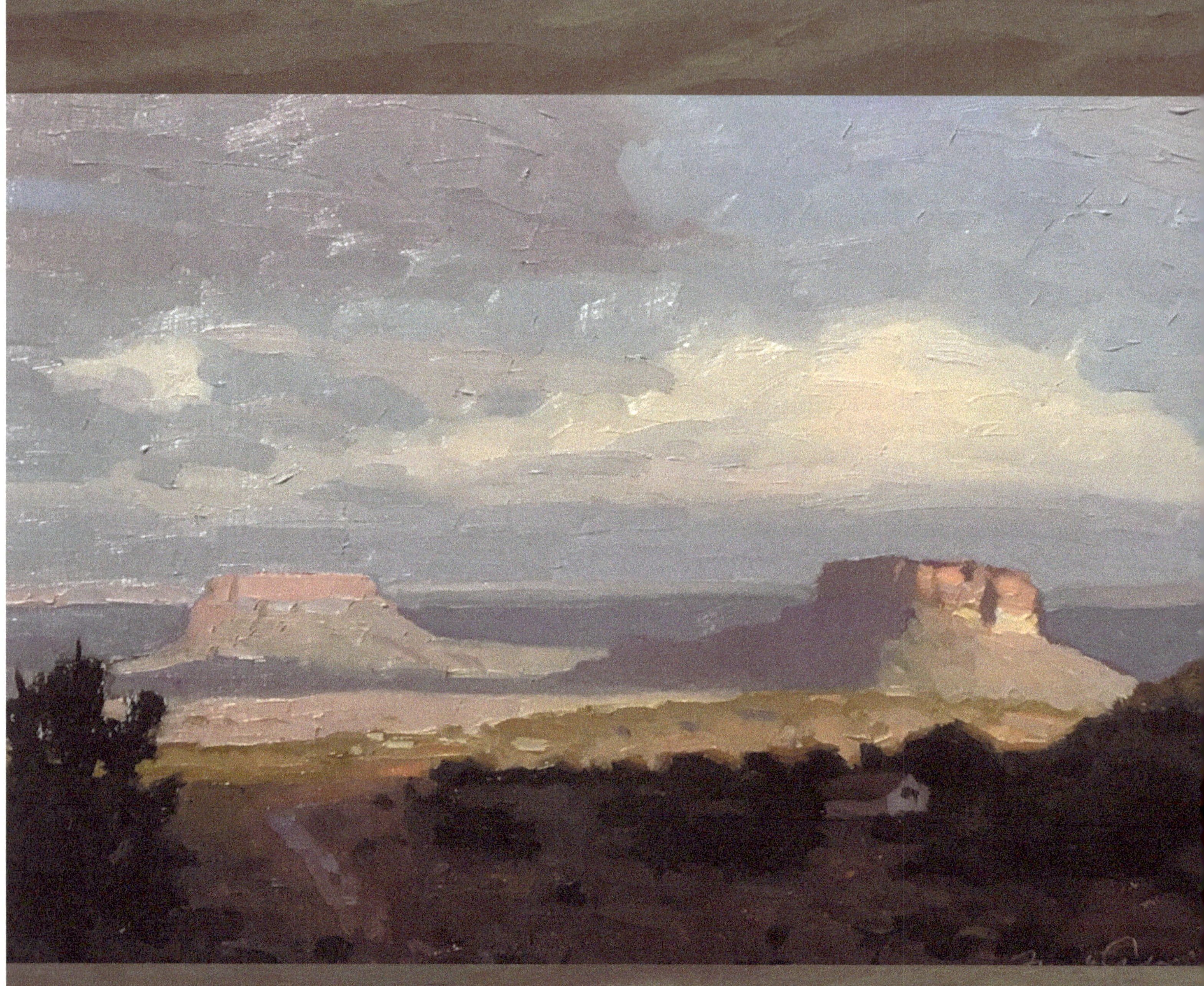

TWO GREY HILLS | Toadlena, New Mexico | 2016 | 8 x 10" | Oil on Panel

Two Grey Hills is famous for a certain Navajo Rug Design. The Navajo women of Toadlena New Mexico are famous for their
unique designs, and when I visited the trading post in 2014, the light mesmerized me as I spoke with Mark Winters,
owner of the trading post and authority on Navajo weavings.

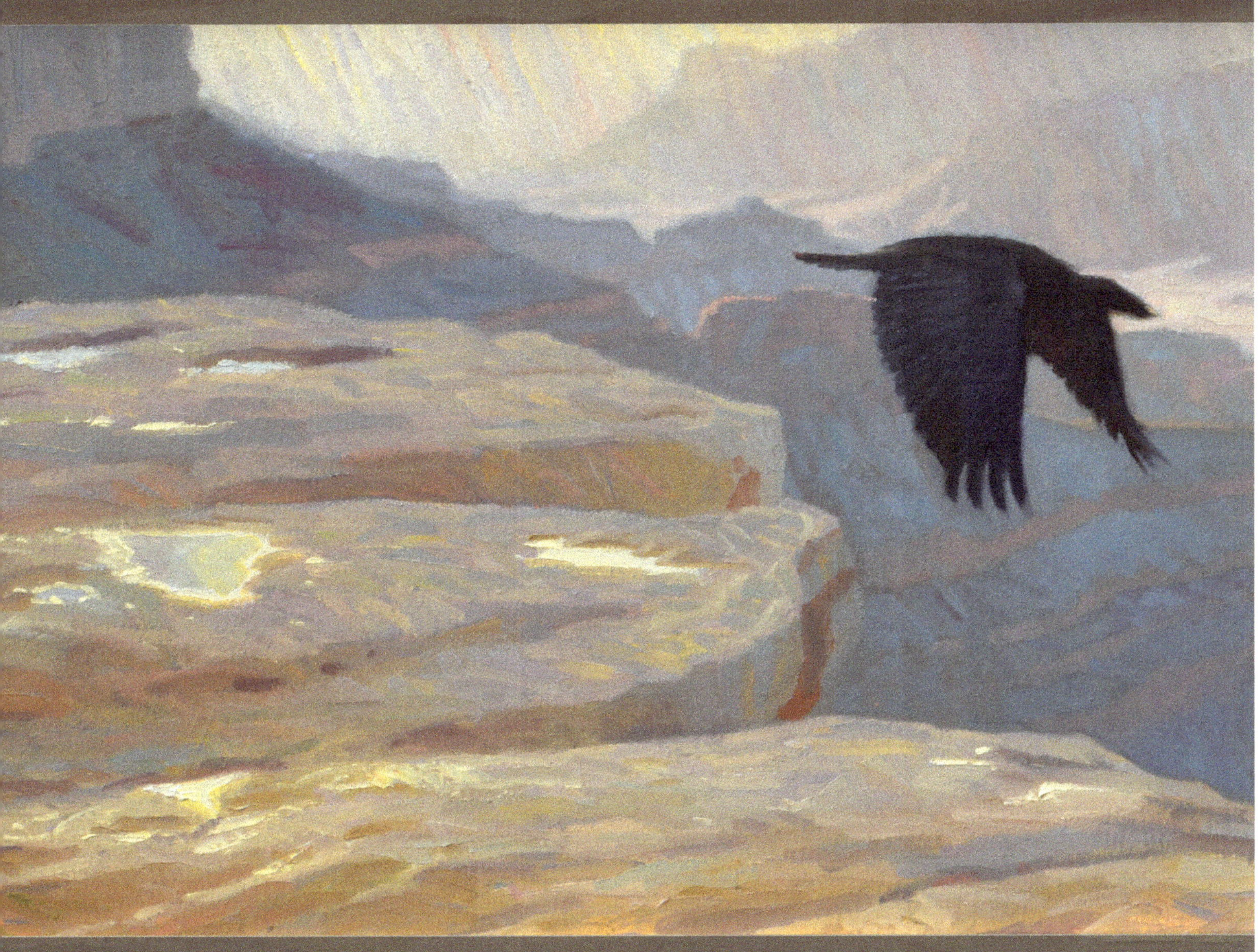

THE WASHING | Grand Canyon, Arizona | 2014 | 14 x 18" | Oil on Canvas

Right after a hard rain at the Grand Canyon, puddles were the only remnants of the cleansing storm. There was a raven that was drinking from the puddles of water and then, without warning, flew away. I marveled at how the light from the sky was reflected by these small pools.

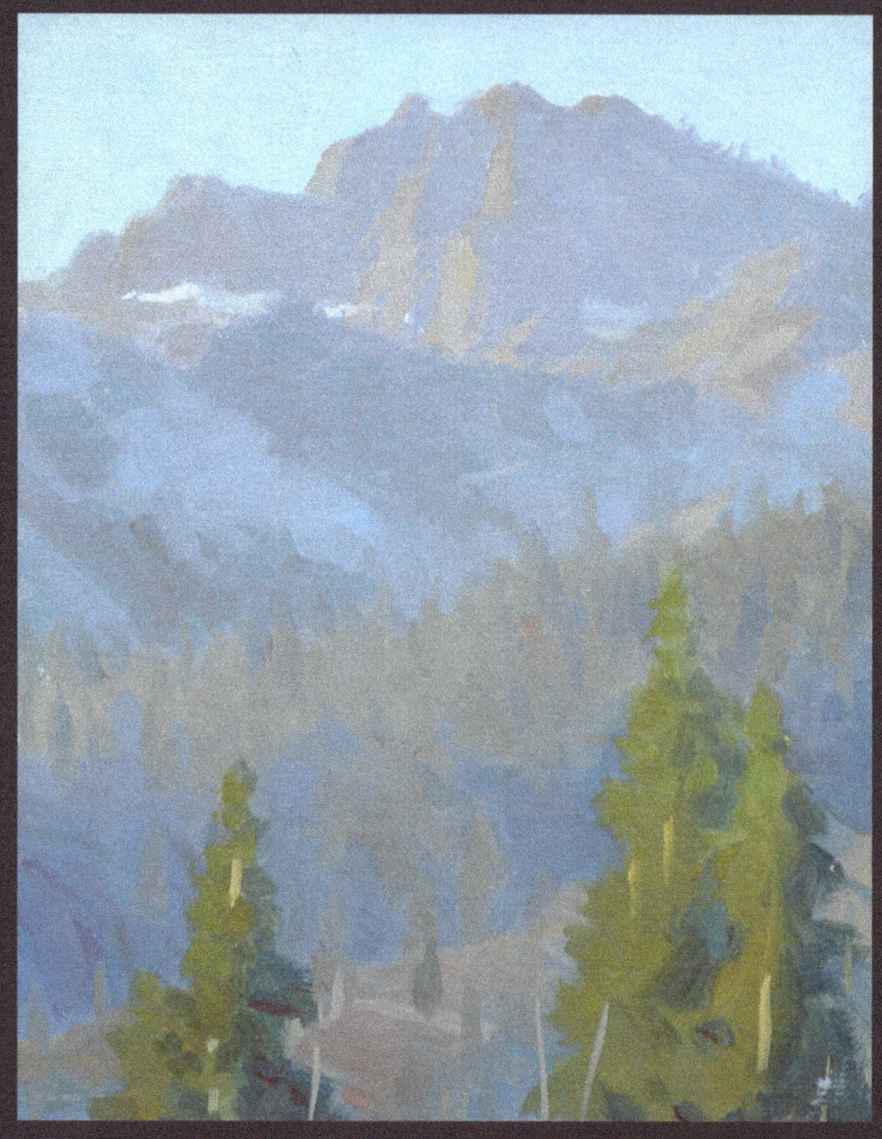

SIERRA BUTTES AT DAYBREAK | Sierra Butte, California | 2009 | 12 x 9" | Oil on Panel

It was oh so cold in the morning, and the light was clear when I painted this small sketch.
My vision of capturing light and a myth-like view of the land was taking shape. Selecting the right view
and time of day was becoming key to making an iconic statement. This view is above Packard Lake.

SIDE OF BUTTE | Sierra Butte, California | 2010 | 7 x 5" | Oil on Panel

*Painted on a journey to the Sierra Buttes, this field study sketch is a view from
Sardine Lake. Every sketch should have a goal and reason for painting. This study was
about capturing the greys, blues and violets on the Butte face.*

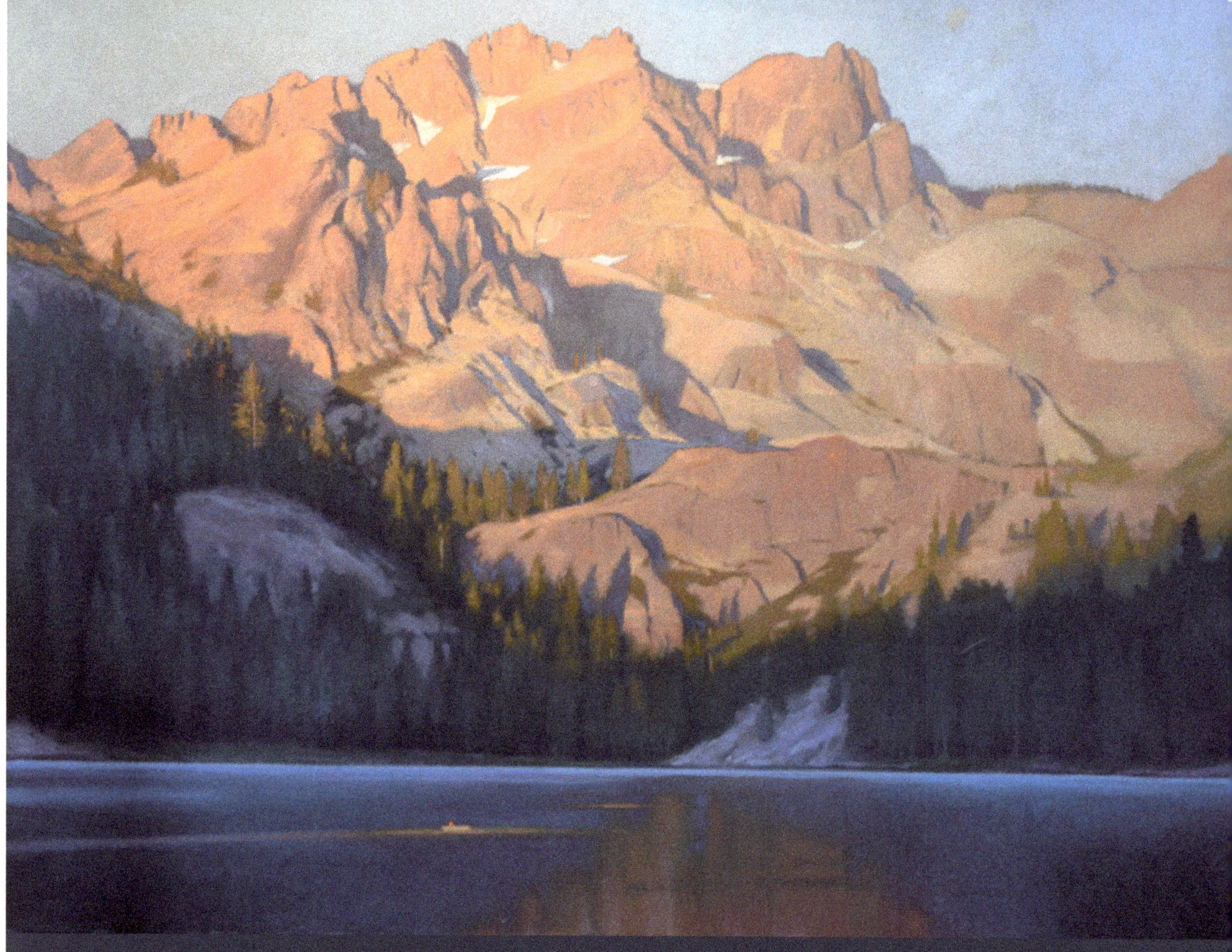

SARDINE LAKE | Sardine Lake, California | 2011 | 30 x 40" | Oil on Canvas

*I was not quite finished with this painting when an art patron walked into my studio and just had to have it.
She made me an offer I could not refuse, as she had wonderful memories looking at the Sierra Buttes above Sardine Lake.
She loved the fisherman beginning his morning catch. This painting was a turning point of translating all of
my small sketches on location to make an important statement of this landmark.*

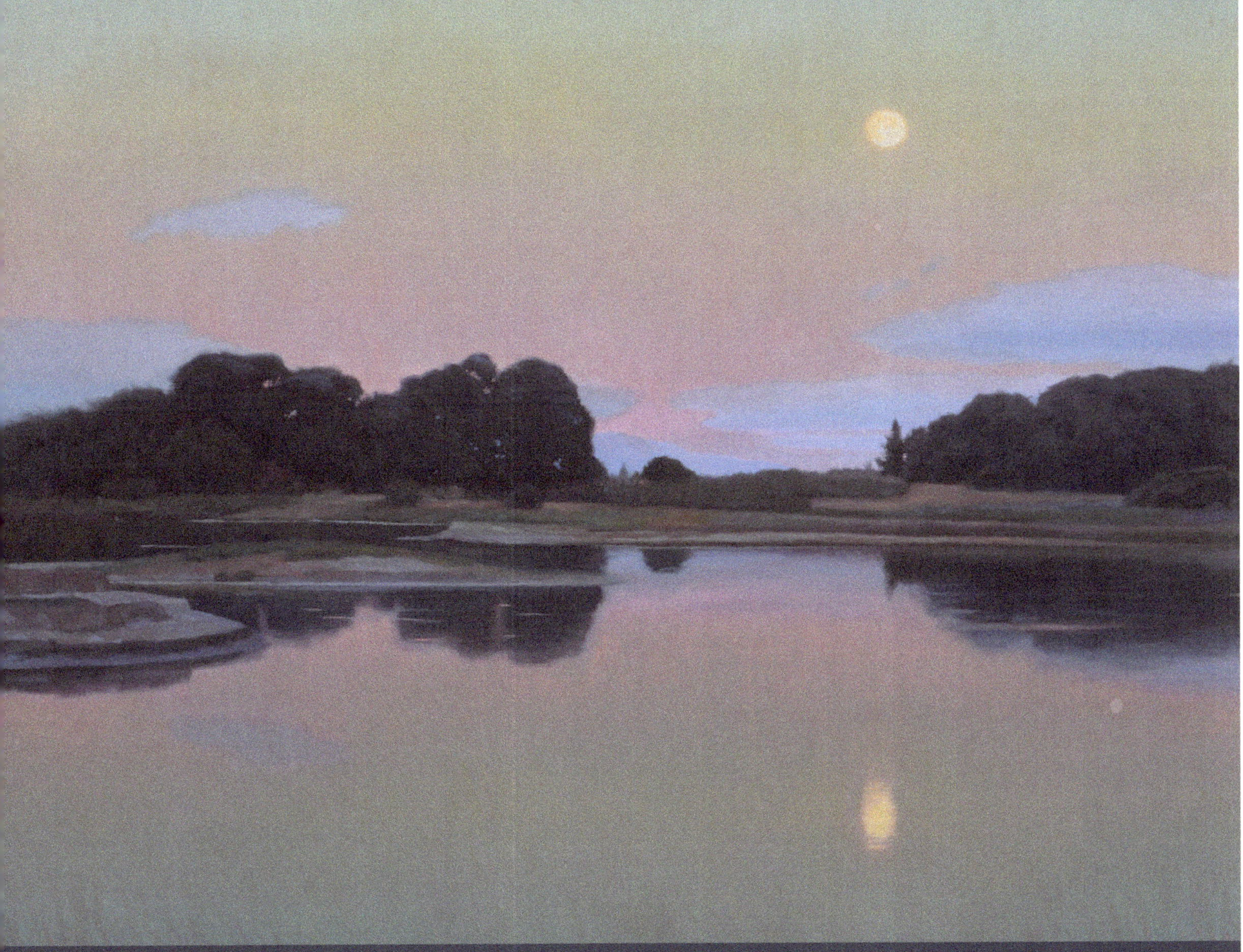

MY HEART DID A LARKSPUR LANDING | Larkspur Landing, California | 2014 | 48 x 60" | Oil on Canvas

I was driving home from a day visiting my friend in Tiburon when I noticed the moon rise
over the bay looking toward Point San Quentin. I turned off the exit in Larkspur Landing
and took several photographs and made mental notes of how wonderful the light felt.
I painted this in a couple days with the memory still fresh in my mind.

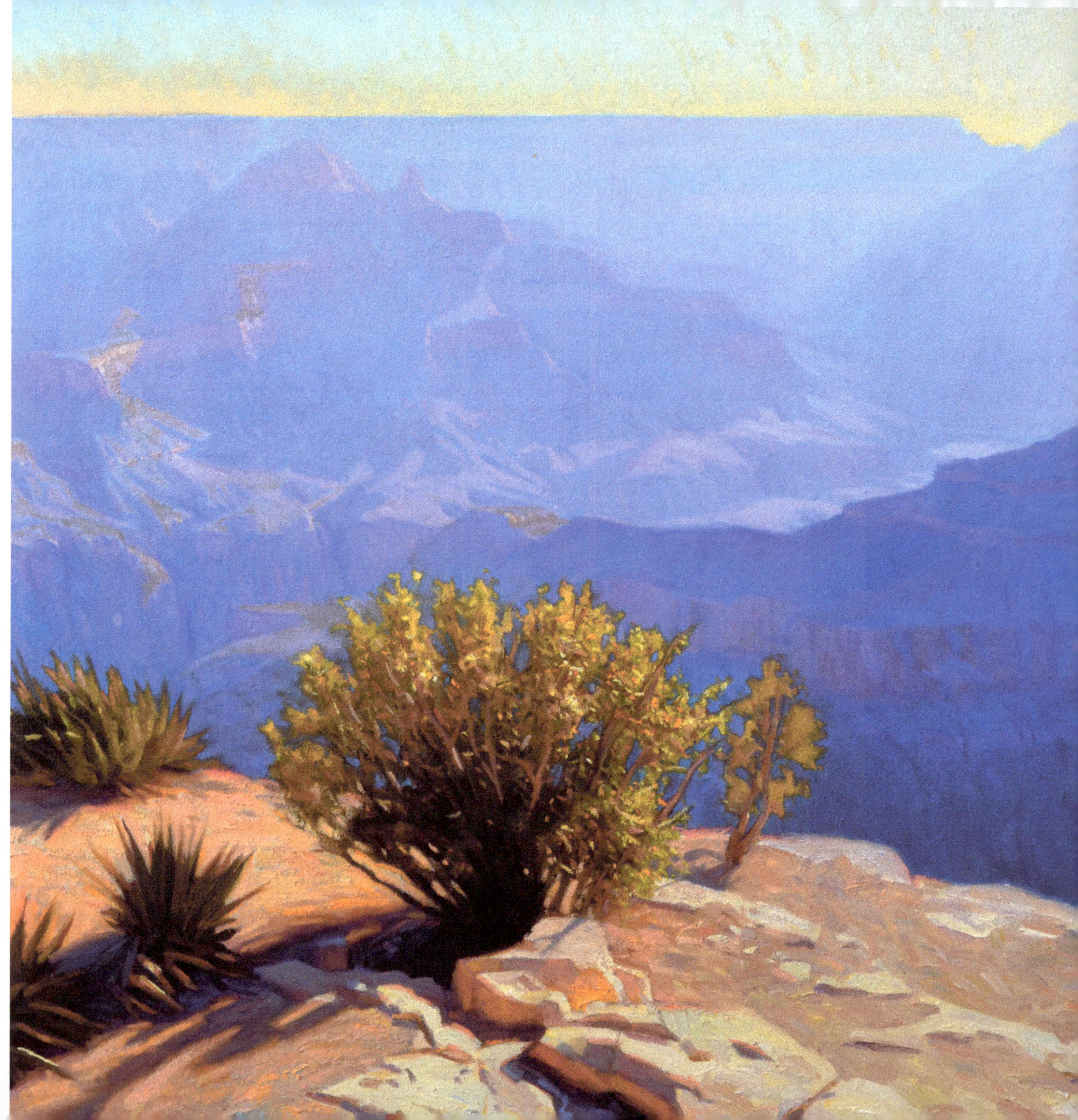

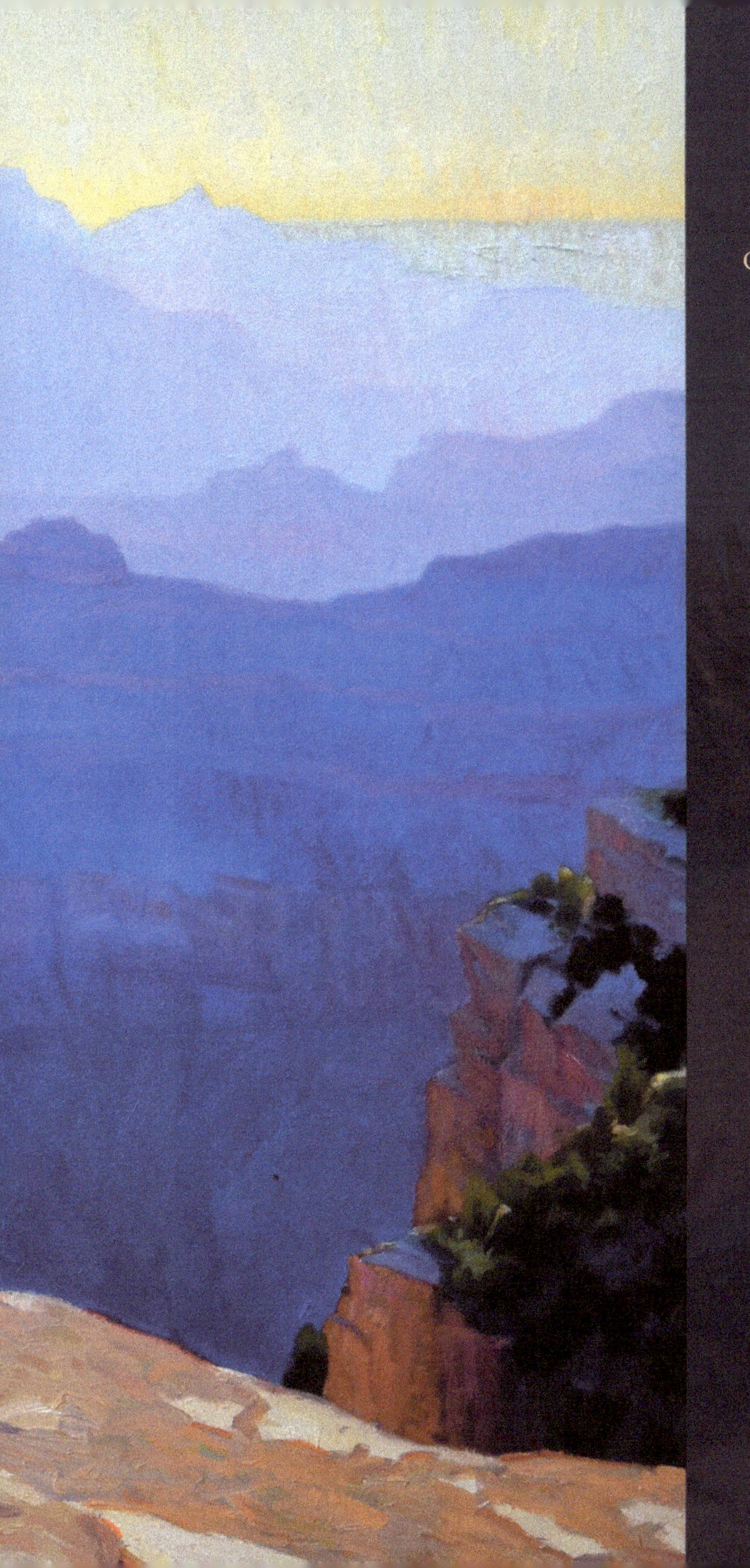

ON THE EDGE OF FOREVER
Grand Canyon, Arizona | 2015 | 30 x 40" | Oil on Canvas

When I saw this bush on the Rim, it reminded me of when
Moses saw the burning bush in the biblical account in Exodus.
As the sun rose at the Grand Canyon, my eye caught this
wondrous light effect. The bush was warm with glowing
yellows and ochres and was set against the blues and violets
of the canyon. What also caught my imagination was that
the foreground was such an abrupt edge. It was as if you
could jump and fly forever into those colors.

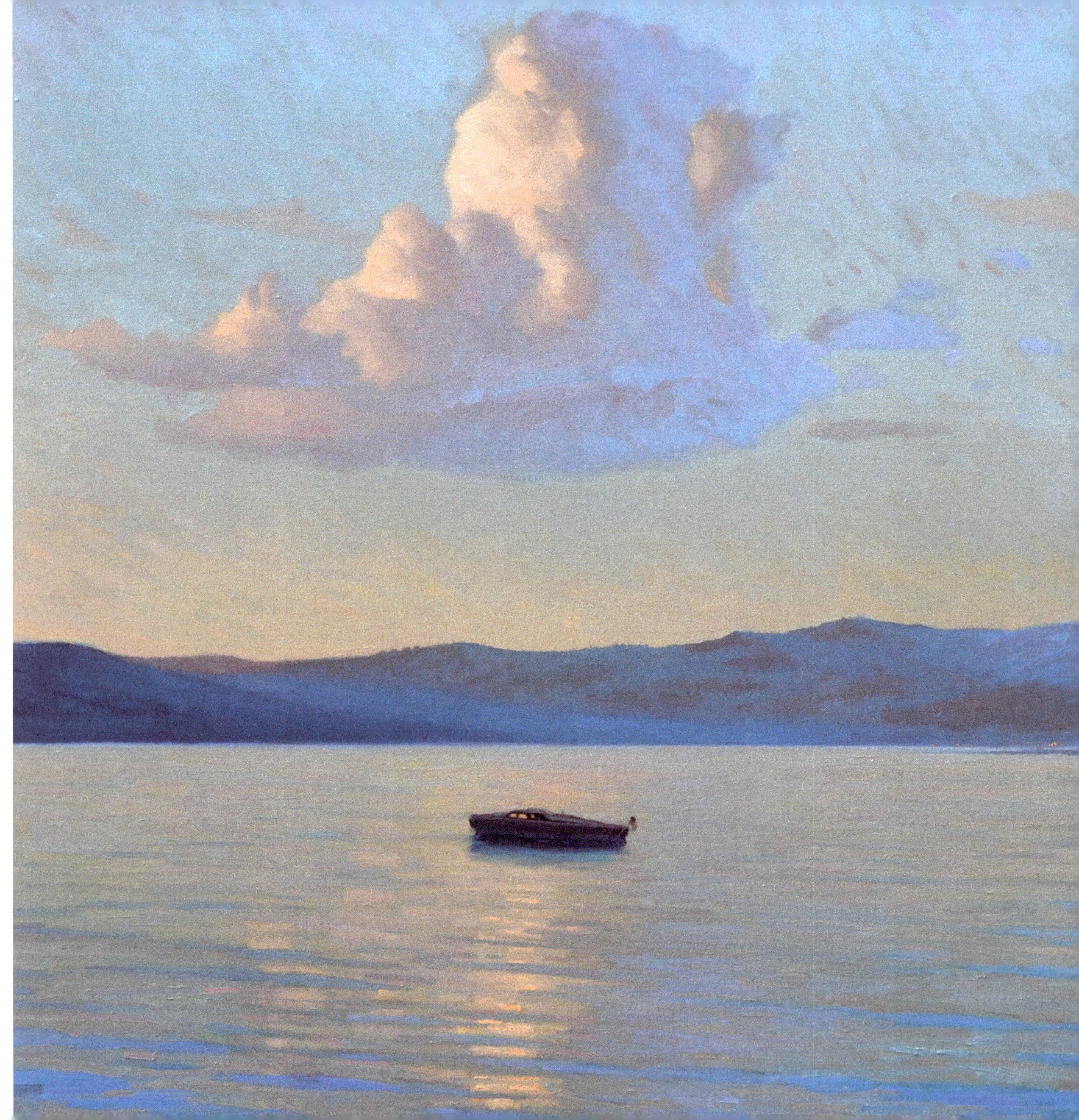

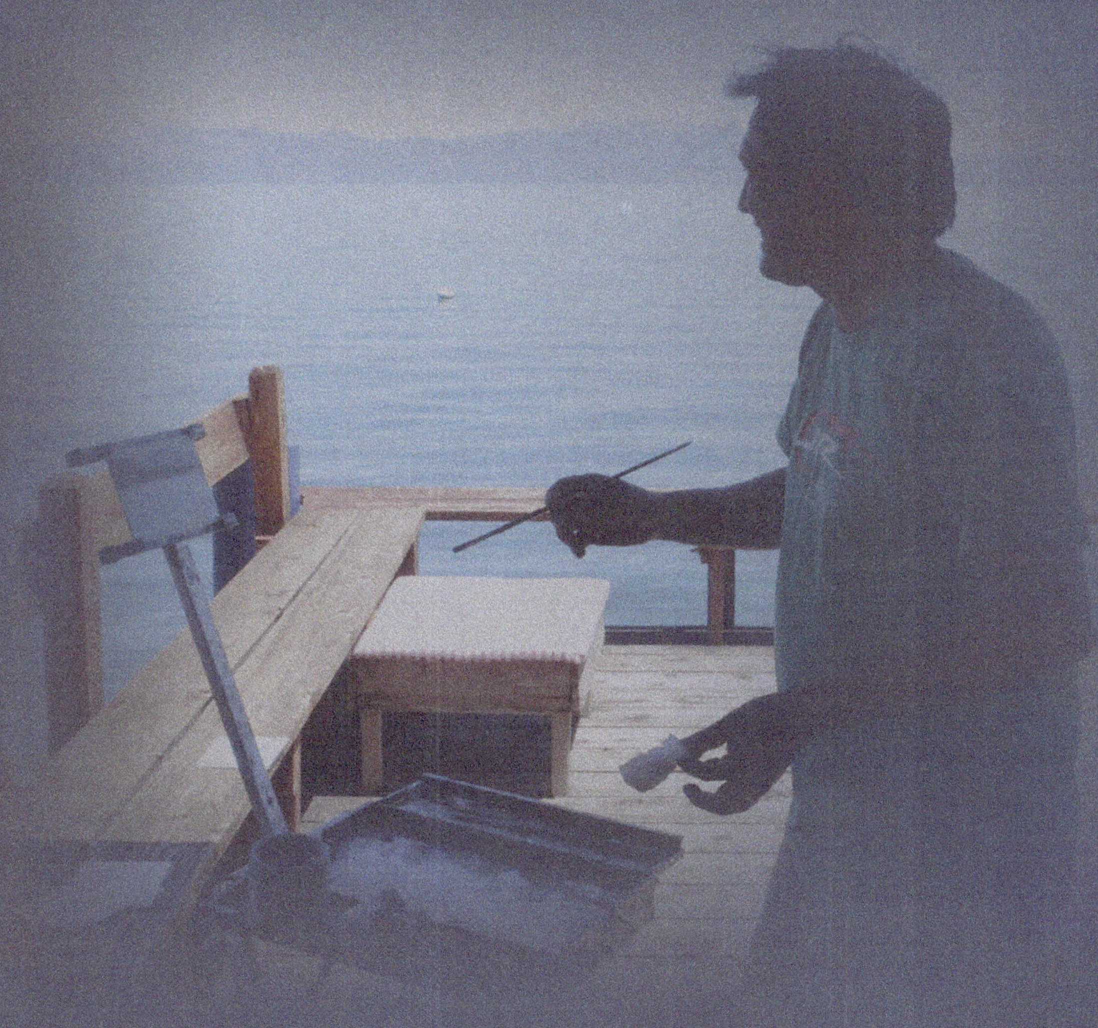

MY SECOND LOVE WAITS | Lake Tahoe, California | 2014 | 30 x 40" | Oil on Canvas

*When Jana and I are at Lake Tahoe we usually stay with a friend at their family compound in Homewood.
They have owned the property since 1934 and it has a wonderful dock that is perfect to paint from. At sunset our
host Kate loves to celebrate 'Pink Time,' and one time this lone cloud gathered itself above the lake and
joined a Chris-Craft anchored. I imagined it waiting for its owner to take it out for a tour.*

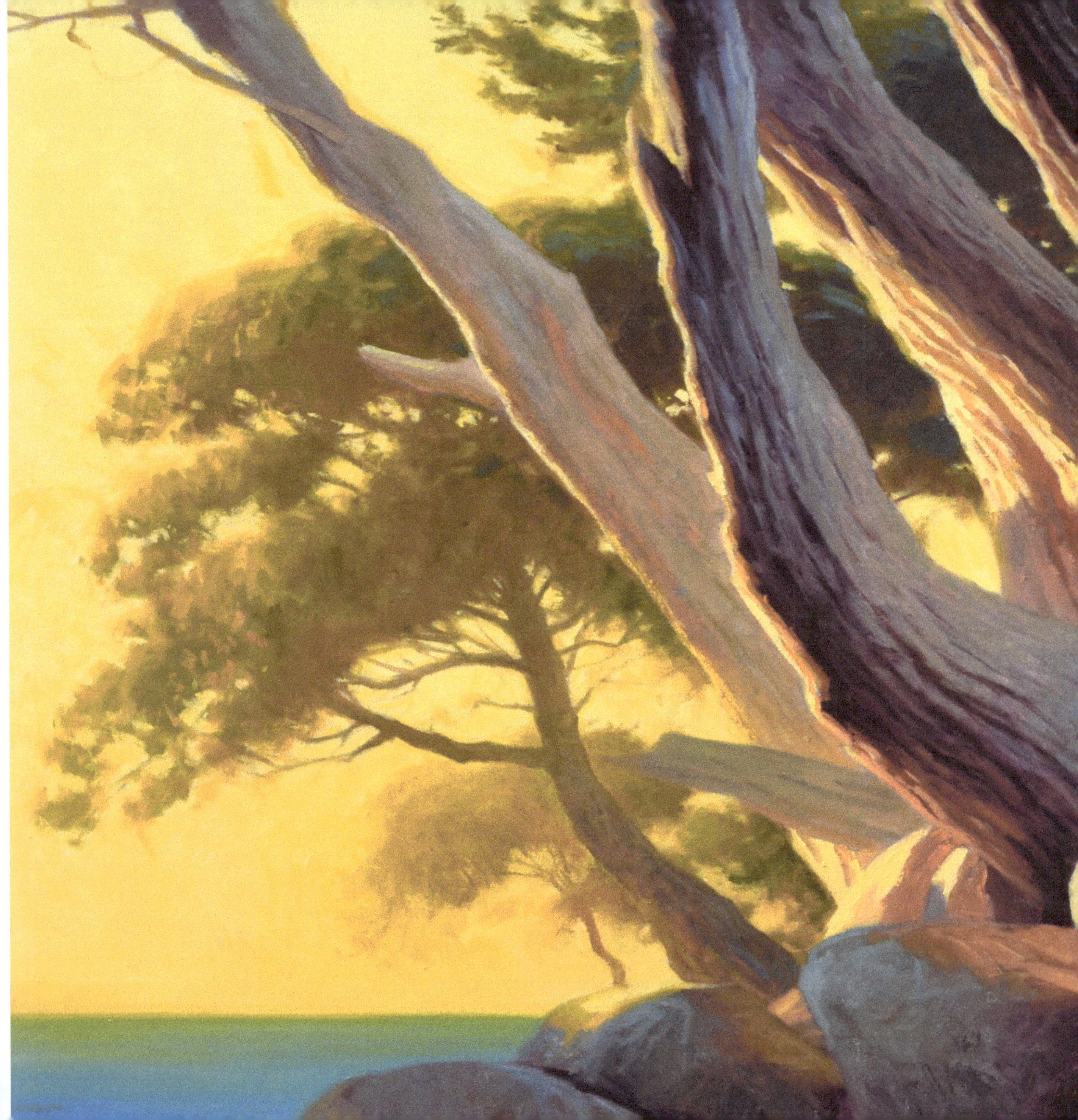

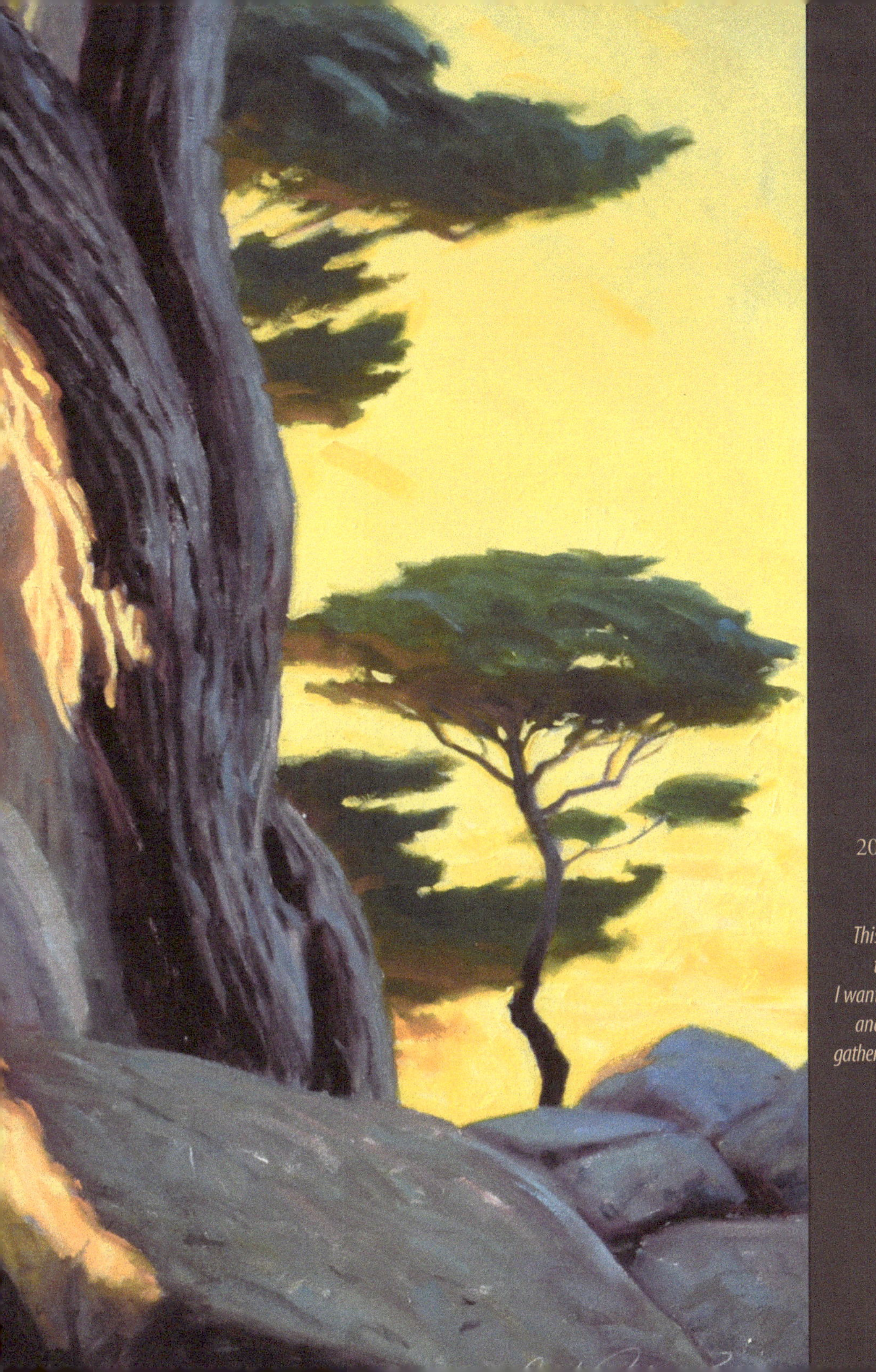

EL LOBO
Point Lobos, California
2015 | 48 x 60" | Oil on Canvas

El Lobo is a favorite painting of mine.
This wonderful old cypress stands guard along
the rim of the Pacific Ocean by Pt. Lobos.
I wanted to idealize its form to capture the romance
and power of these magnificent trees that are
gathered in groves at Point Lobos State Park, California.

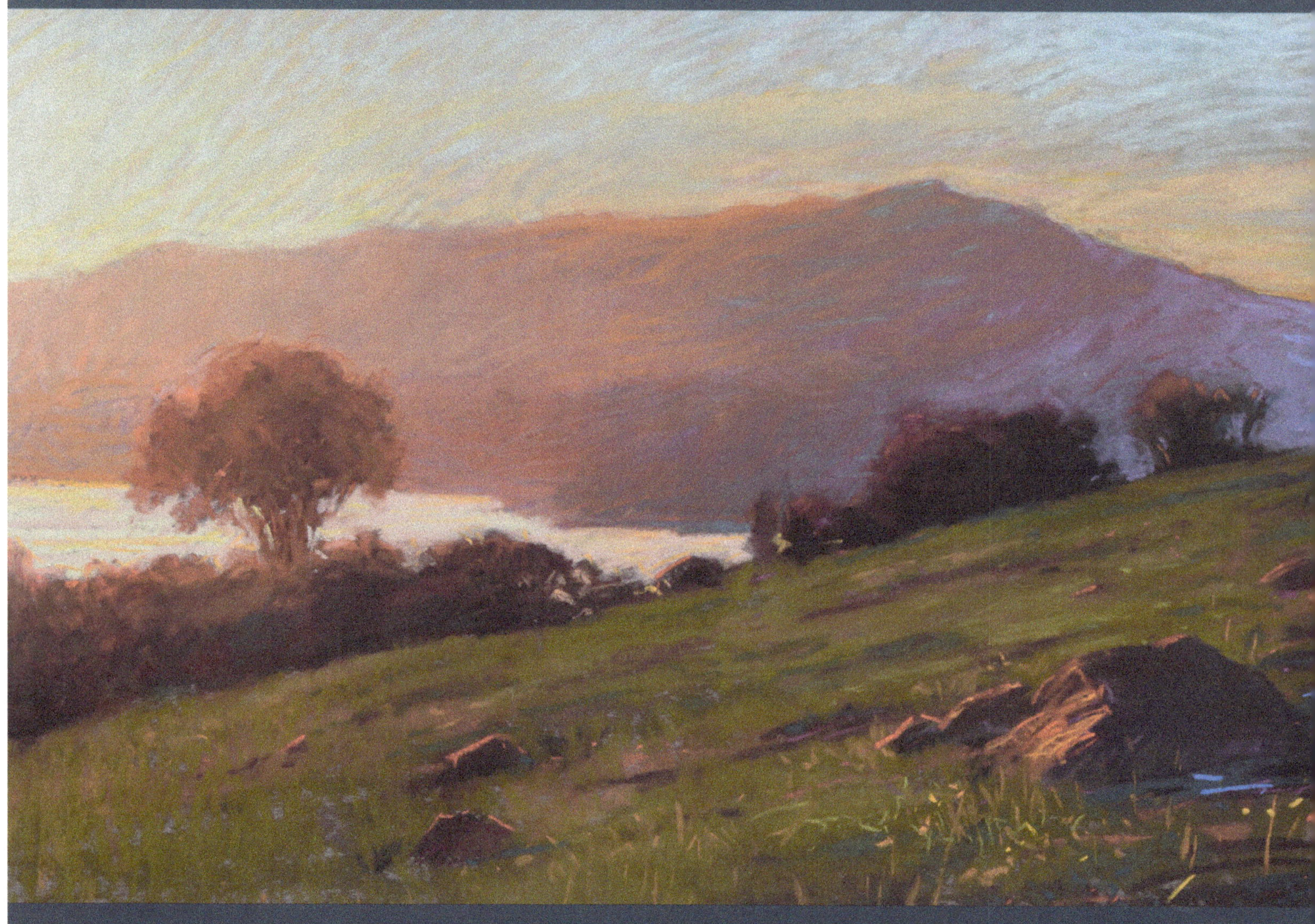

END OF DAY | Tiburon, California | 2014 | 12 x 18" | Pastel on Paper

The end of a day in Marin. A view of Mount Tamalpais from a hillside in Tiburon.

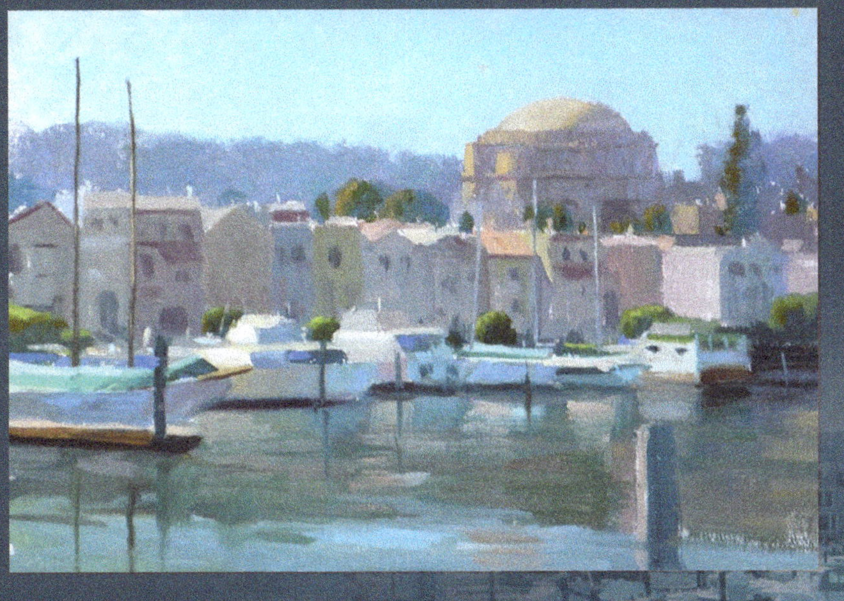

THE MARINA
San Francisco, California | 2014 | 9 x 12" | Oil on Board

On a hot and balmy day, I painted along the dockside at the Marina in San Francisco facing the Palace of Fine Arts Building. I was in heaven. I just took my time and loved the emerald greens bouncing around the boats and inlet. Is there a better life?

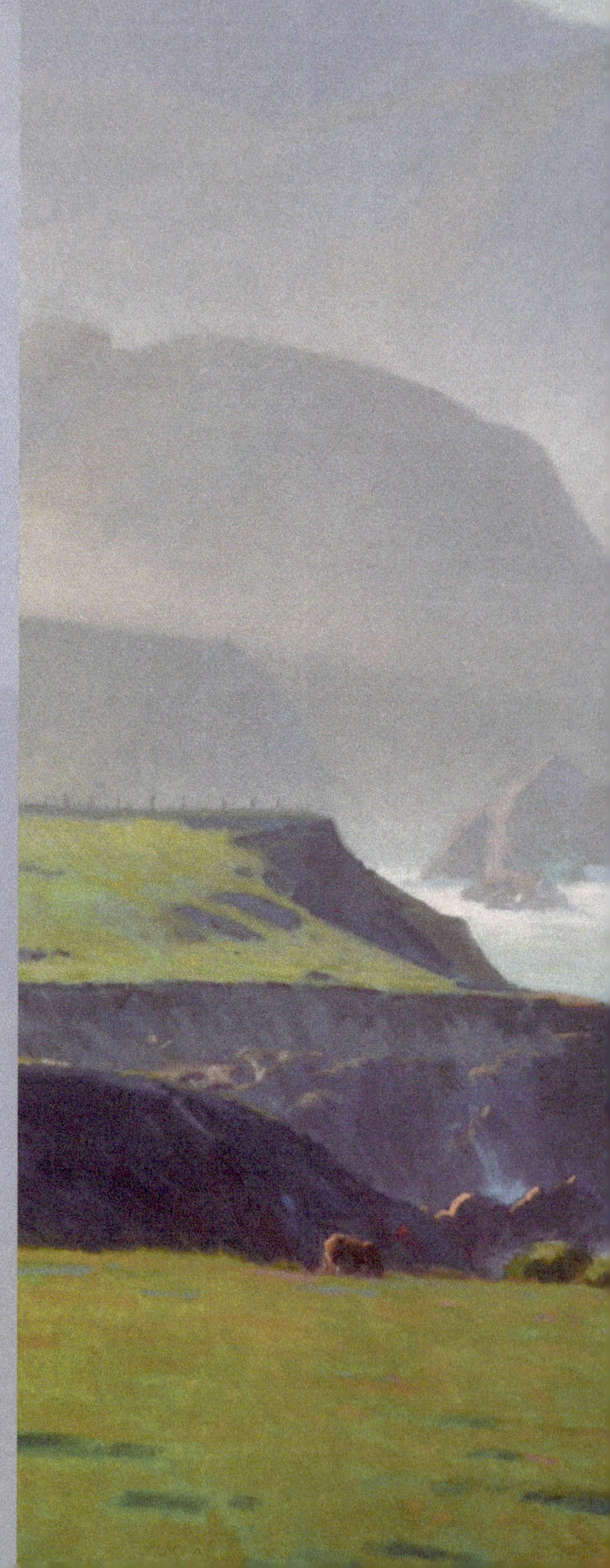

SHE FOUND HERSELF AMONGST THE MIST
Big Sur, California | 2015 | 48 x 60" | Oil on Canvas

*When you travel to Carmel, you are amazed
and enthralled by the beauty of this cypress-rich hamlet.
Further down California Highway 1 you then will experience the
rugged coastline known as Big Sur. As you round a one particular curve
on this winding road, this jaw-dropping scene serenades you with the
harmonies of crashing waves and swirling mists. Upon feeling a deep
connection to the land, a friend of mine made Big Sur her home.*

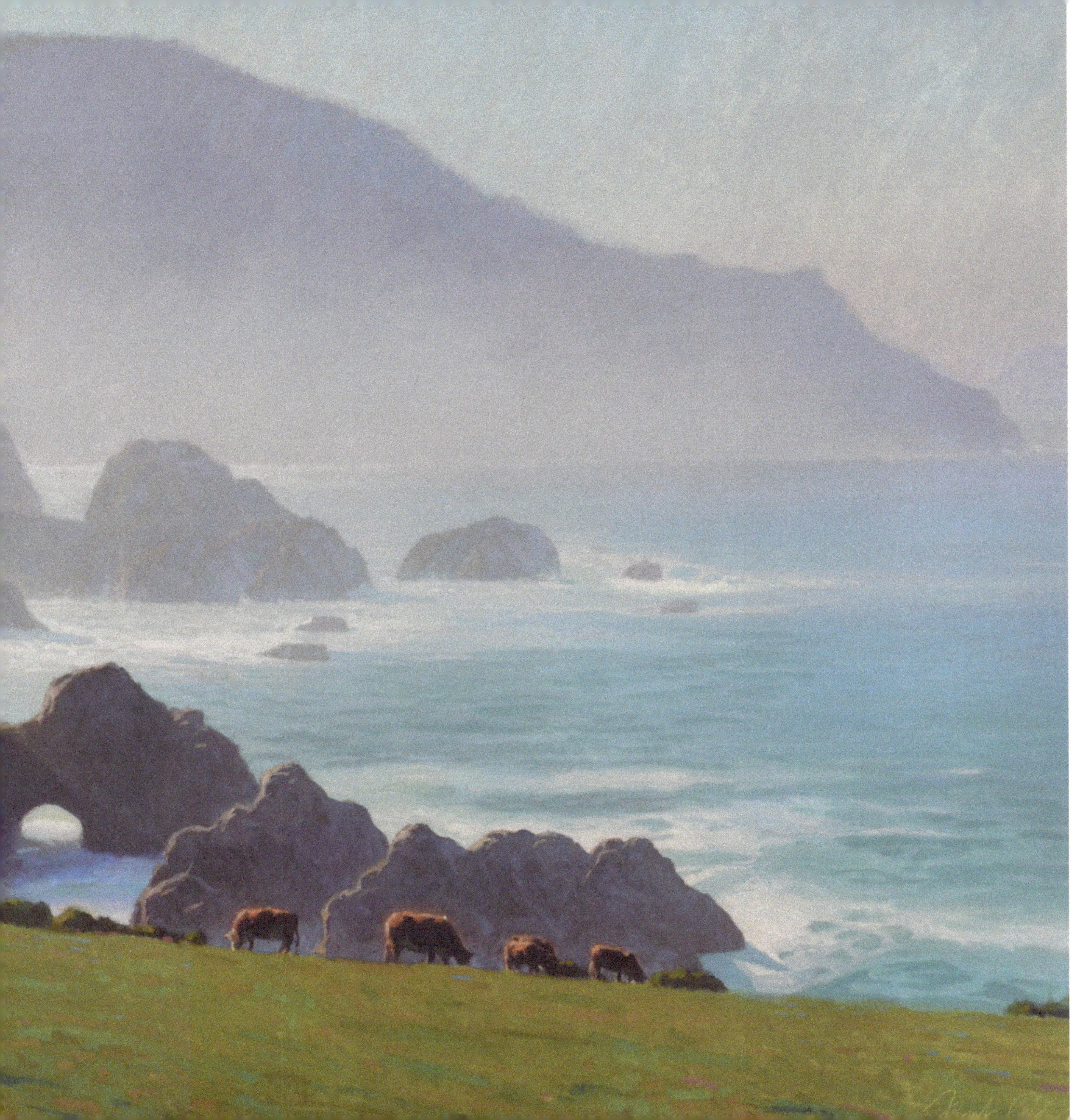

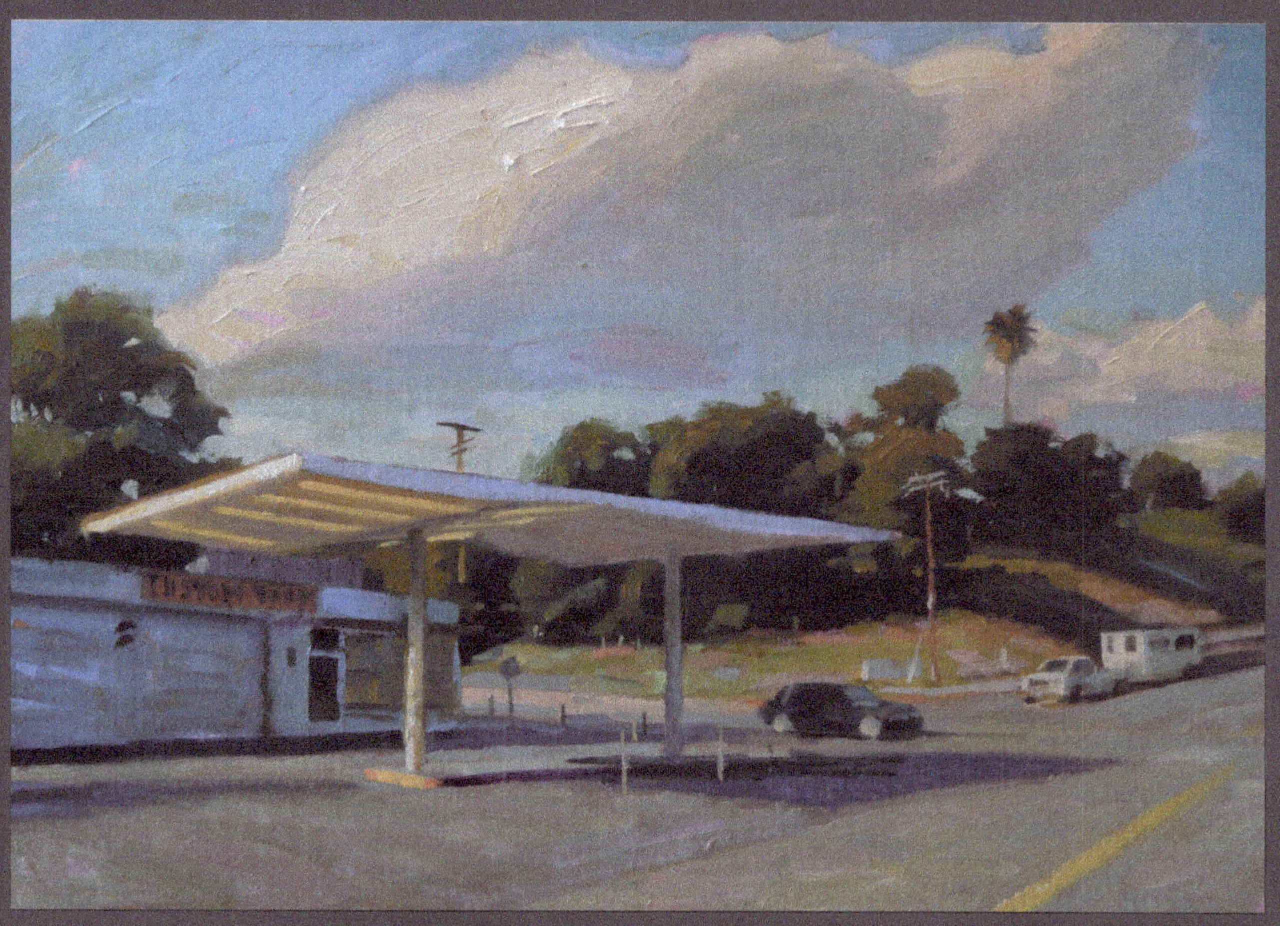

REPURPOSED | Auburn, California | 2015 | 11 x 14" | Oil on Panel

You've got to love a repurposed gas station that is now a business that sells camper shells. Oddly enough this station is right off the 80 freeway coming down from Tahoe. You would think it would be a great spot for the sale of gasoline.

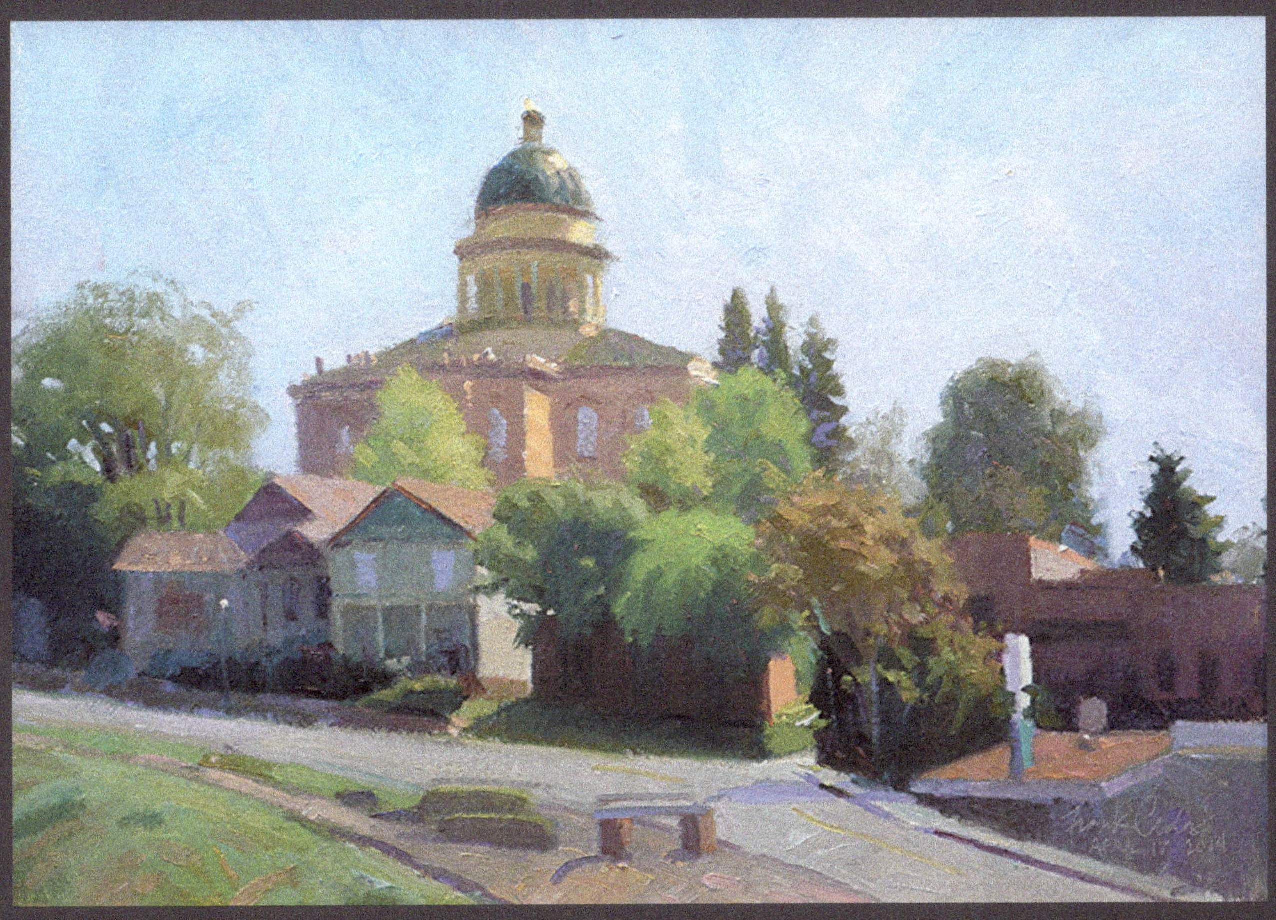

MORNING TIME IN AUBURN | Auburn, California | 2014 | 14 x 18" | Oil on Canvas

I really do love my town. Through every season, in every light, I find beautiful, cinematic scenes to capture. Painted on location with the aid of carbon monoxide inhalation.

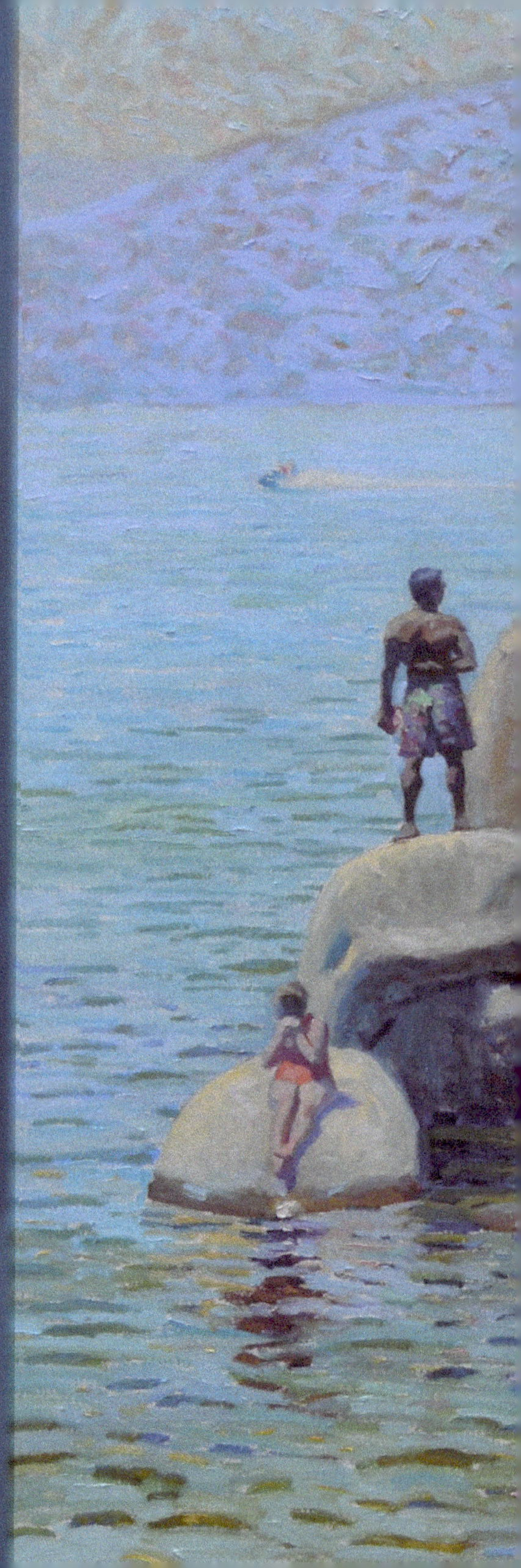

THE MATING SEASON
Sand Harbor, Nevada | 2015 | 48 x 60" | Oil on Canvas

In many ways, this work was inspired by a famous Thomas Eakins painting where we
see youths around a swimming hole. It is a rite of passage for young people as they display
their physiques and prowess in and around the water. Like colorful peacocks,
the young men try to get the attention of pretty ladies in bikinis.

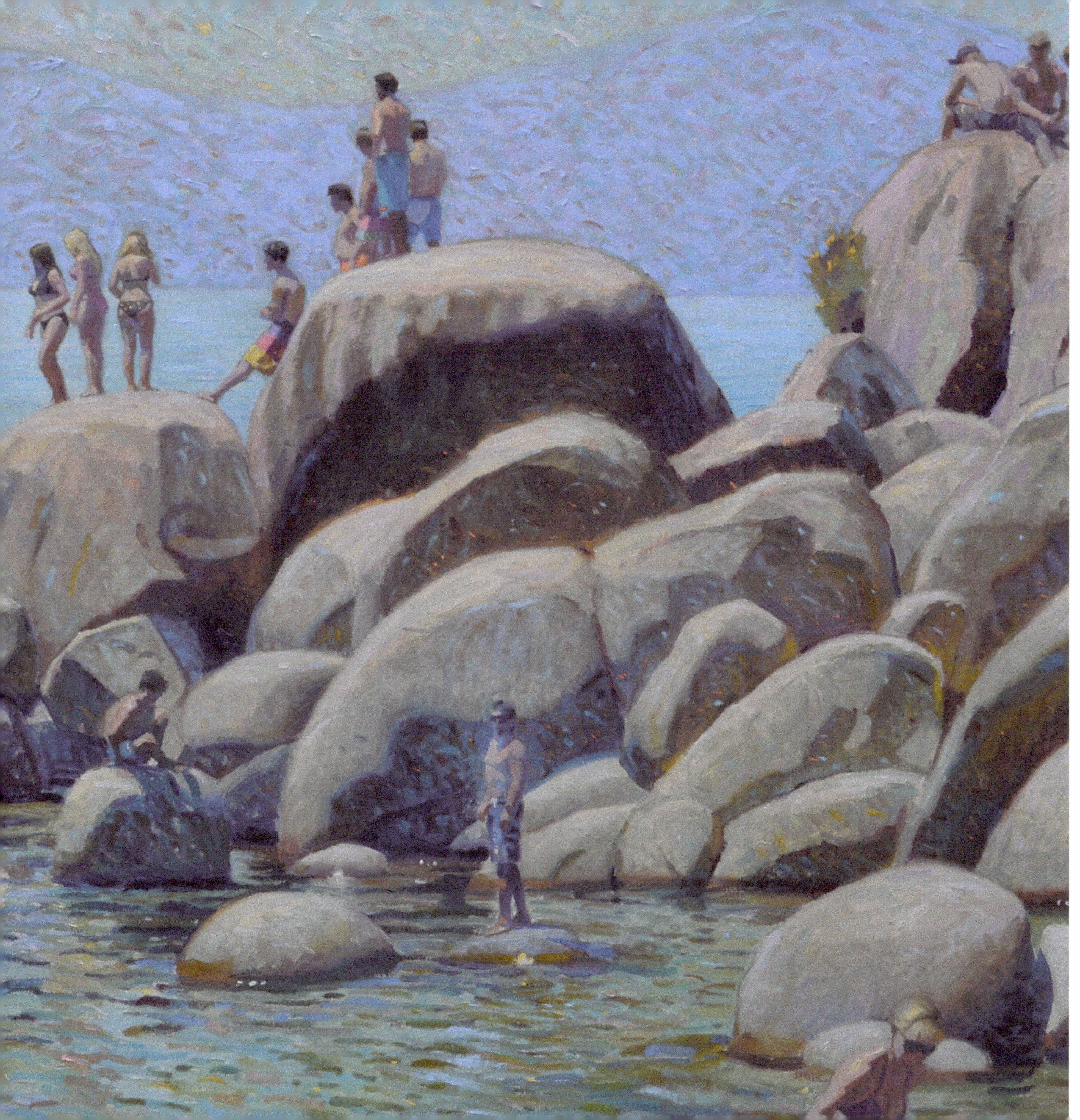

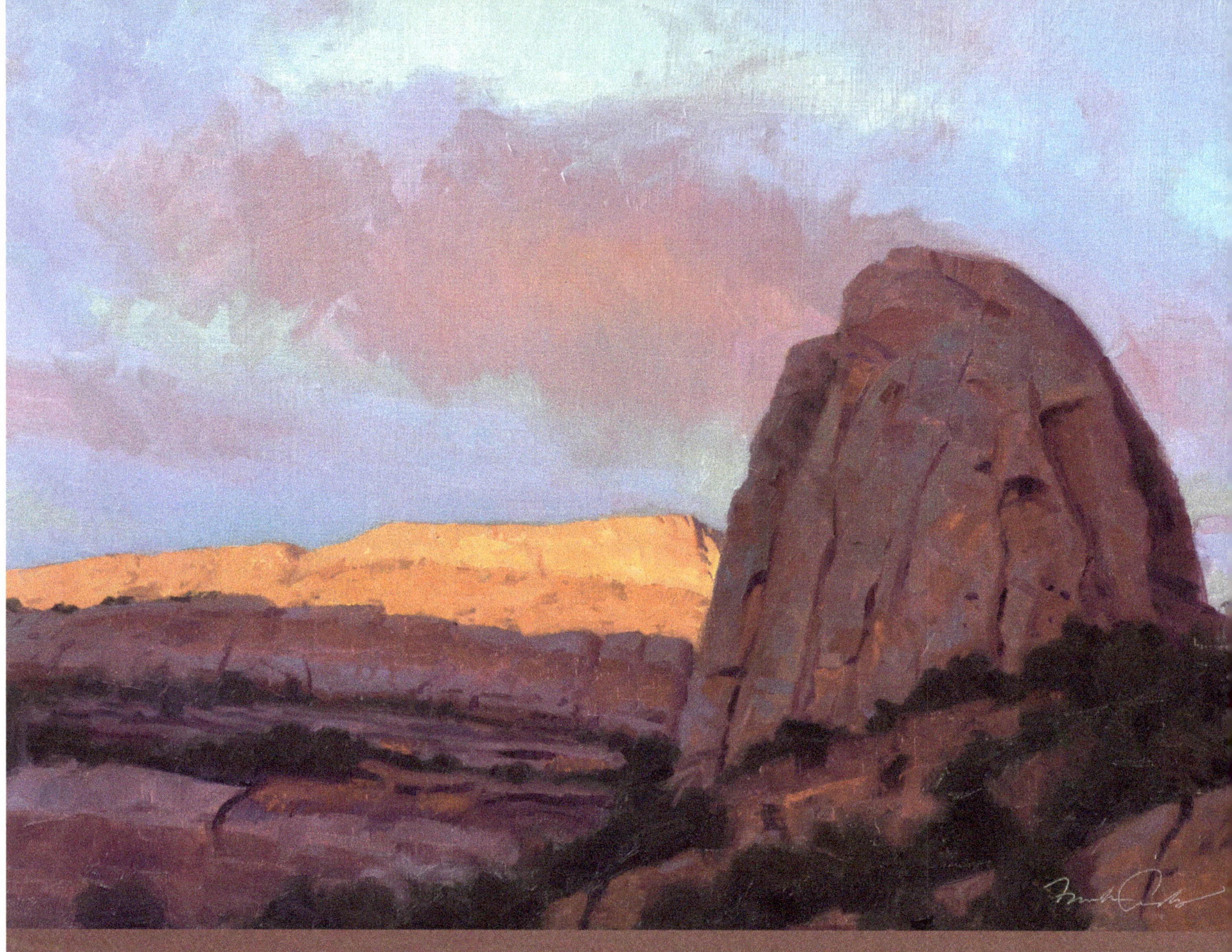

END OF DAYS, NAVAJO NATION | Navajo Nation, New Mexico | 2015 | 16 x 20" | Oil on Panel

End of Days. Last Days. All tribes have end times prophesies. Markers on the land like this red rock are symbols of robed prophets who spoke blessings and curses to their people. Redemption and a gathering of the broken-hearted were promises when their people repented with a broken and contrite spirit. This spot is north of Gallup, New Mexico on Navajo Land.

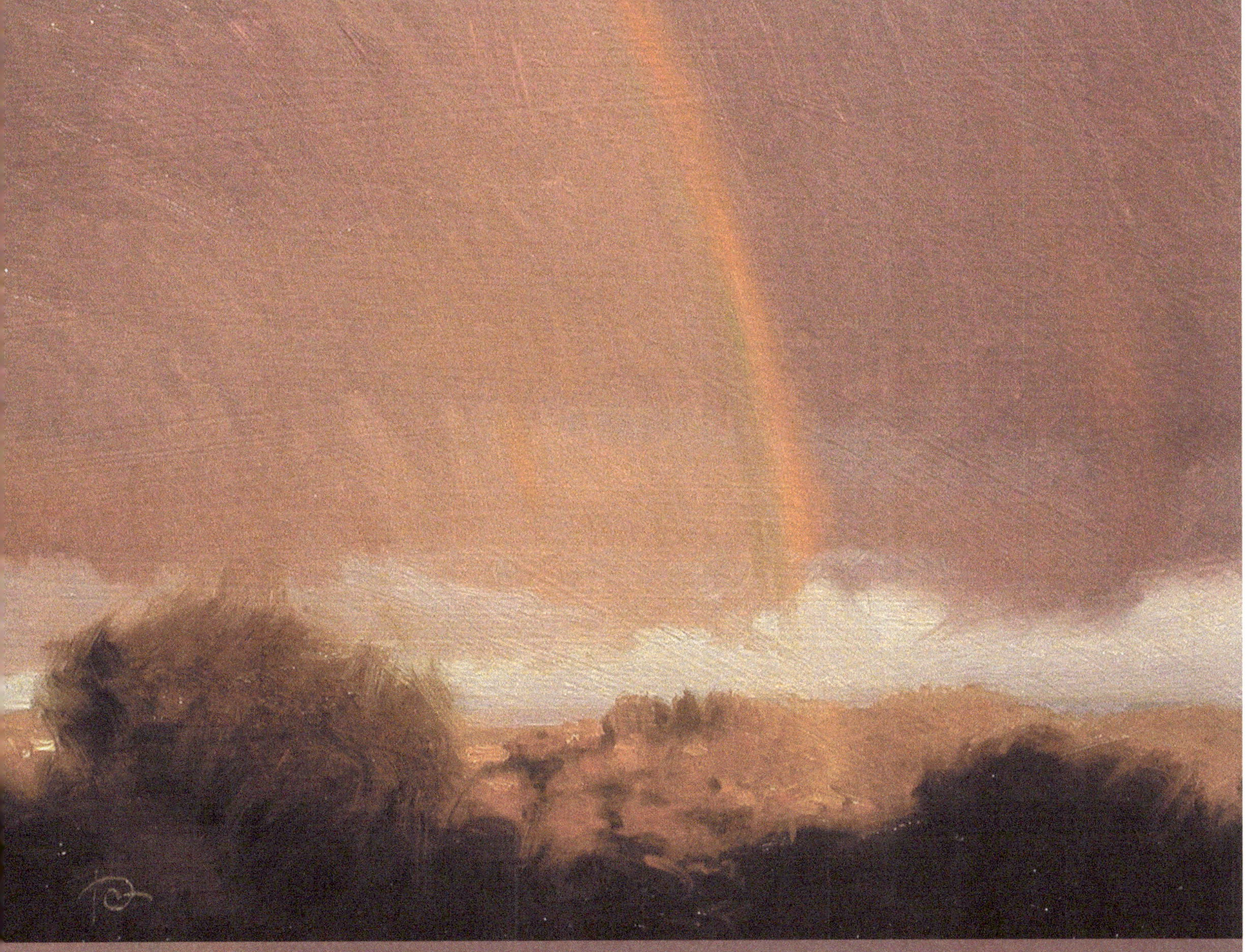

*Red Rainbows are rare. They occur when it is dusk and the sun is at the horizon.
This effect occurred while I drove home one day in Auburn.*

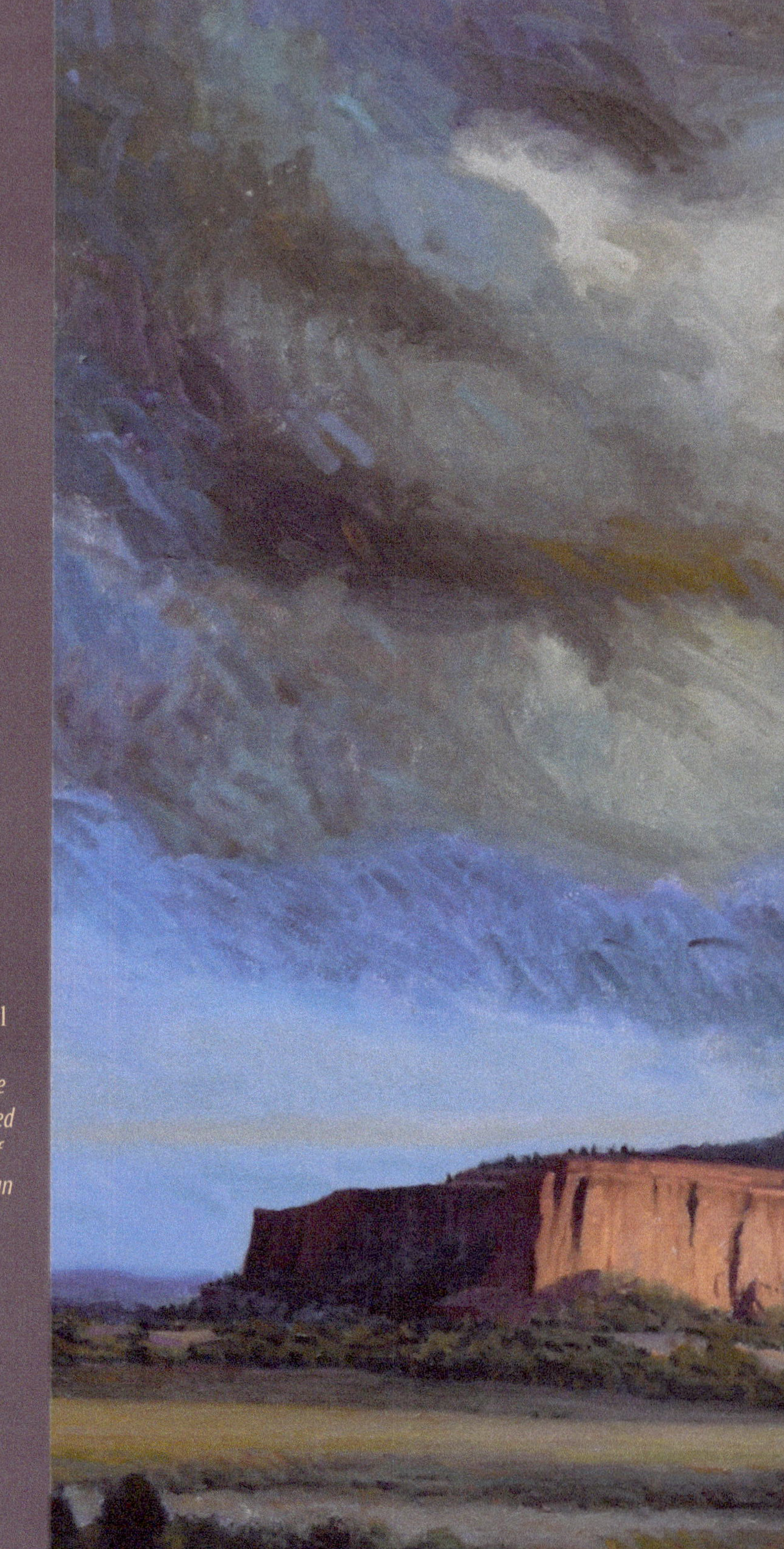

Inspired by my travels thru Navajo Nation above Gallup, New Mexico, the rock formations go back to an aboriginal time where the elements dictated the course and character of its inhabitants who followed the rhythms of the seasons. I not only paint from life and photo reference but also from an intentional memory of my experience and reaction to this sacred Land.

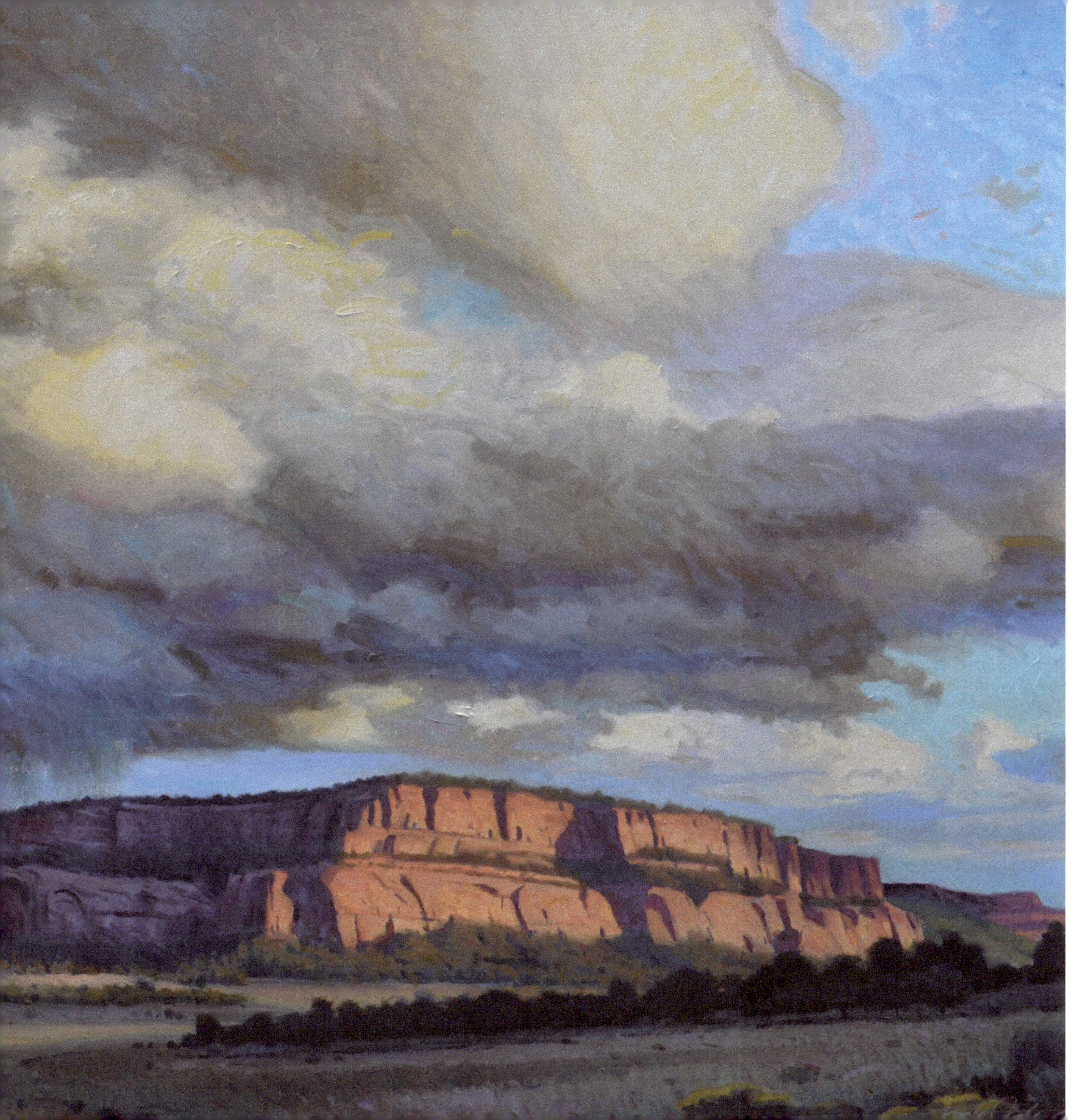

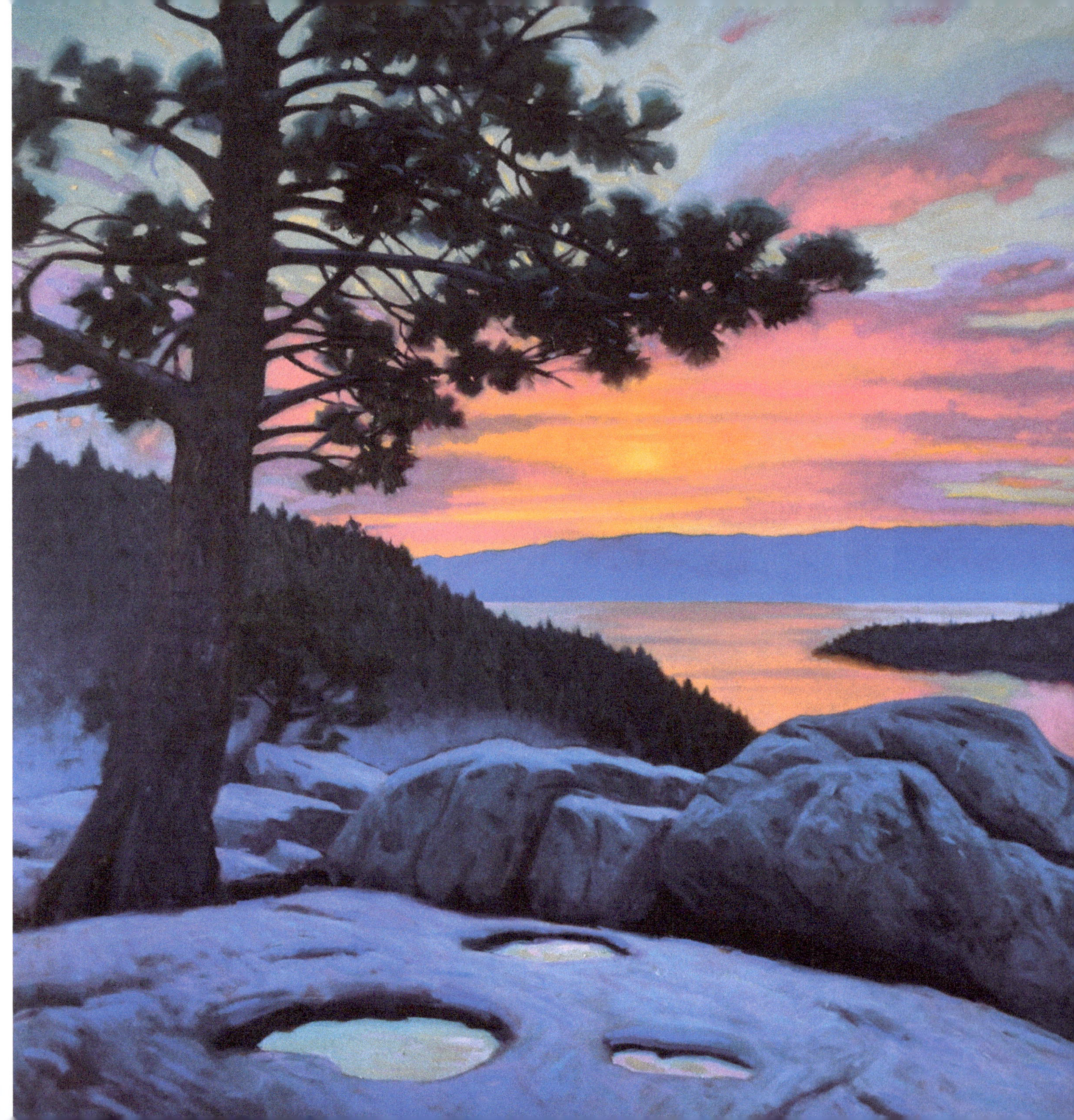

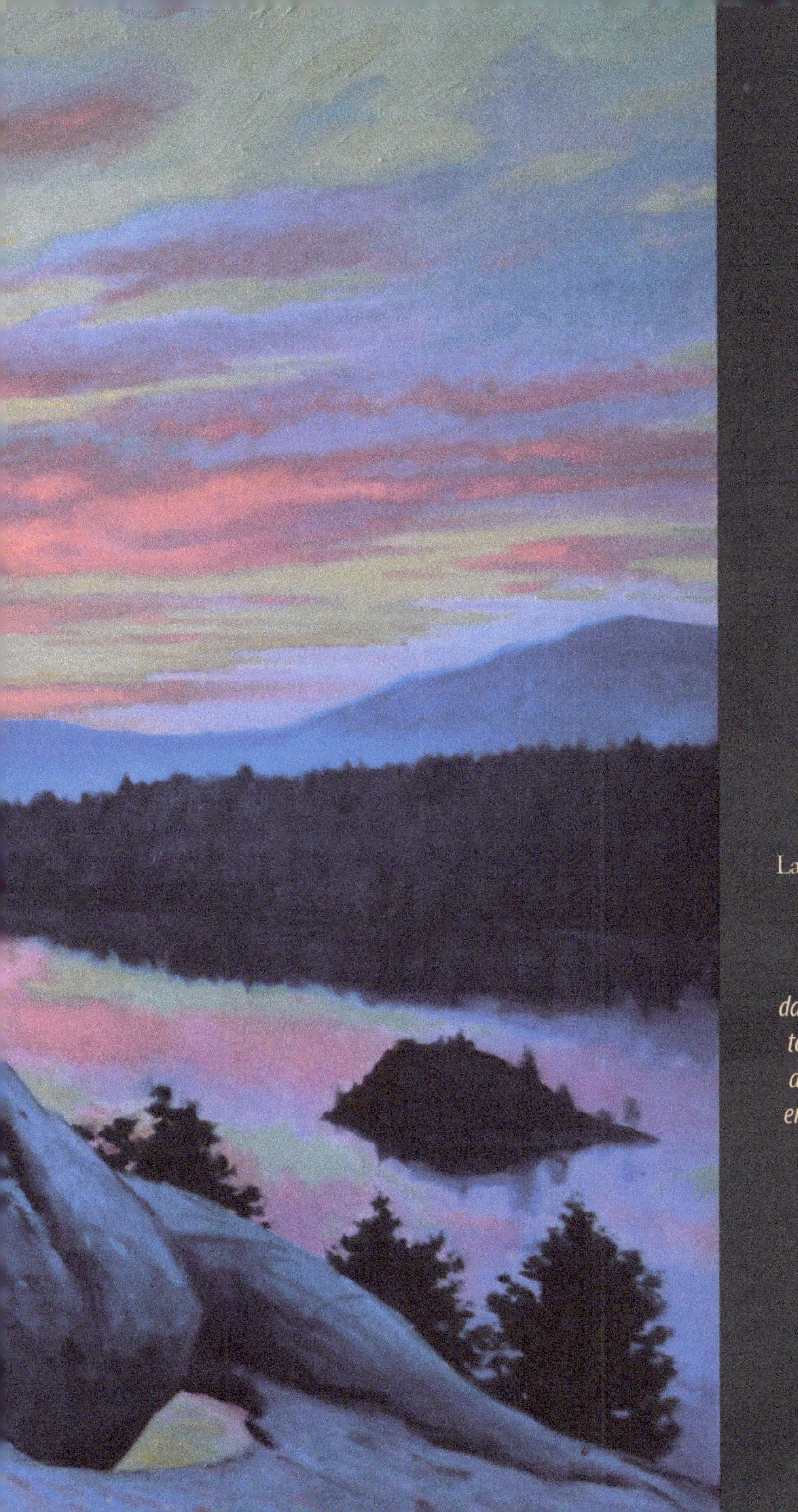

PINK OVER EMERALD

Lake Tahoe, California | 2015 | 48 x 60" | Oil on Canvas

I've spent some GOOD times up at Homewood in Lake Tahoe. I would venture to Emerald Bay early in the morning to catch daybreak. I was rewarded one day with this spectacular scene that took me to another realm. Emerald Bay is visited by tourists from all over the world, and capturing just the right view that visually embodies the idyllic quality of Emerald Bay is quite the challenge.

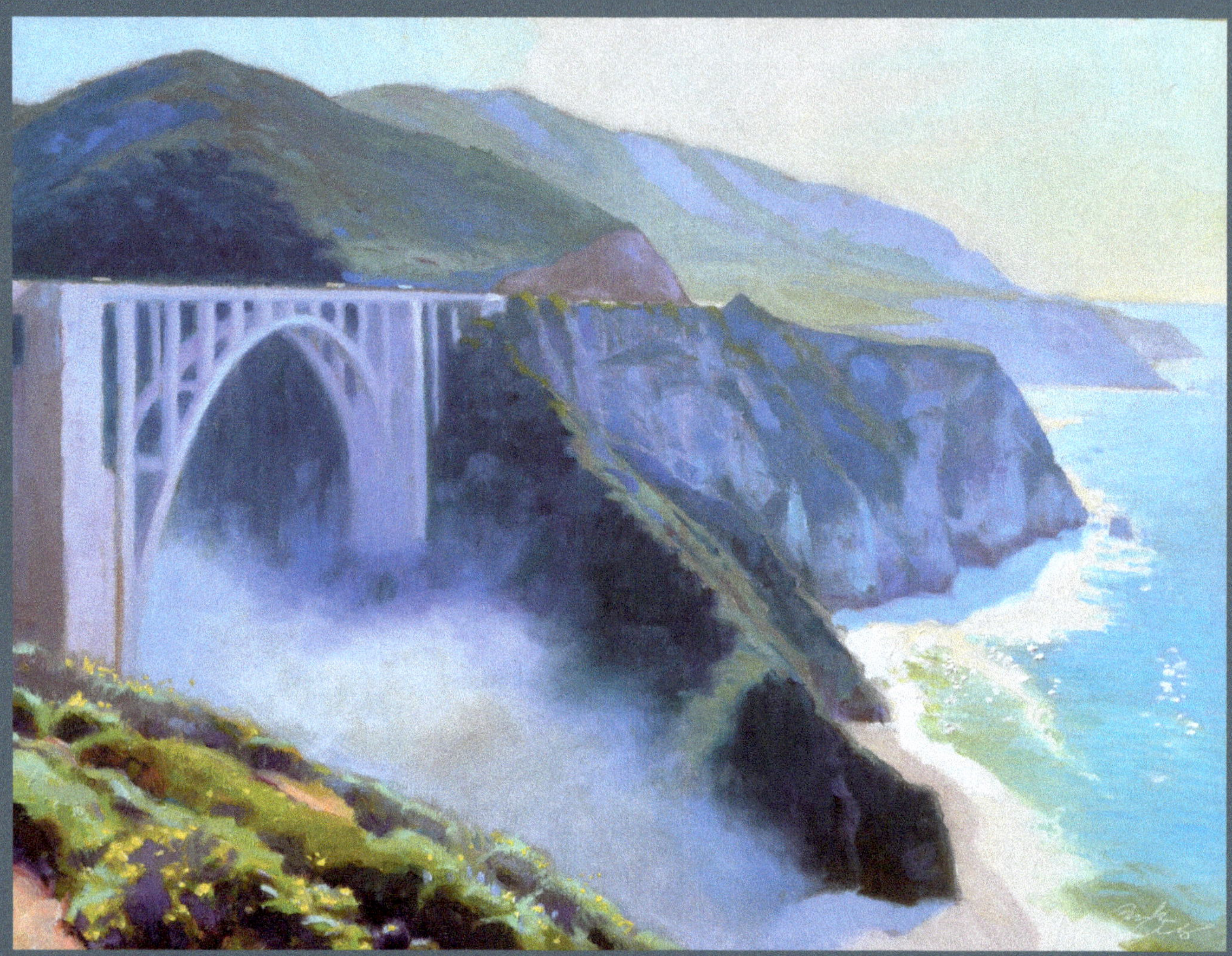

NOTHING BEHIND ME, EVERYTHING AHEAD OF ME,
AS IS EVER SO ON THE ROAD, JK
Big Sur, California | 2015 | 16 x 20" | Oil on Panel

Though Jack Kerouac spent little time in Big Sur, I still sense his presence as I drive over the concrete bridges along
the Pacific Coast Highway. I'm on the road and the spirit of the poet and the Beats are reminders of passing rhythms and
adventures that happen on wandering hearts that dare to risk. The title is from his ground-breaking novel On the Road.

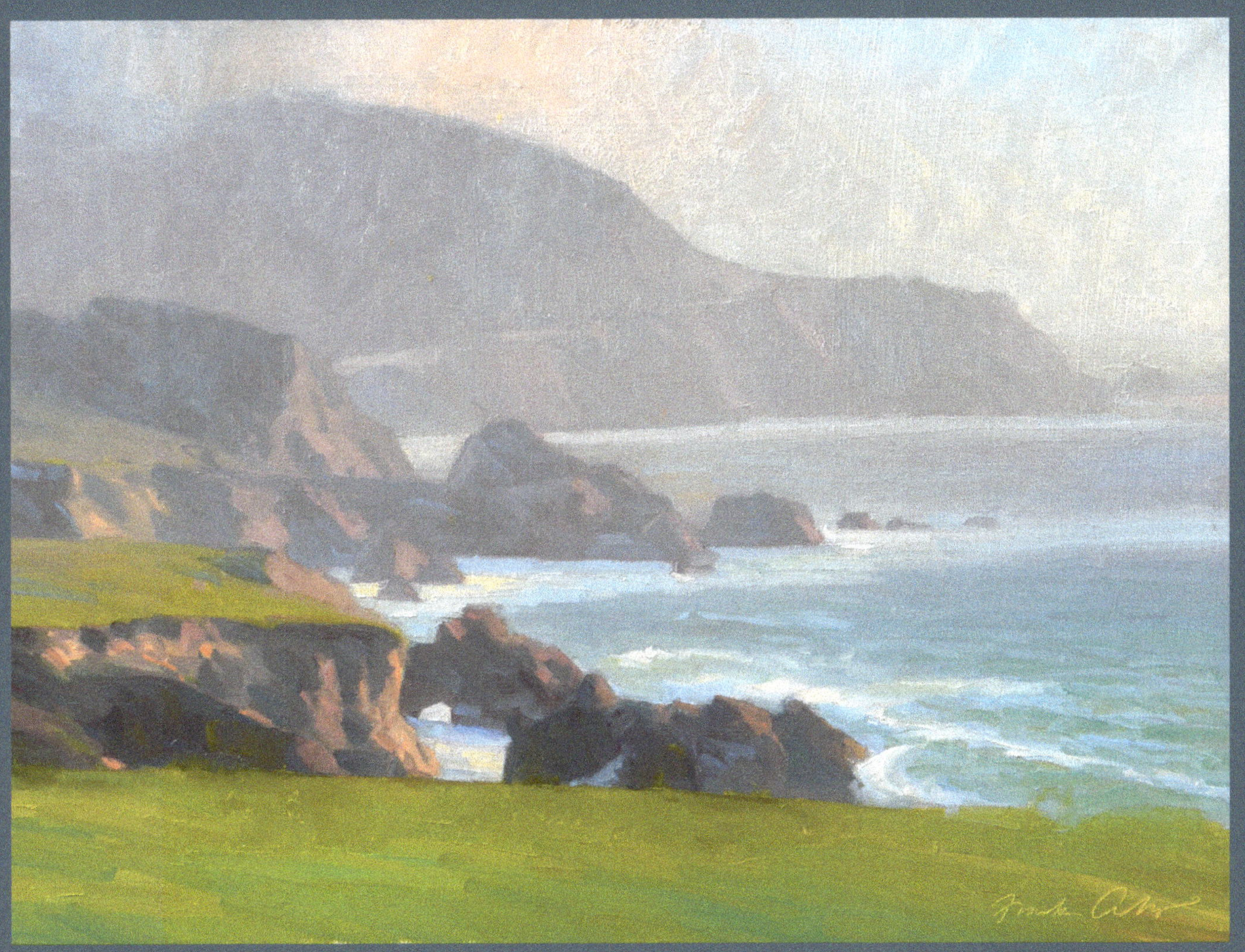

EVEN WITH THE MIST, I FEEL EVERYTHING
Big Sur, California | 2015 | 16 x 20" | Oil on Panel

I love the mist that creates this veil-like transcendence at dusk whereupon, like an expressionistic painting, my mind feels what is there. As mountains recede they become silhouette-like forms that take on these muted greys. What I am trying to capture is a travelogue-like image very similar to a postcard.

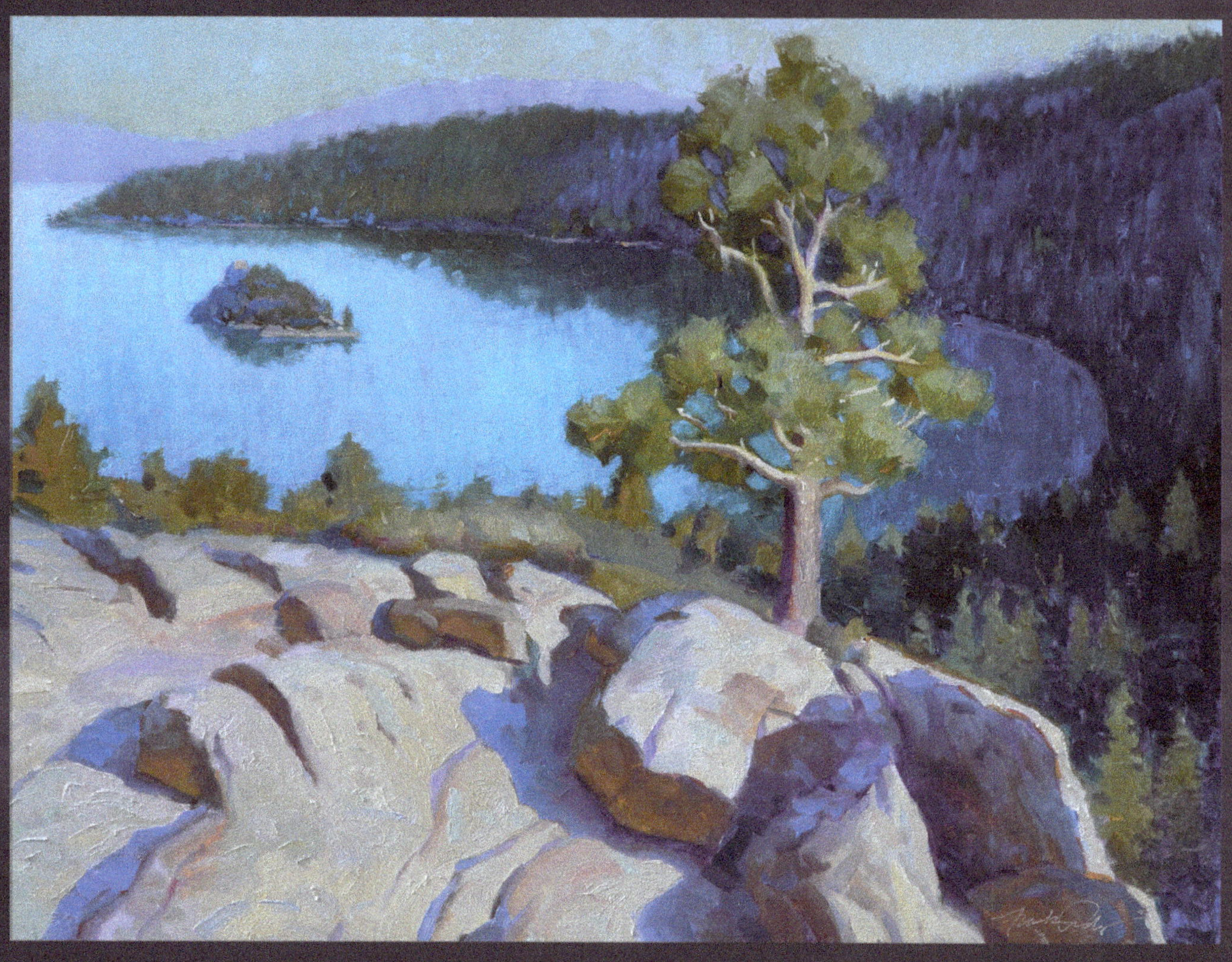

I HAVE CALMED AND QUIETED MY SOUL | Emerald Bay, California | 2015 | 18 x 24" | Oil on Panel

The tree in this painting represents a man who stands on a high place firmly rooted on a rock.
Only one voice is going to be listened to before the storms of life arrive.

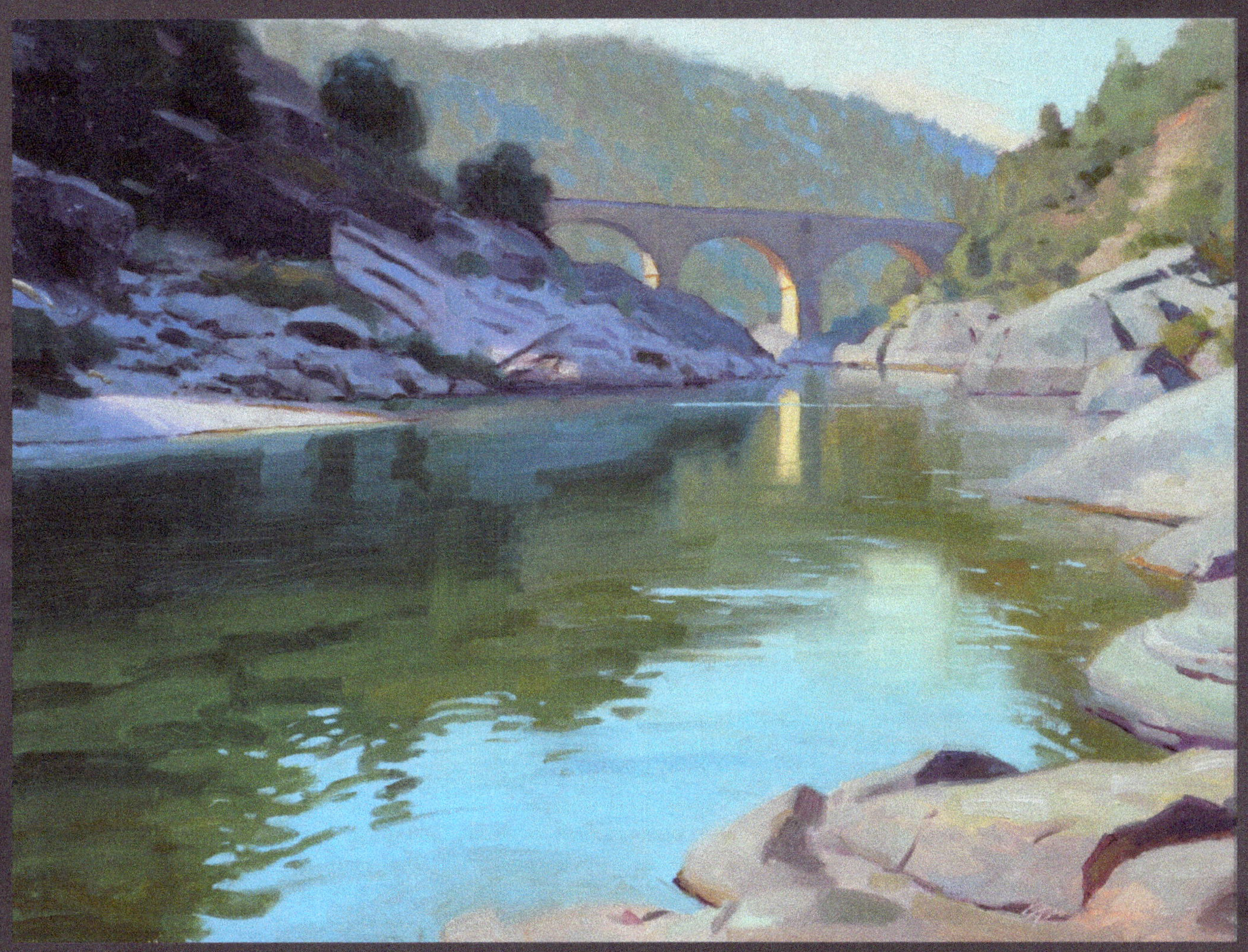

MY RESTING PLACE | Auburn, California | 2015 | 16 x 20" | Oil on Panel

There have been times when I first moved to Auburn that I would get away from the madness and hike down to the American River by the confluence and sit on a rock looking at No Hands Bridge. I could hear the slow movement of the water as it made its way toward the Sacramento basin. It was at these alone times that I felt closer to God and could quiet a restless heart. Finding rest is a blessing.

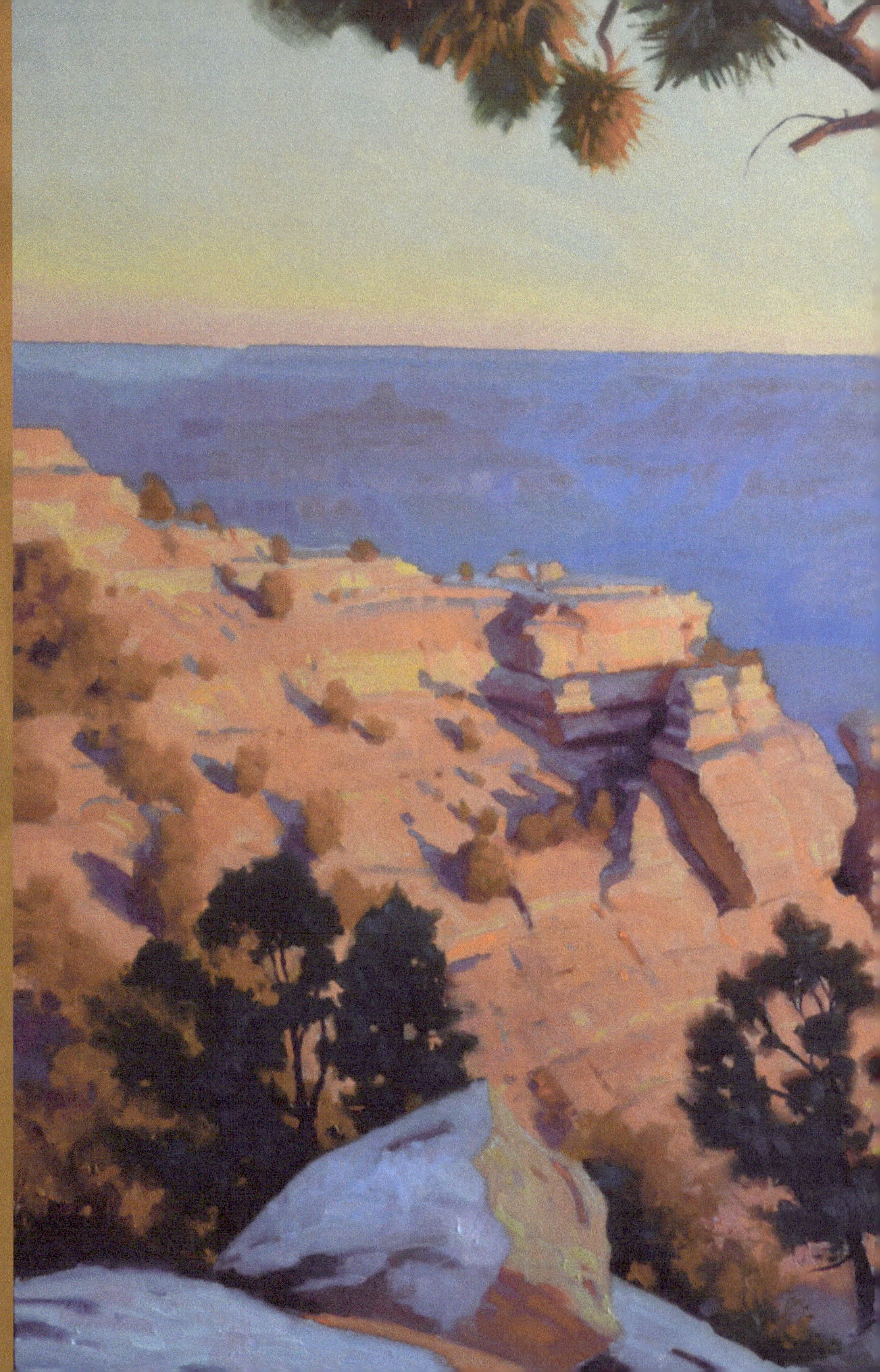

THE RED SENTINEL
Grand Canyon, Arizona
2015 | 30 x 49" | Oil

I just love seeing the sun rise over the plateaus of the Grand Canyon. Hordes of tourists line the edge of the rim and welcome the new day and cheer. It's really a wonderful, wholesome experience. Having returned many times over the years, these gnarled trees are like old friends that I visit every year. I should probably give them names. This chap is like a guard or sentinel who warns of the power and beauty of the Canyon.

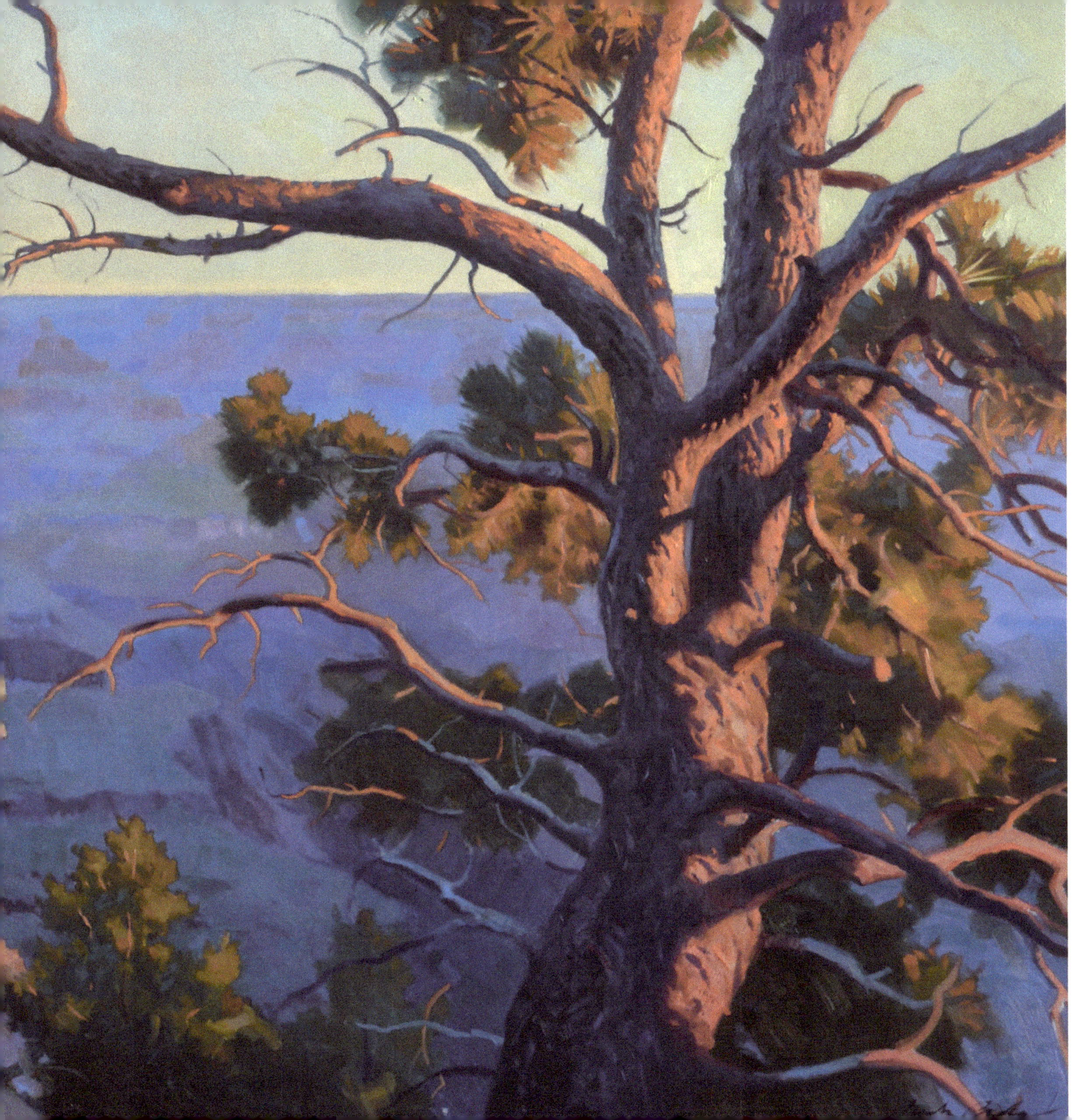

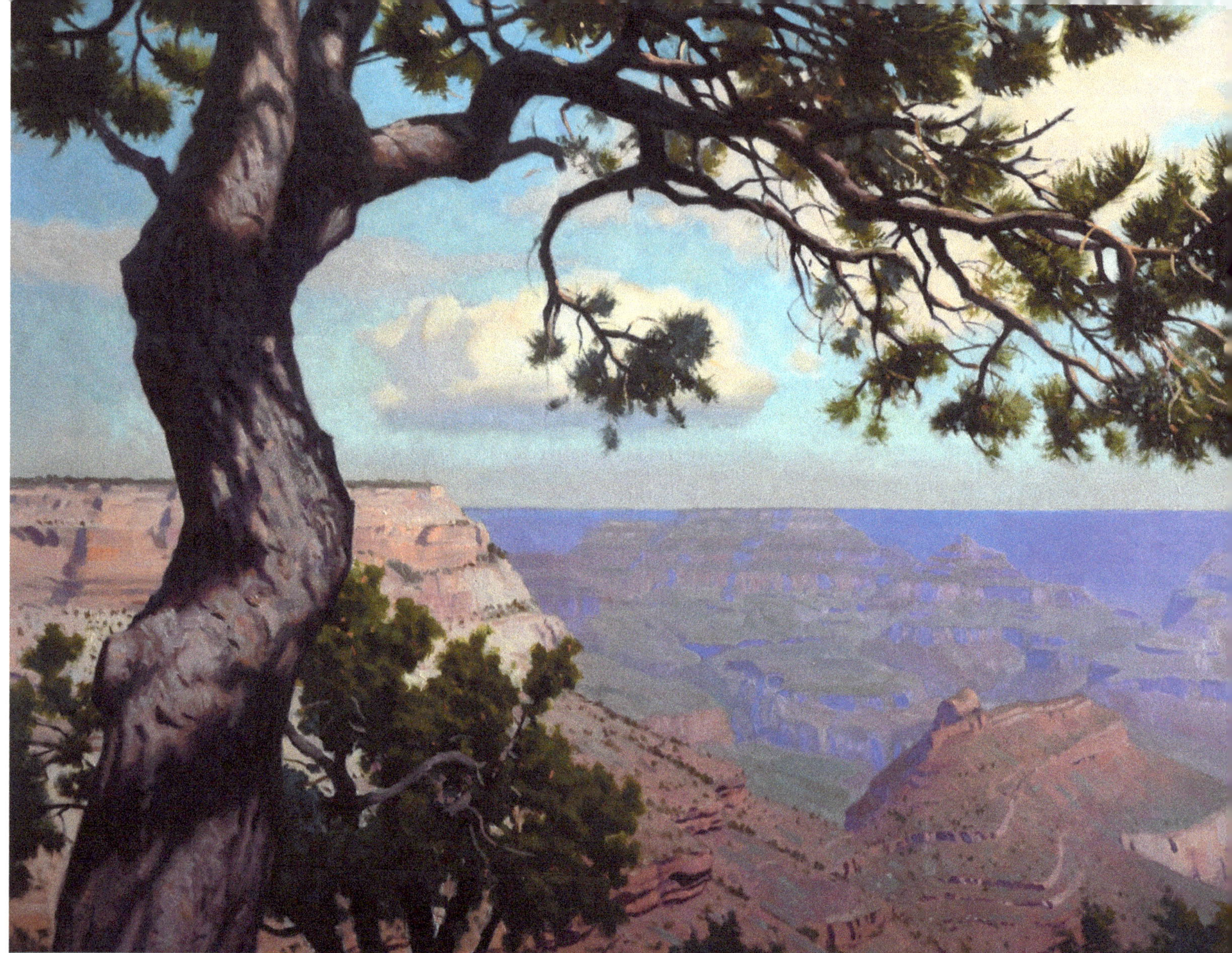

ANCIENT SENTINEL | Grand Canyon, Arizona | 2015 | 30 x 49" | Oil on Panel

As you walk along the Grand Canyon rim you are struck by the vast stretches of time that are revealed by the many layers of sediment carved by the Colorado River. These sentinels remind me that I am only here for a breath and that they will continue to silently remind future generations of the brevity and value of our existence. I like to use a large foreground tree to symbolize a relationship with the Land.

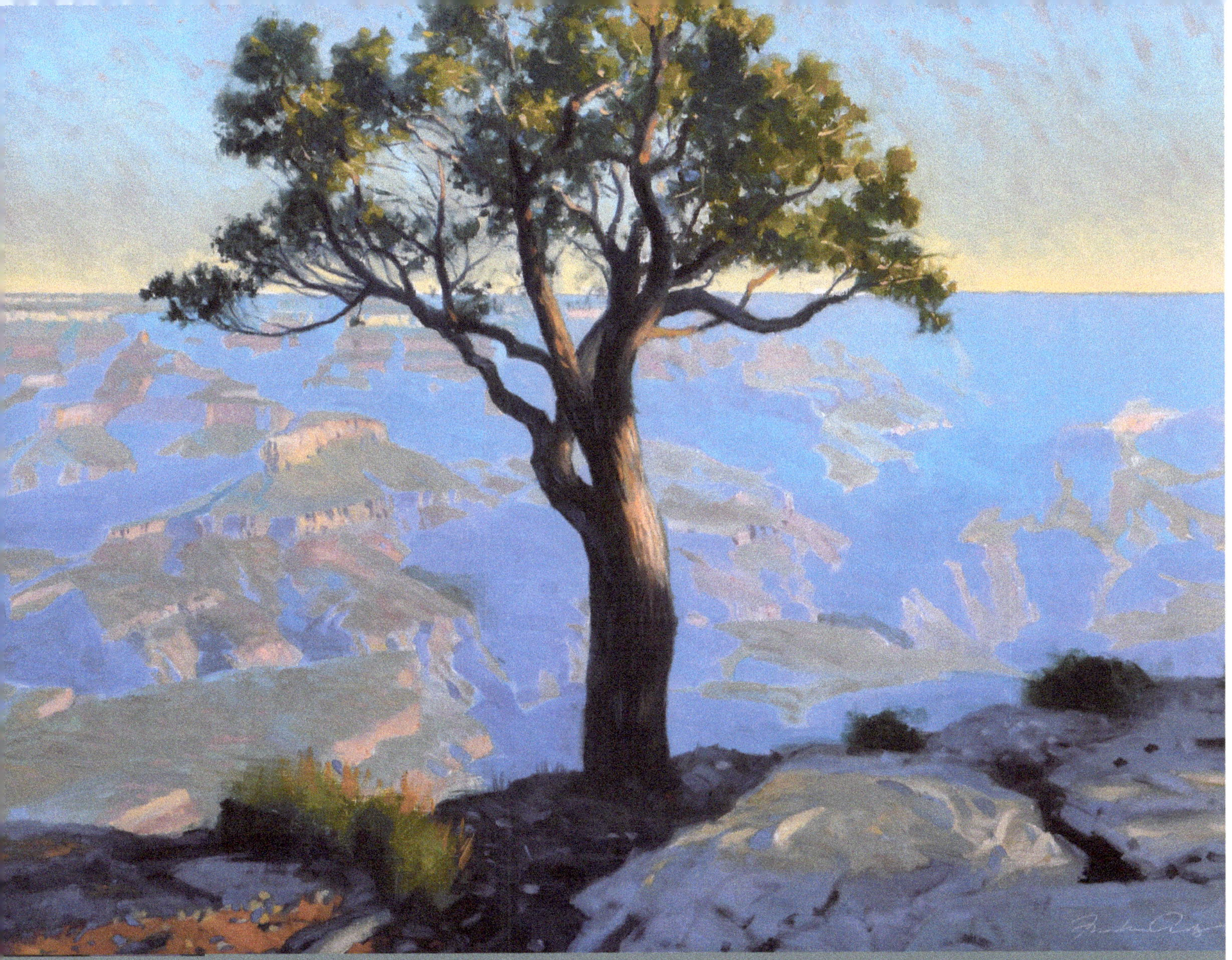

TREE OF LIFE | Grand Canyon, Arizona | 2015 | 16 x 20" | Oil on Panel

A collector recently commissioned a painting from my travels around the Grand Canyon. I focused on a single tree as a philosophical and spiritual anchor point. Taken from Genesis, it is a symbol on reliance on God and walking with him regardless of our doubts. It is a life of Faith. The man who commissioned this piece had his life changed while rafting down the Colorado River at the Grand Canyon.

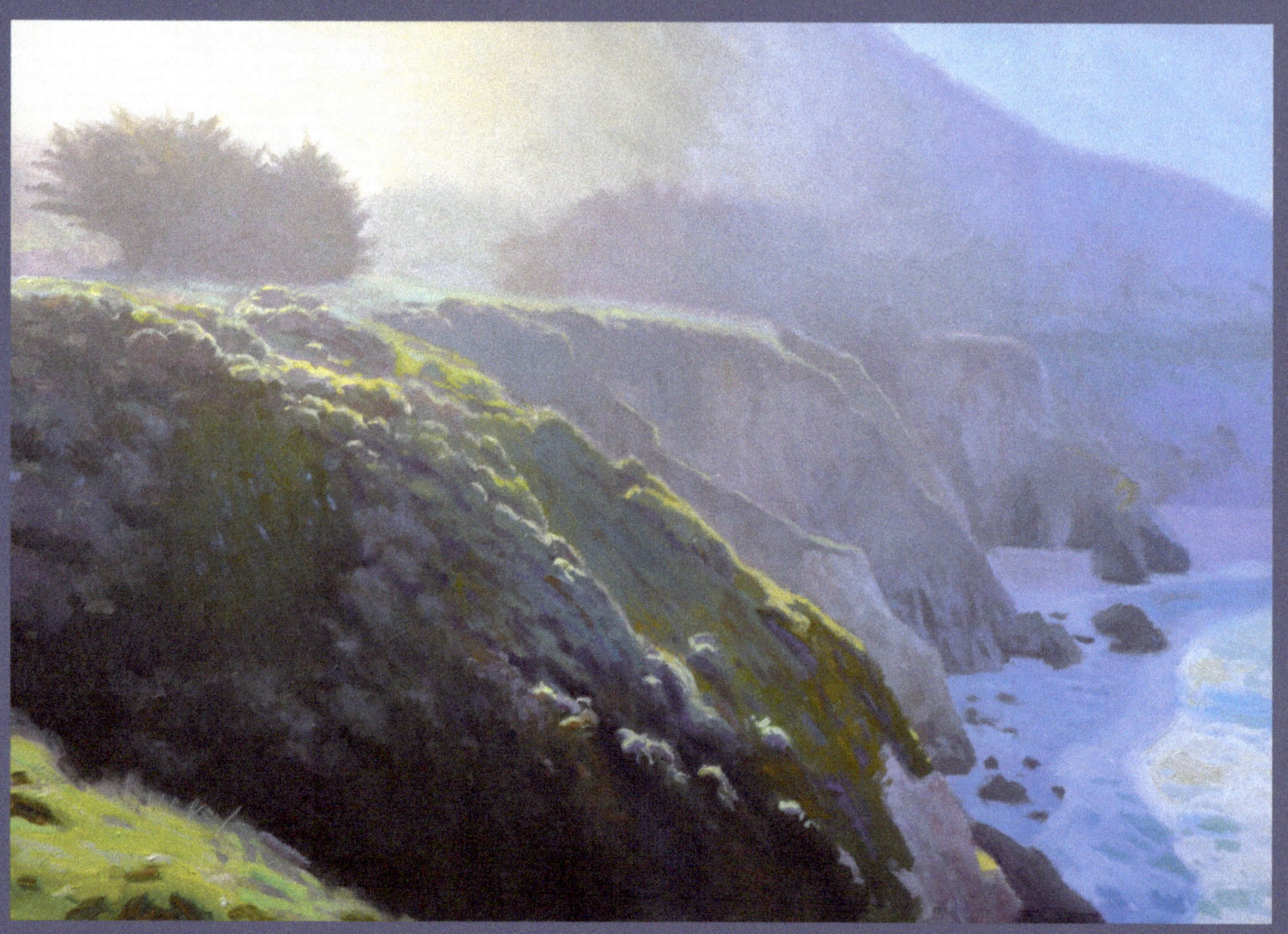

SPRING MIST BIG SUR | Big Sur, California | 2015 | 14 x 20" | Oil on Panel

Big Sur in February is special in its own way. The ice plant is green and the early morning fog blankets the coastline and shrouds the hills until finally the sun starts to reveal the beauty hidden from sight. It's magic and Nature's sleight-of-hand makes one just stop and enjoy the reveal. I usually stay with my friend in Big Sur and study the Land for a week to capture an iconic statement of her beauty.

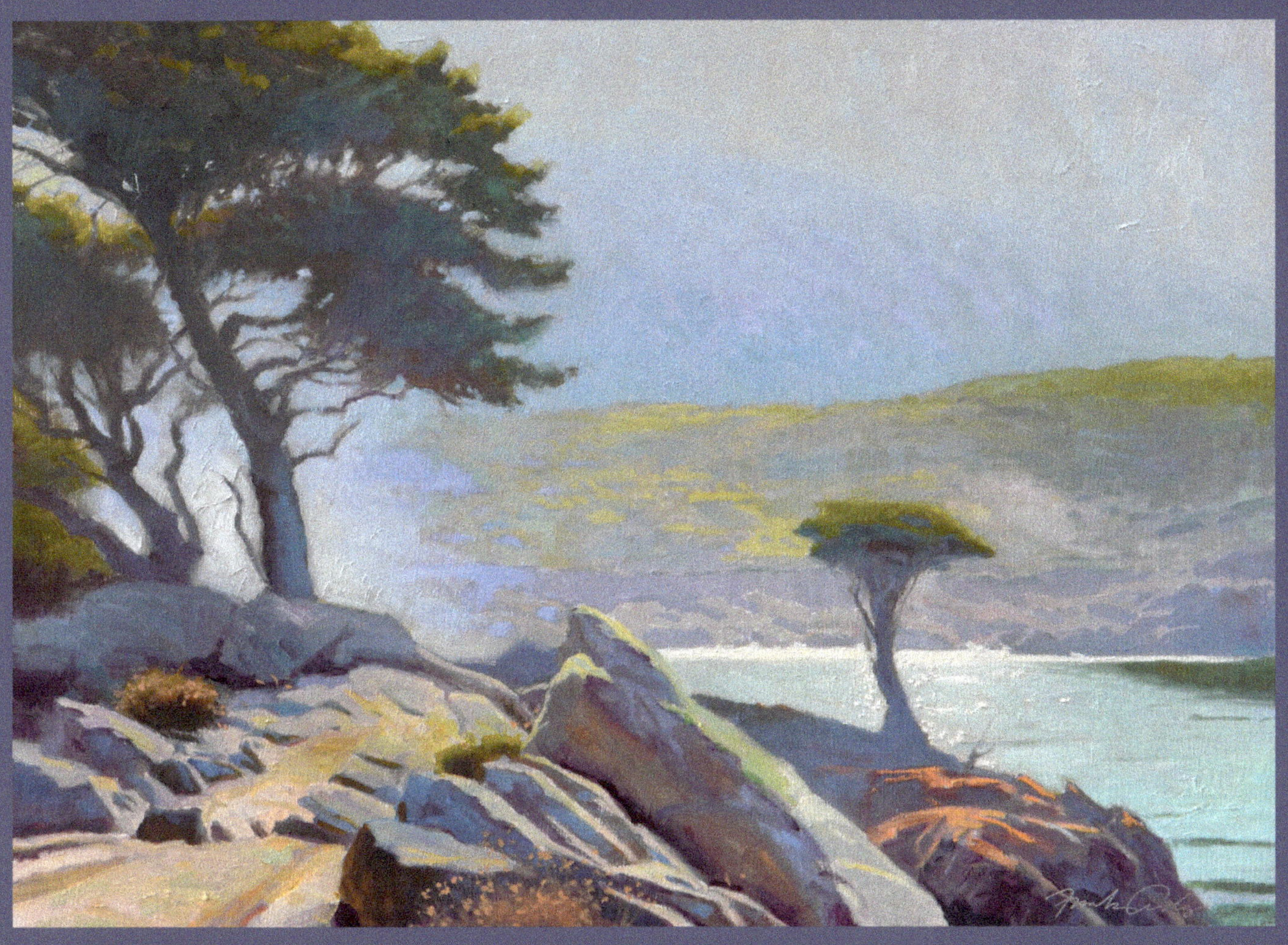

ON THE STILLNESS OF WILD GREY | Point Lobos, California | 2015 | 16 x 20" | Oil on Panel

The fog has lifted and the wild coastline prepares to glory in another day. Visitors from all
over the world walk along the cypress trails at Point Lobos State Park and enjoy the preserved
ruggedness of this idyllic coastline along the Pacific Ocean near Carmel, California.

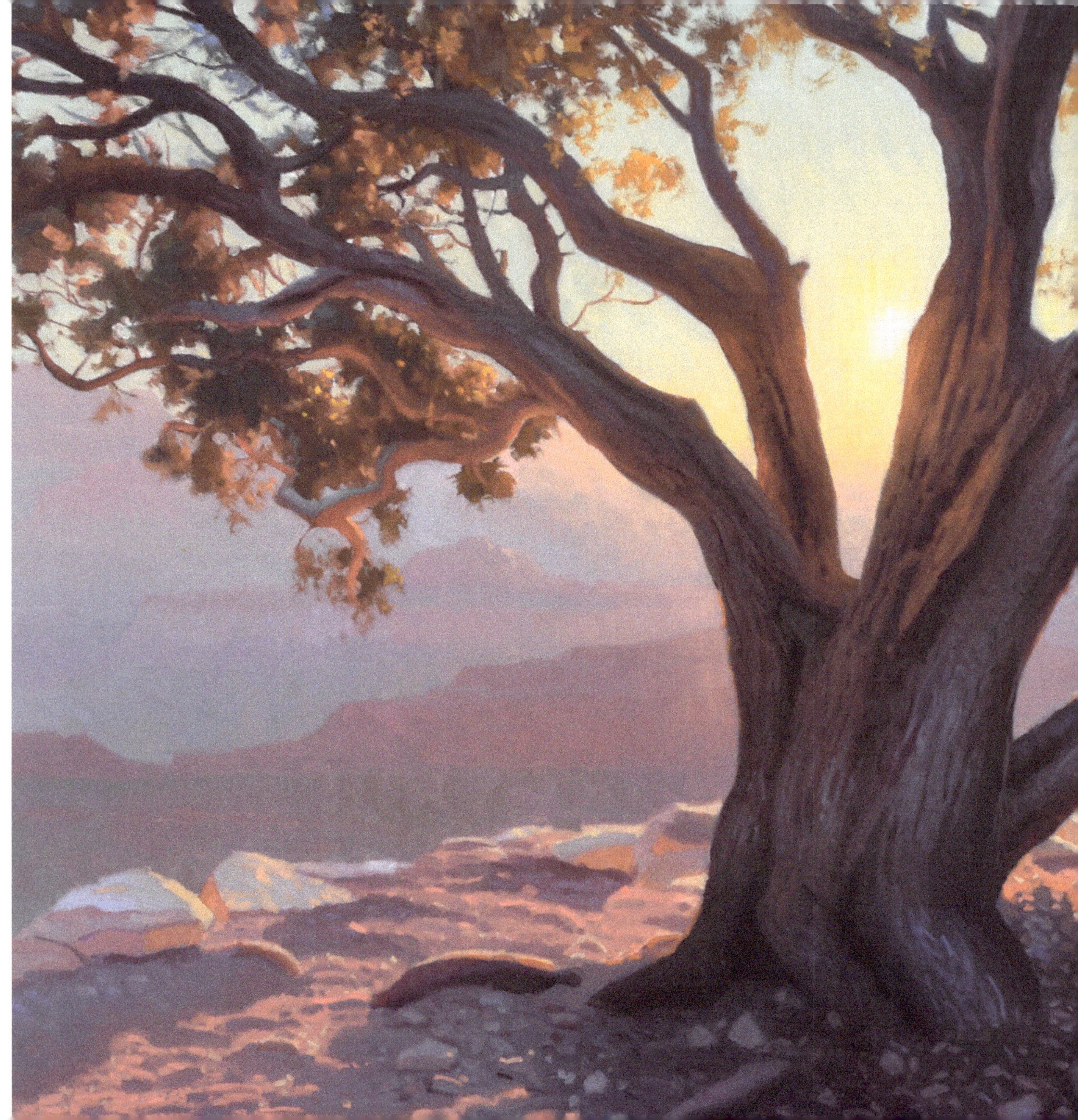

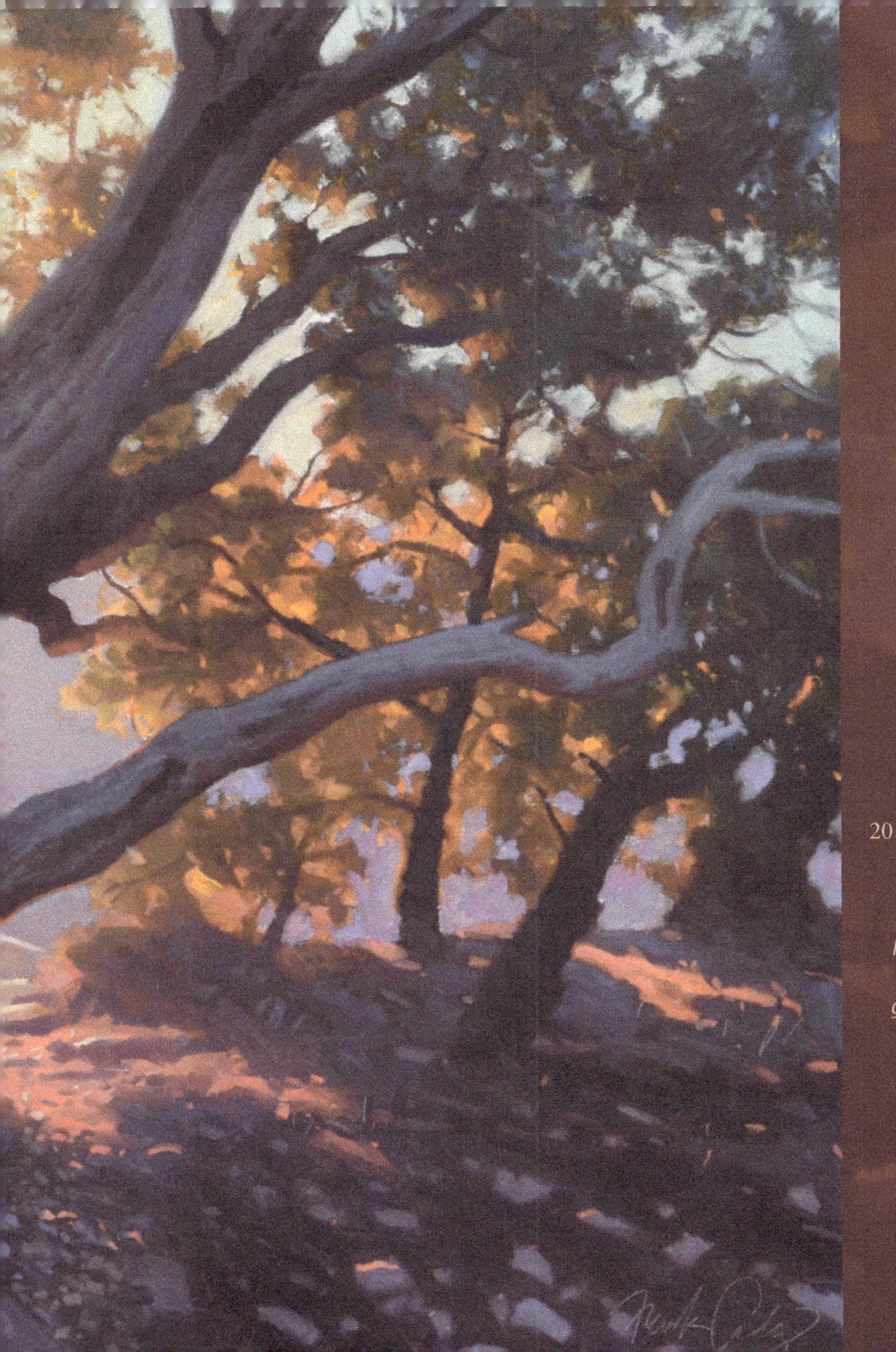

BISHOP OF
THE CANYON

Grand Canyon, Arizona
2015 | 30 x 49" | Oil on Panel

*This remarkable tree reminded me
of an old sage who had seen it all.
He stood still and watched the world
around him move and stir. Old and
gnarled with the passing of years yet
wise to the movements of man.*

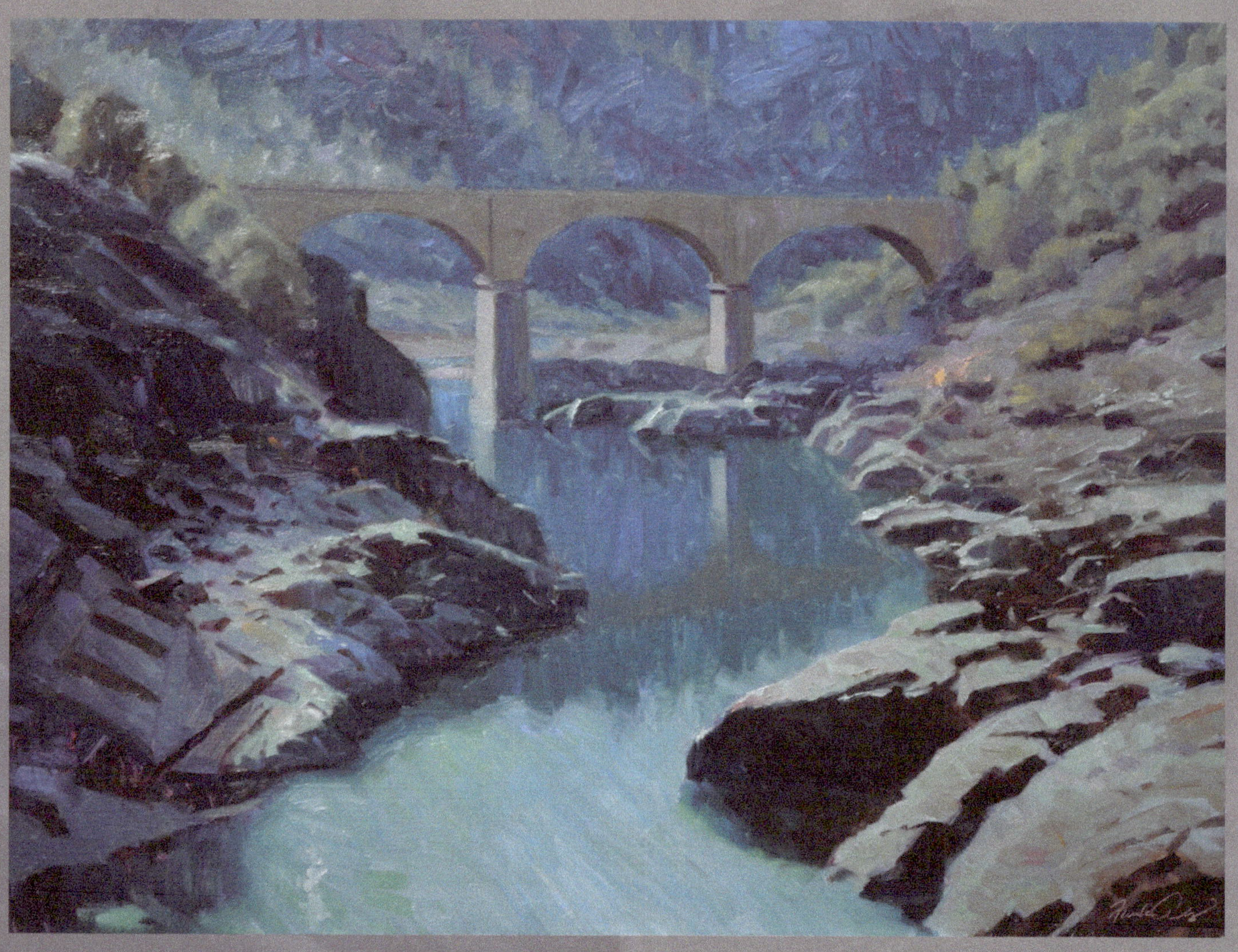

NO HANDS NOCTURNE | Auburn, California | 2016 | 16 x 20" | Oil on Canvas

A lot of early Hollywood movies filmed night scenes during the day and transposed the
coloration to look like moonlight. It was called "Day for Night." You can spot these shots in early Westerns.
I did the same here, using a day shot and just eliminated warms in the light area and diffused the reflected light.
One of my favorite subjects is No Hands Bridge on the American River in Auburn.

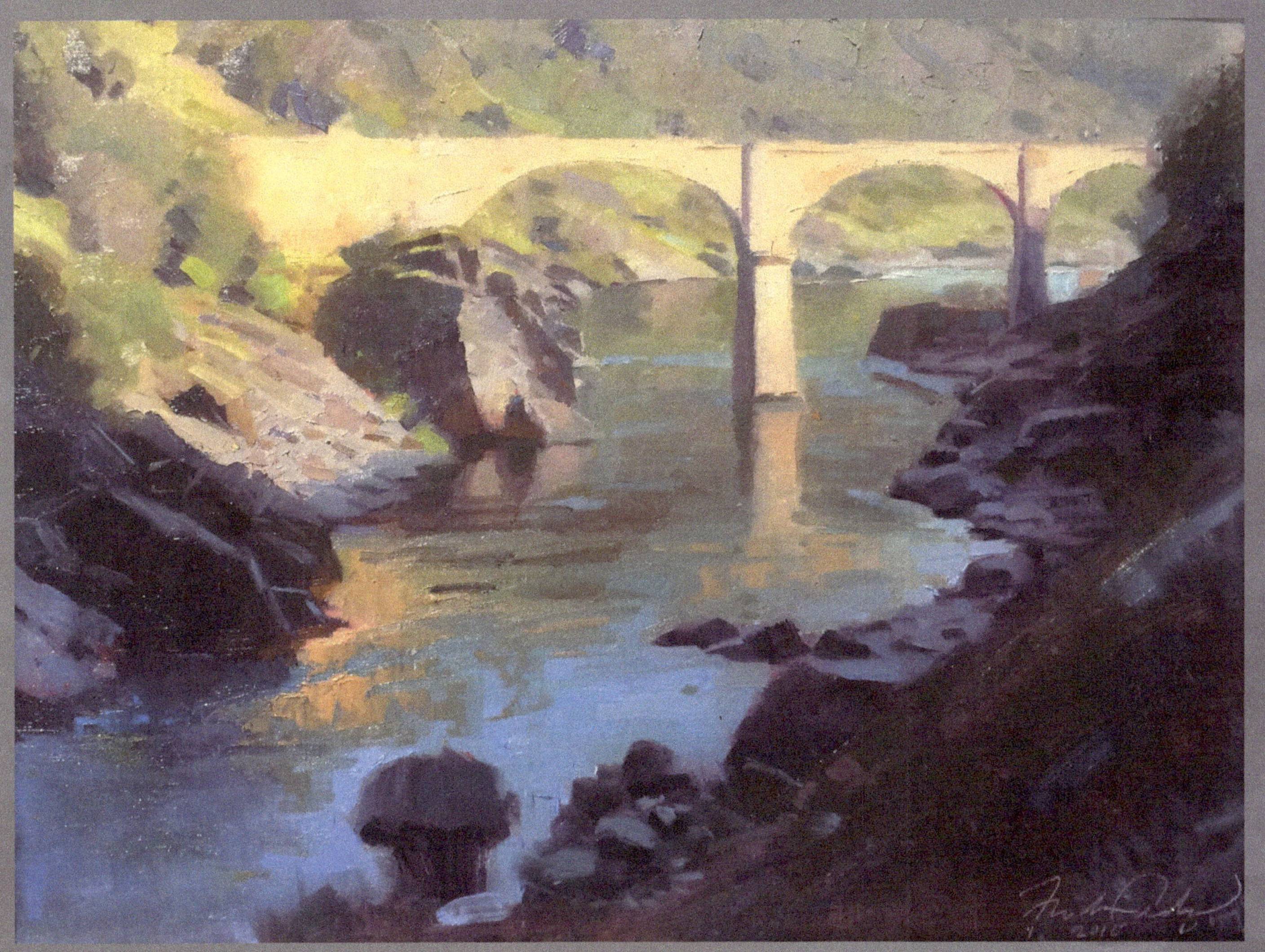

INTO THE LIGHT | Auburn, California | 2015 | 11 x 14" | Oil on Panel

One of our friends has a beautiful young daughter stricken with a rare strain of Lyme disease. One day, the mother walked into my gallery and said she would love to have one of my No Hands Bridge paintings for her home. She mentioned it was a location where her whole family would go and enjoy the American River. It was the last time she can remember that her daughter ran and played like any other child. I gave her this painting in hopes that it would help her remain hopeful for her daughter's healing.

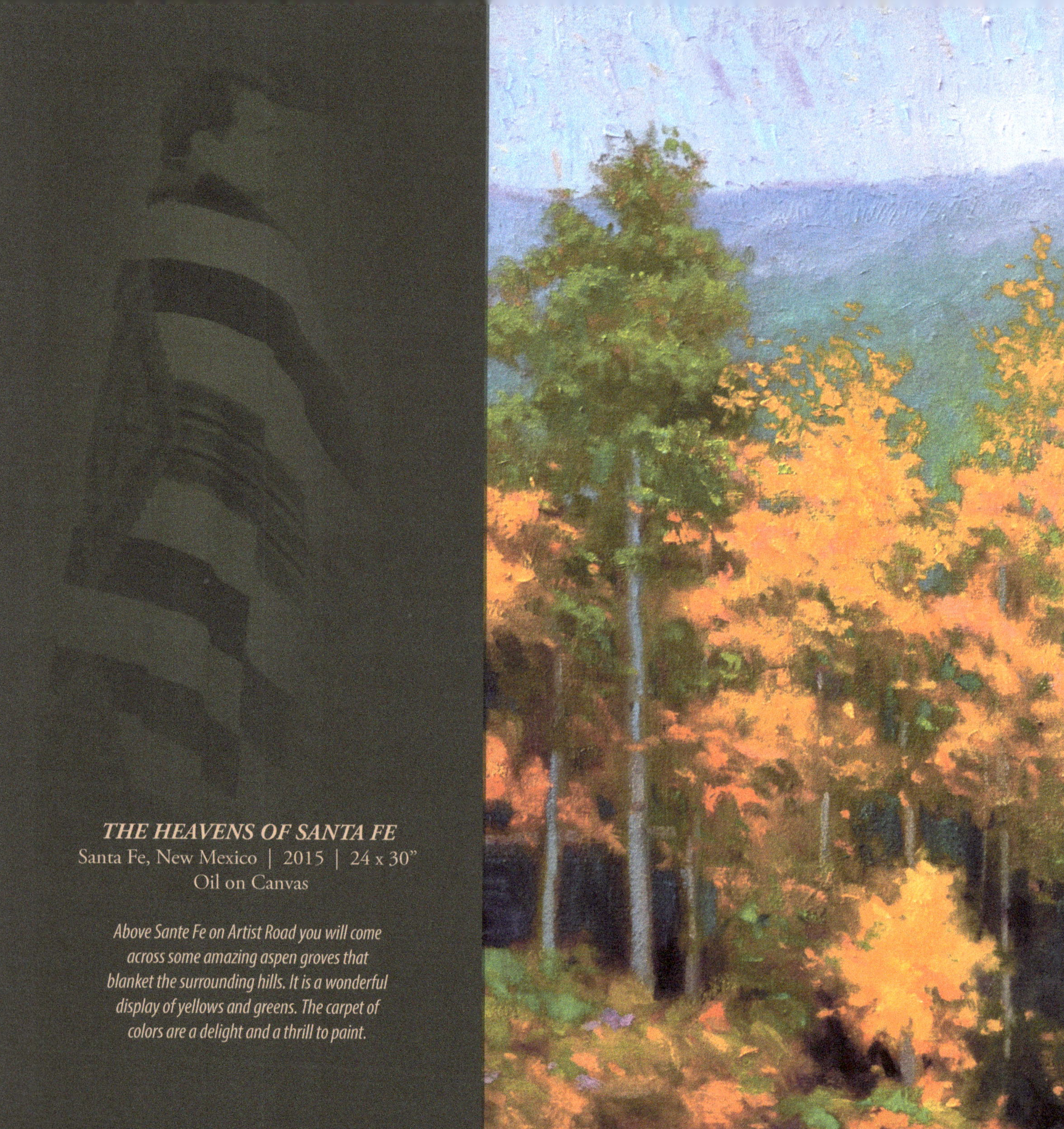

THE HEAVENS OF SANTA FE
Santa Fe, New Mexico | 2015 | 24 x 30"
Oil on Canvas

*Above Sante Fe on Artist Road you will come
across some amazing aspen groves that
blanket the surrounding hills. It is a wonderful
display of yellows and greens. The carpet of
colors are a delight and a thrill to paint.*

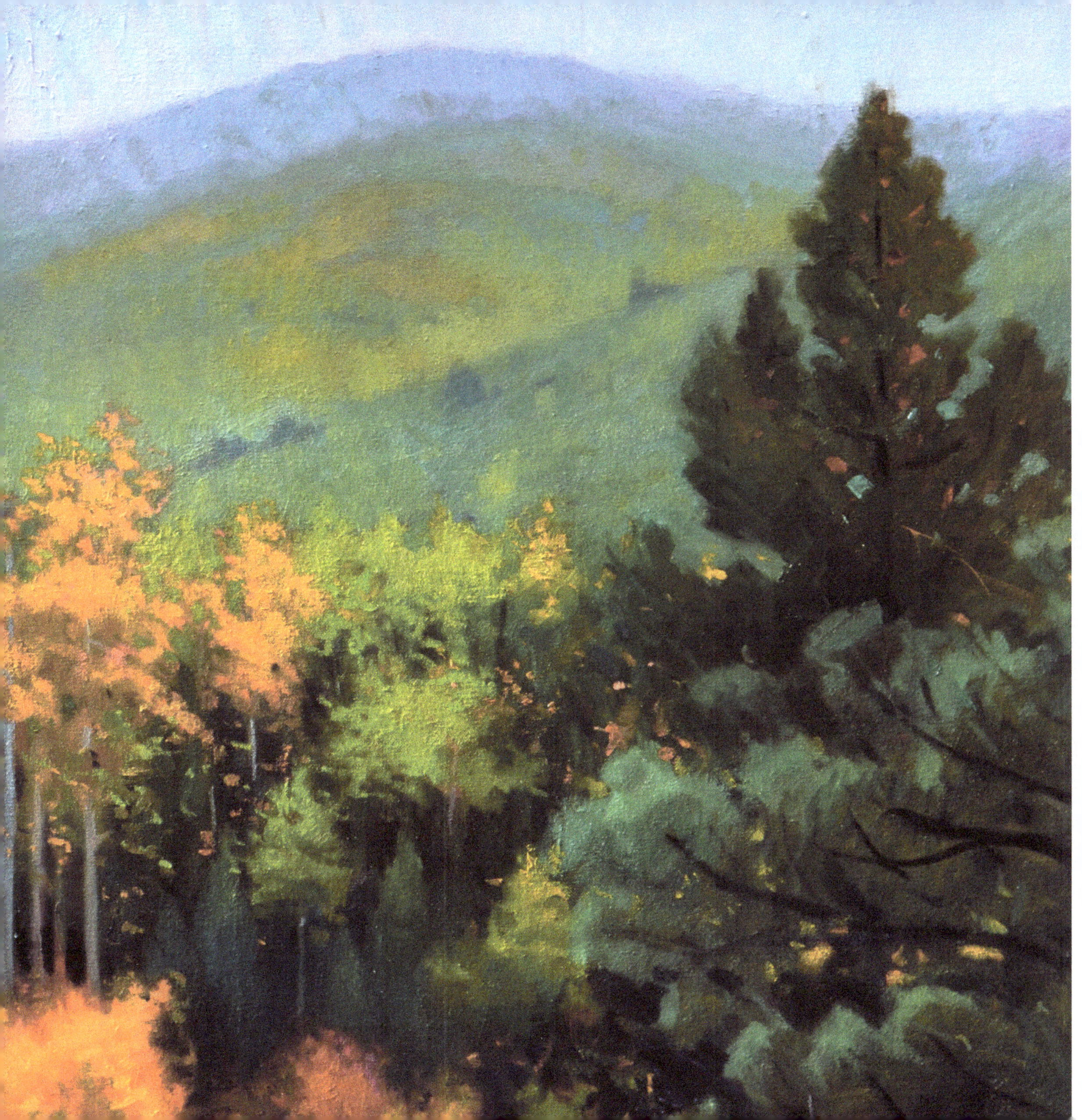

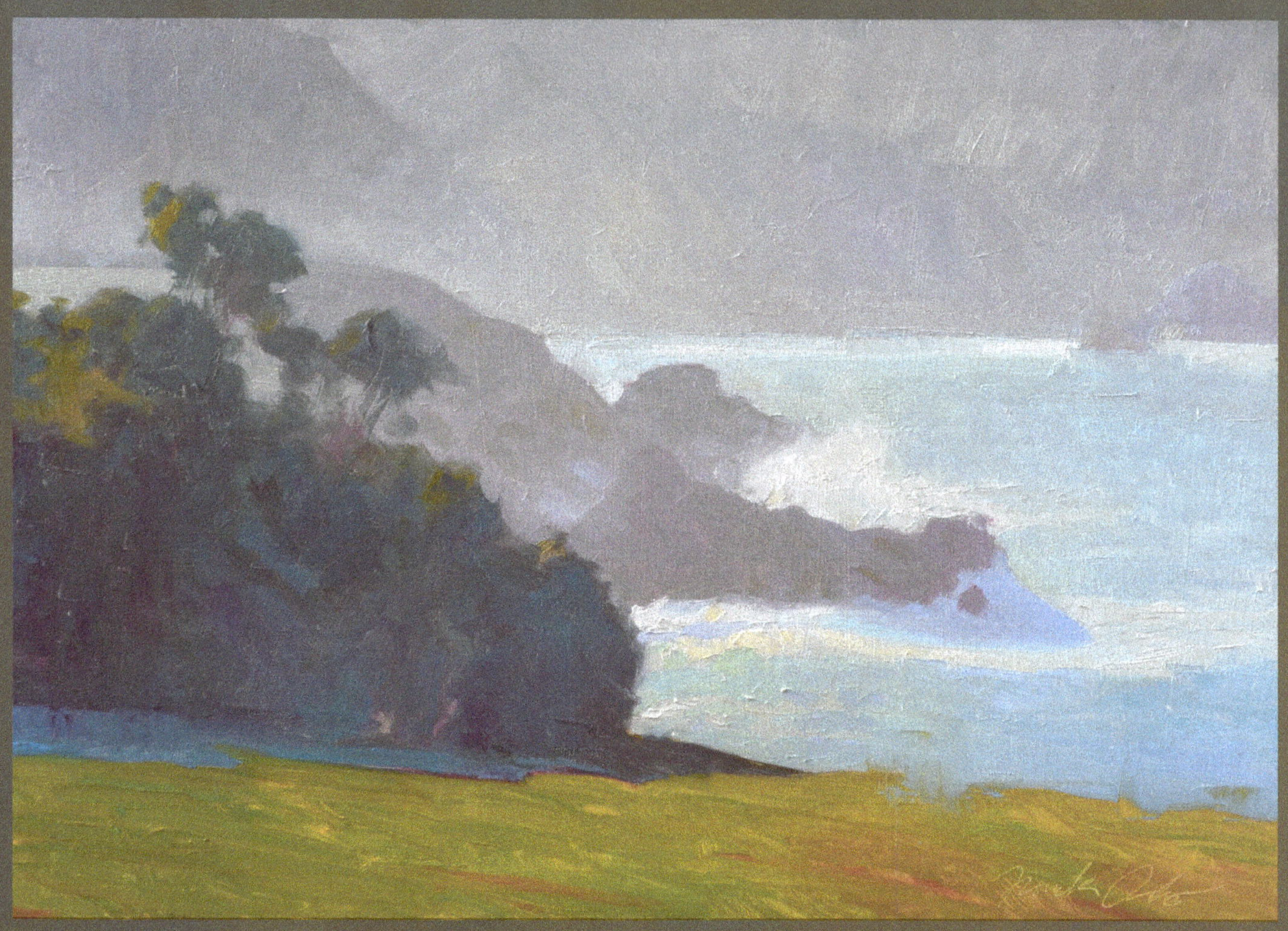

WIND AND WISK | Big Sur, California | 2015 | 16 x 20" | Oil on Panel

This painting is my reverting to a state of just sheer delight in the ability to put paint on canvas and marvel at the colors and feeling of light. I saw this scene around Big Sur, and I can still breathe the air and remember the wind pushing me back away from the sea. The mist swirls, and if you wear glasses like I do, you tend to return to your car with a bit of the Pacific Ocean on them.

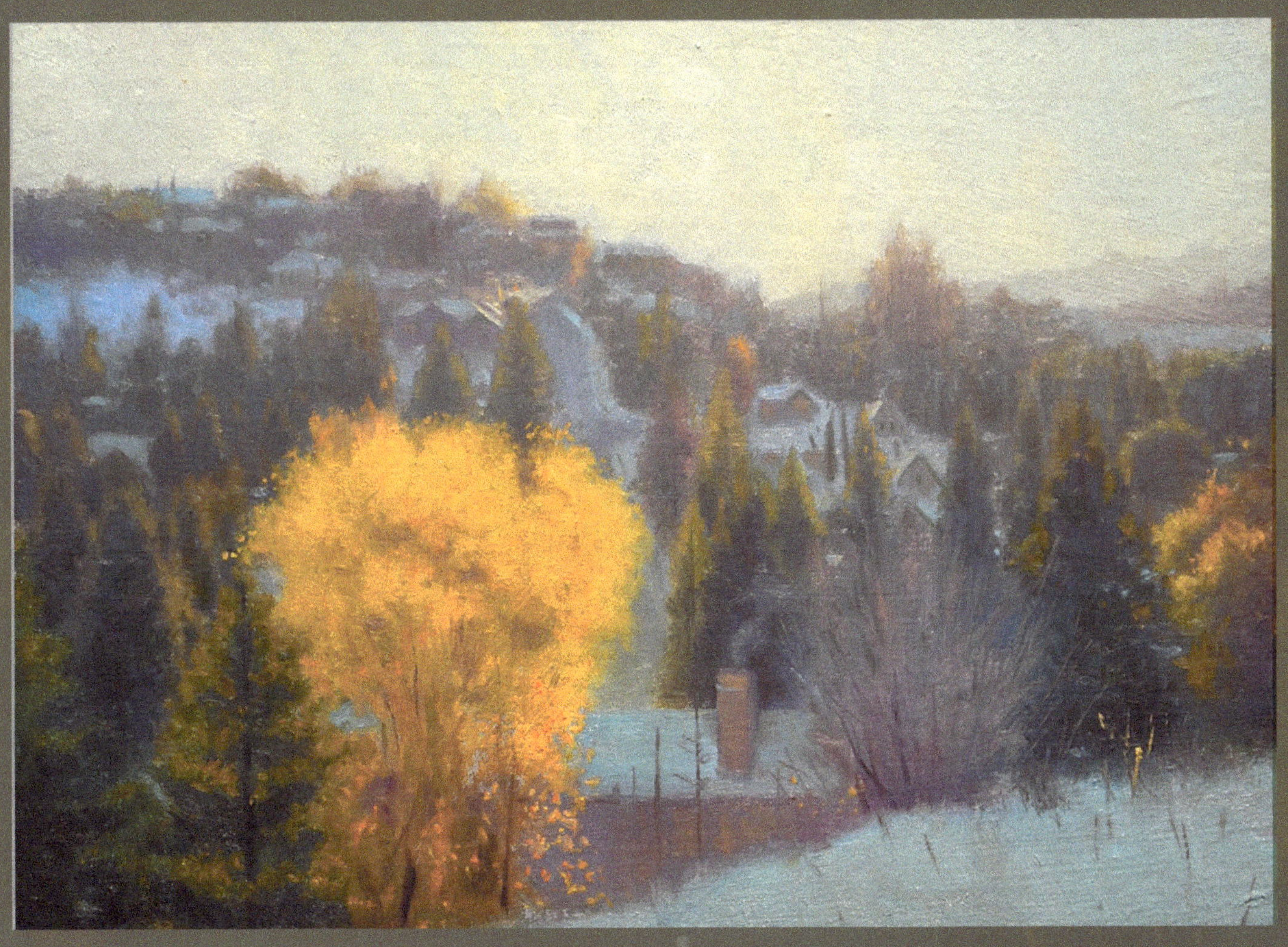

AUBURN DUSTING | Auburn, California | 2009 | 11 x 14" | Oil on Panel

It snowed in Auburn back in 2009 and this small painting was a record of the dusting, looking from
Auburn Folsom Road down into the valley. The single tree in the foreground is the beginning of
my fascination with having them stand like a person in their relationship to the Land.

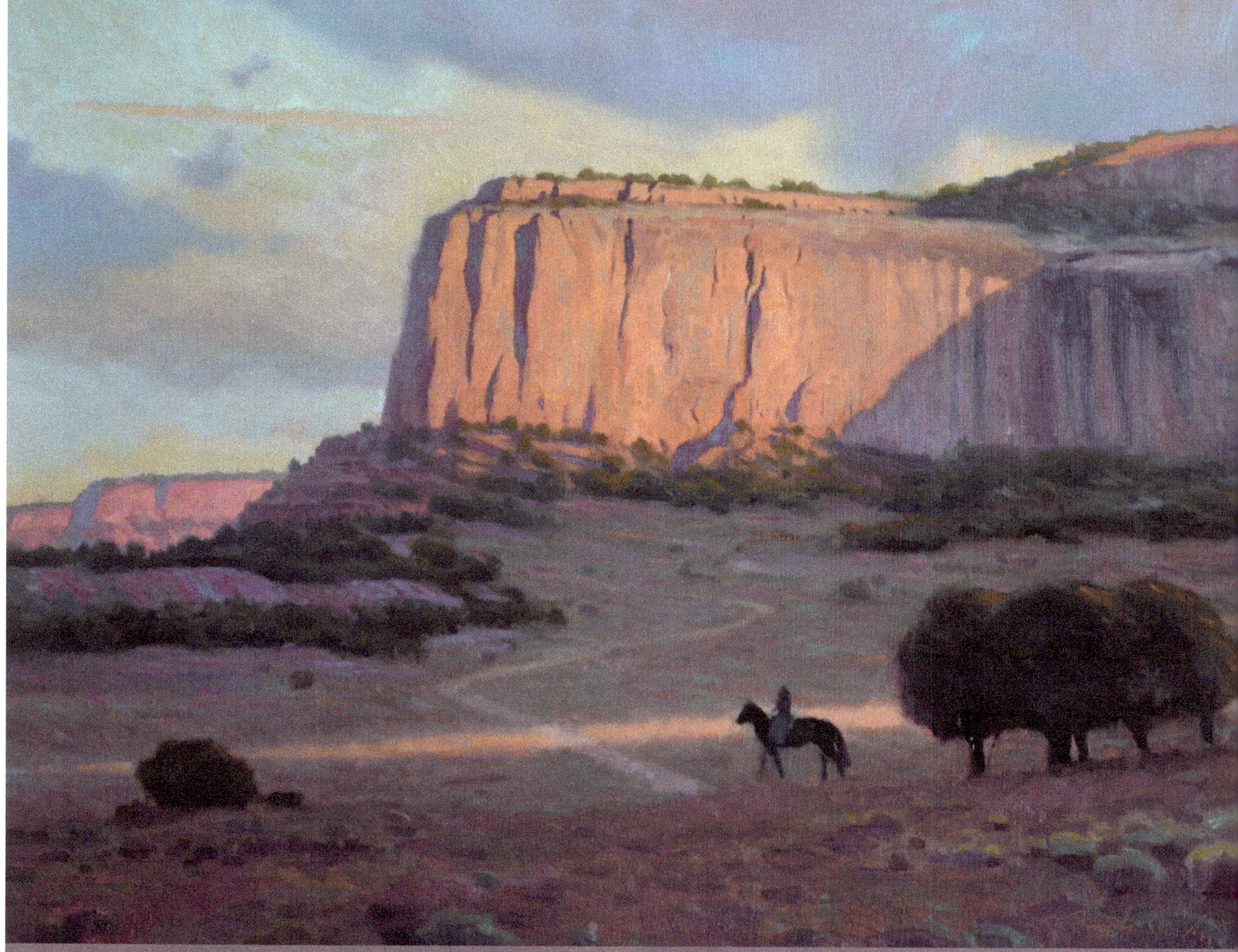

LAST RITE | Navajo Nation, New Mexico | 2016 | 16 x 20" | Oil on Panel

The last light, like a a call to worship, reveals a silent glory painted on stone colored with light from God's brush that is there for the moment and then taken away. Those that see it and are still. . . worship at this amazing gift that money can never fulfill.

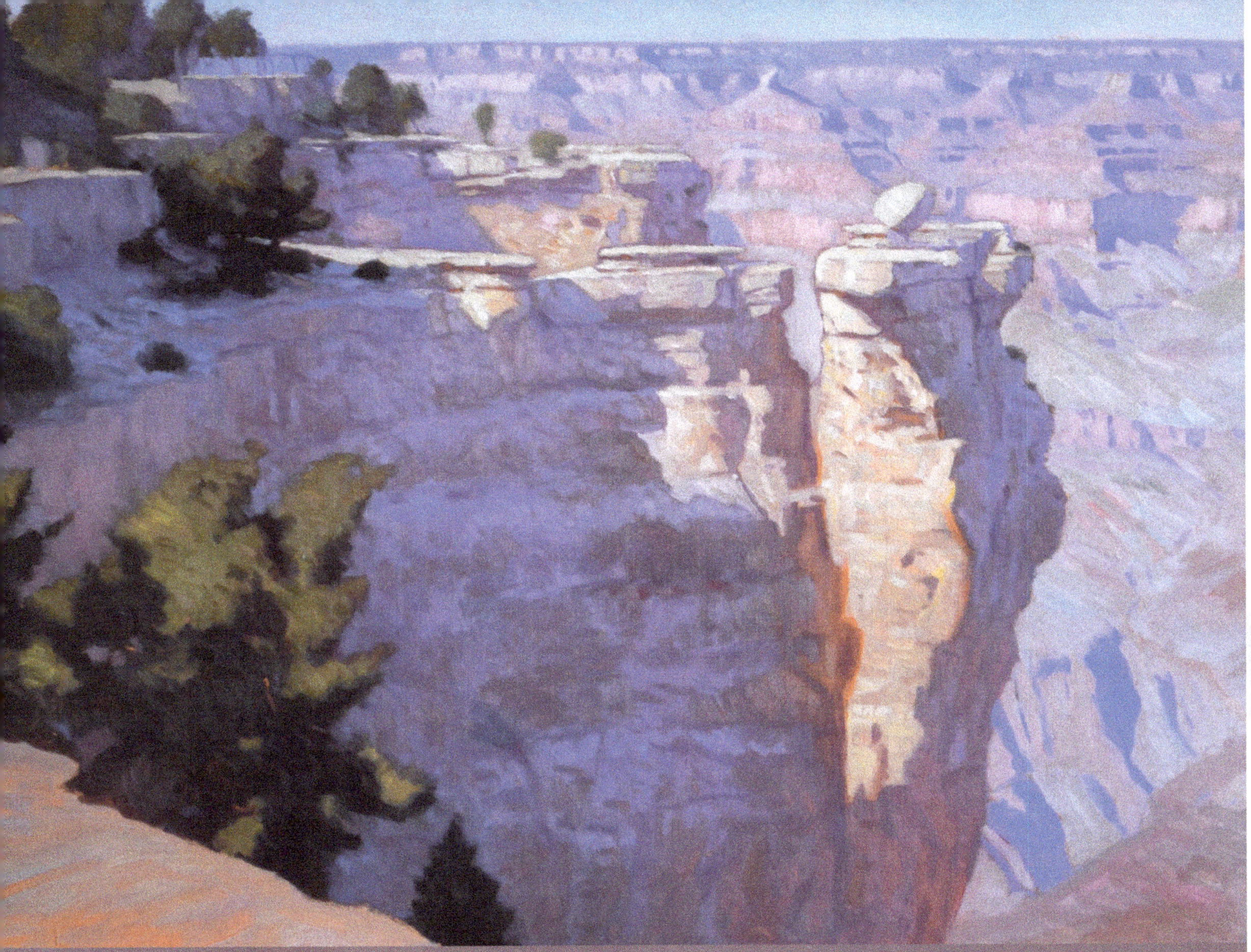

A SUNDIAL FOR TIME | Grand Canyon, Arizona | 2016 | 16 x 20" | Oil on Panel

I loved this view which was around Mather Point at the Grand Canyon.
The rock at the edge, which looks like it is ready to fall over, reminds me of Nature's sundial.
Weather-beaten and wind-torn yet still reflecting the light of the sun.

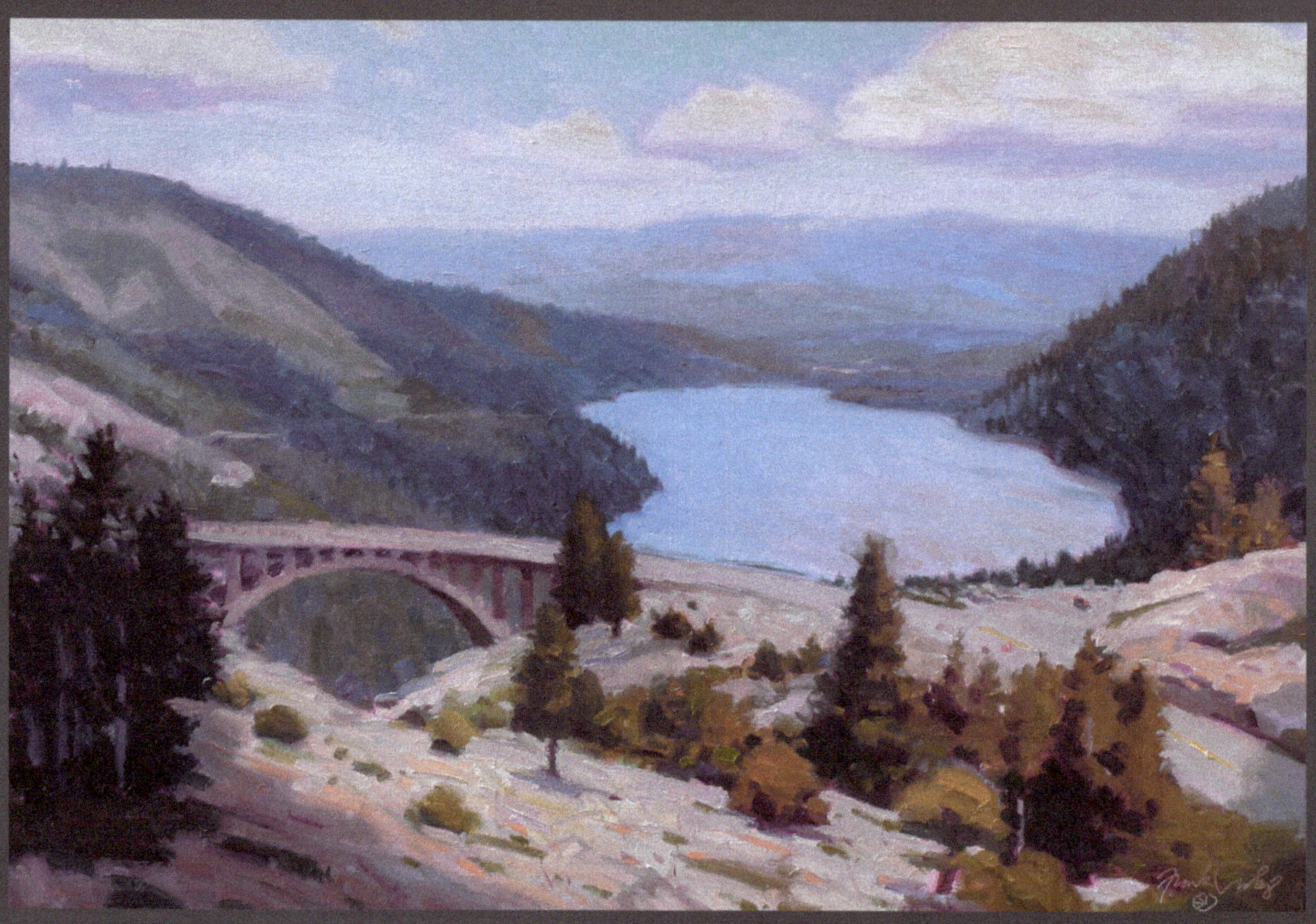

DONNER IN JUNE | Auburn, California | 2016 | 16 x 20” | Oil on Canvas

In June 2016 on our way back from a stay in Tahoe, we ventured over to Donner Bridge. As you drive
past it and park, you will have a wonderful view of Donner Lake. It had snowed the week before and the clouds were just
magnificent and added this wonderful dappled light effect to the landscape below. This area is great for hiking and rock climbing.

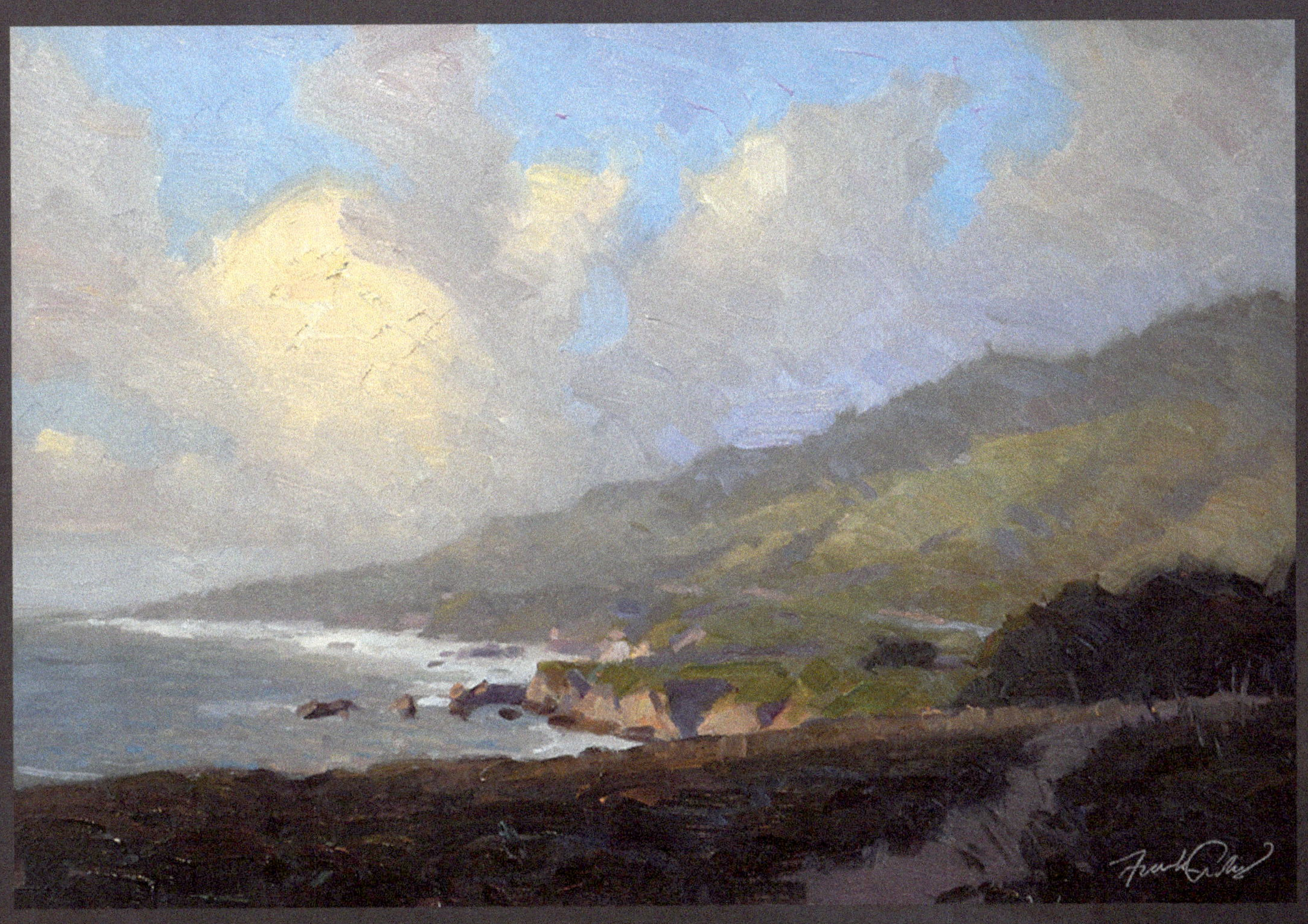

ALONG THE ROAD REDEEMED | Carmel, California | 2016 | 9 x 13" | Oil on Panel

As you pass Carmel and Point Lobos, you will navigate south along State Highway 1. The coastline view will take
your breadth away, especially around sunset time. Years ago, this part of the Pacific Coast Highway was really beat up.
Now, it is a great drive that all can navigate in all climates. Best enjoyed on a motorbike or convertible.

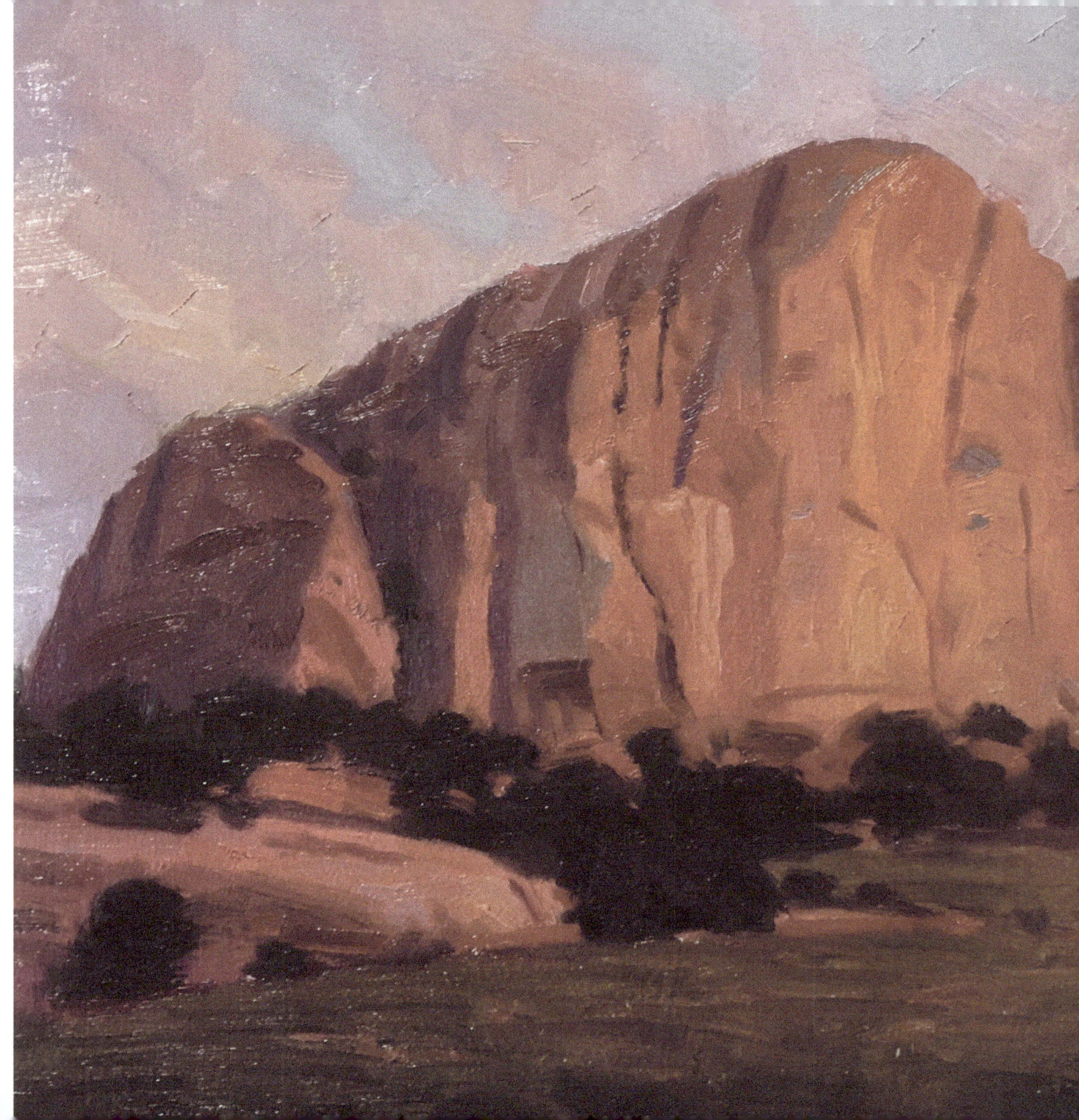

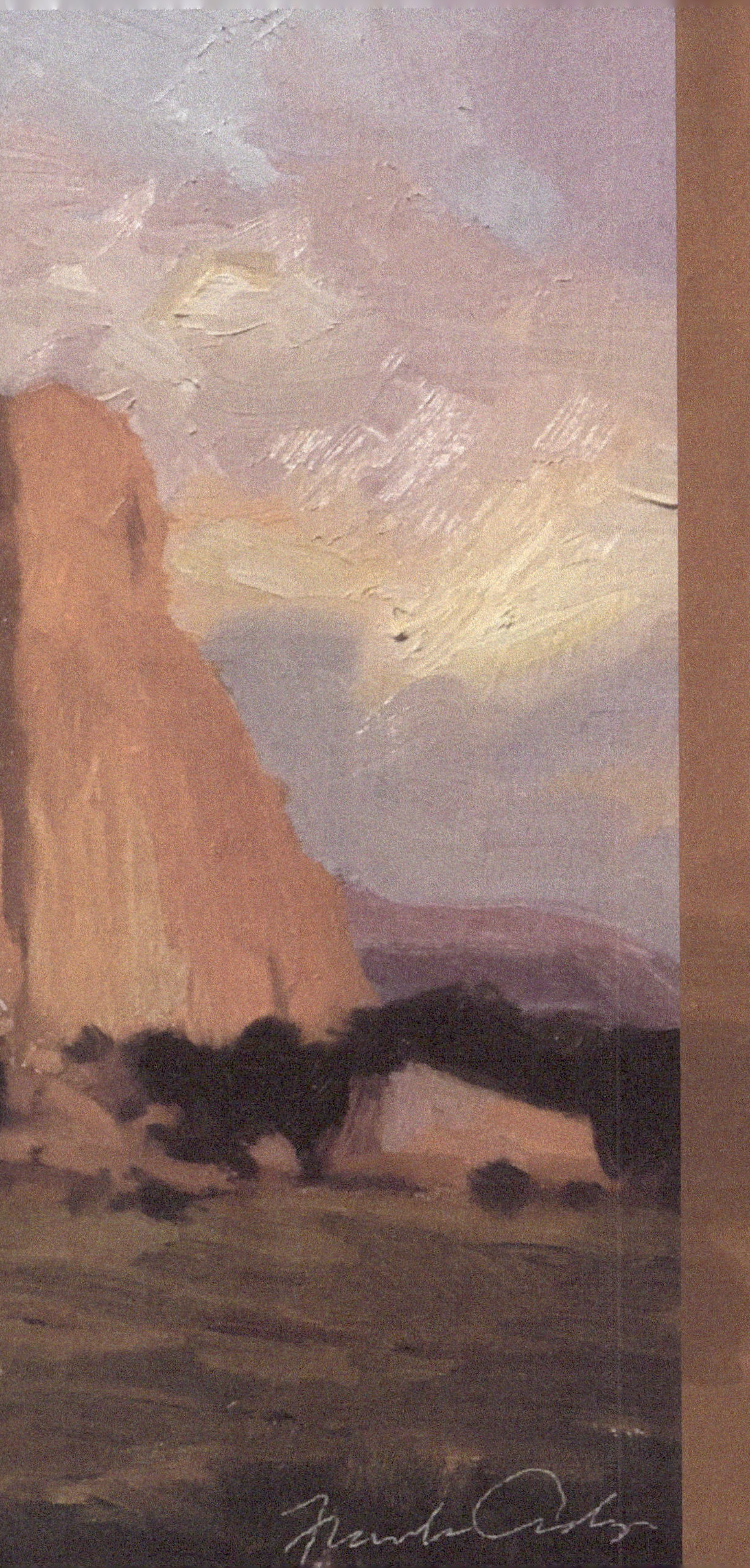

PILLAR OF FIRE
Navajo Nation, New Mexico
2016 | 8 x 10" | Oil on Panel

*As I traveled across Navajo Nation
above Gallup, New Mexico there were many buttes and
mesas that jigsawed through the land, creating a sense
of Nature's temples. I had to stop and give thanks to
God for such beauty and majesty on this Earth.*

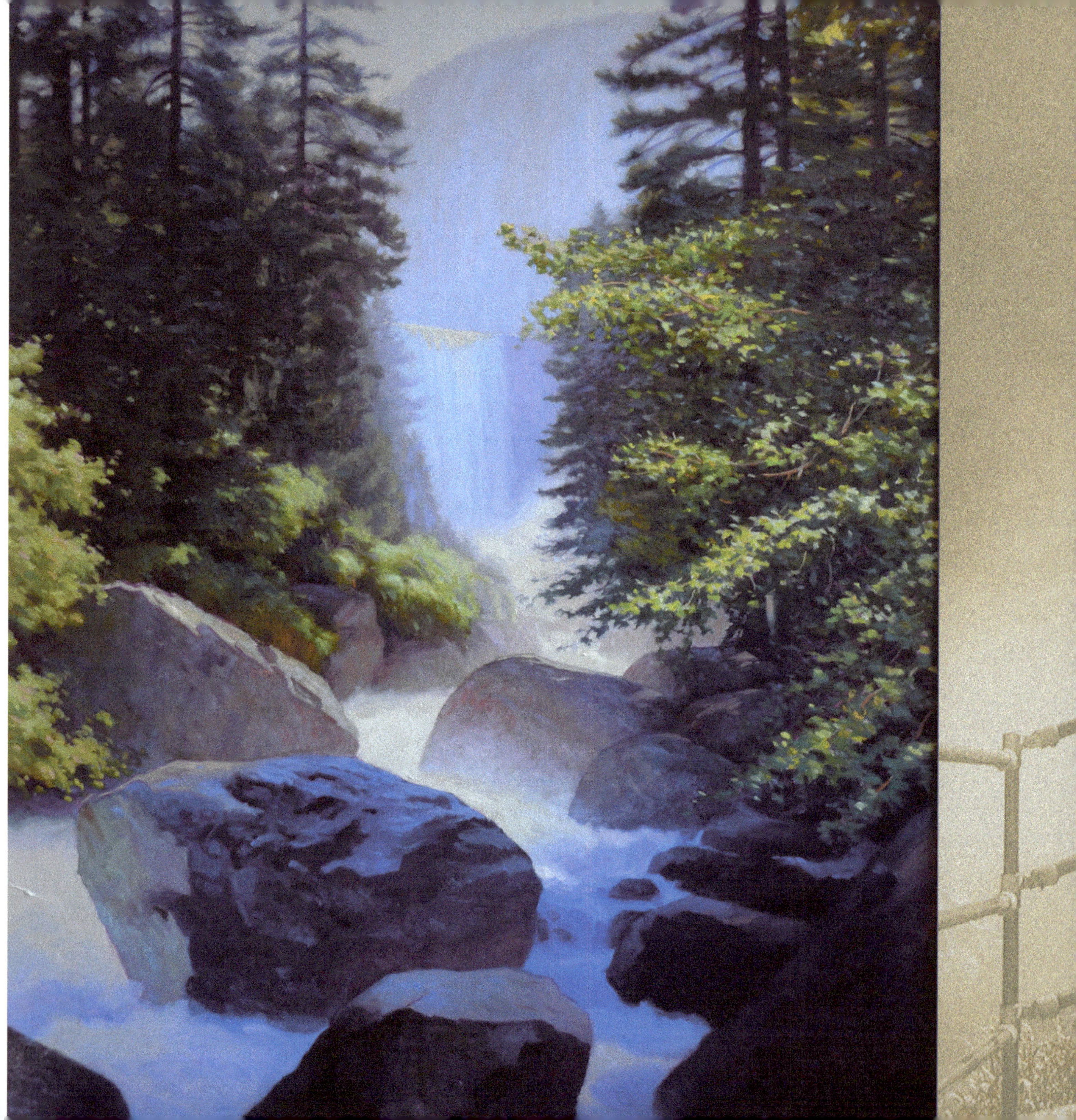

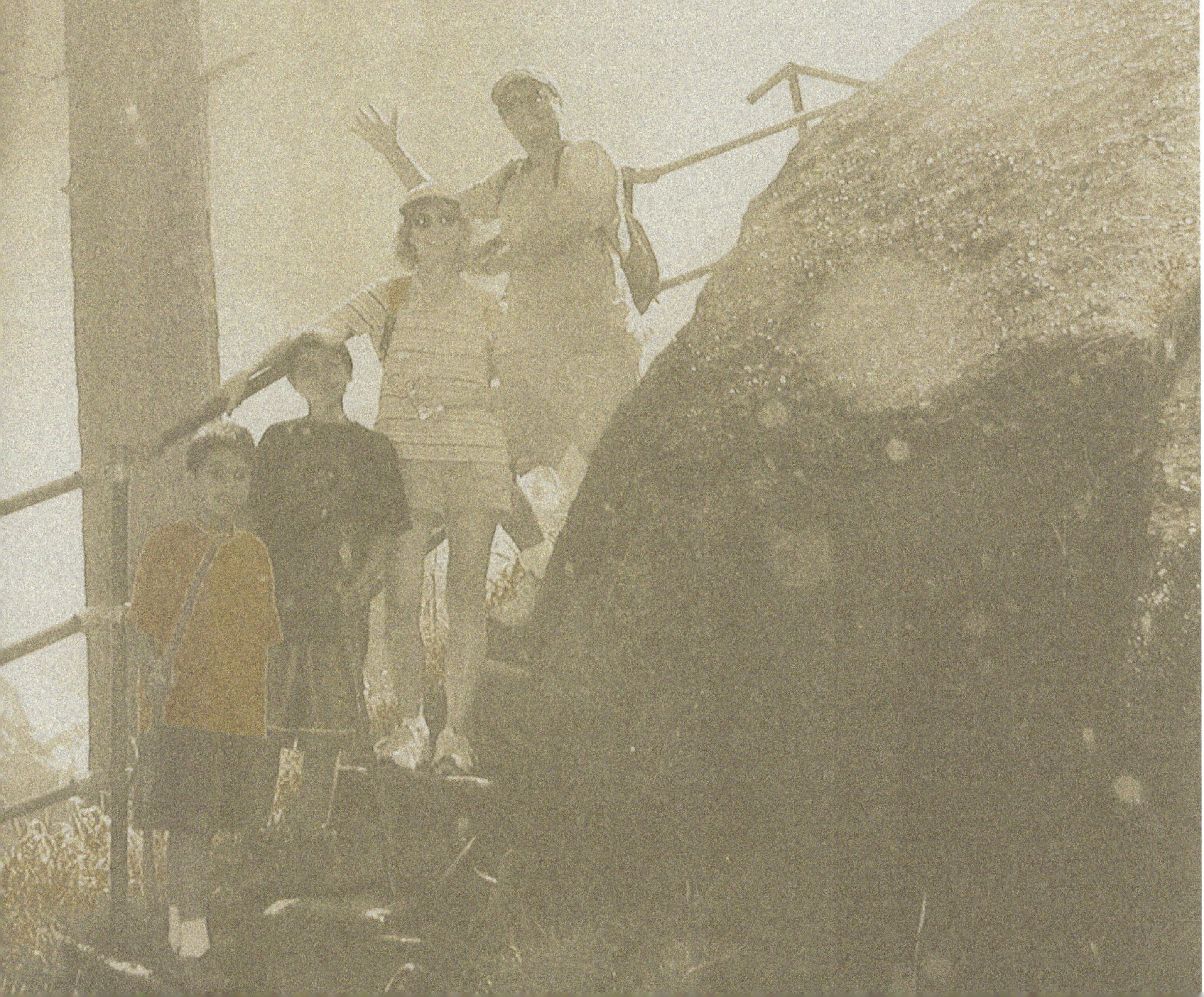

THE WONDROUS ROAR OF MIST | Yosemite National Park, California | 2016 | 49 x 34" | Oil on Panel

This painting that depicts the majestic power of Vernal Falls at Yosemite was etched onto the Ordaz Family Myth. When my boys were young, we all walked the arduous granite steps up to the top of Vernal Falls where a perpetual rainbow greeted us. On our way down we stood by the river and were in awe at the power and beauty of the river that was fed by the granite rock above. The memory is forever part of our story and this painting has special meaning. I can still see my boys running by those dangerous currents, unaware of its power for life and death.

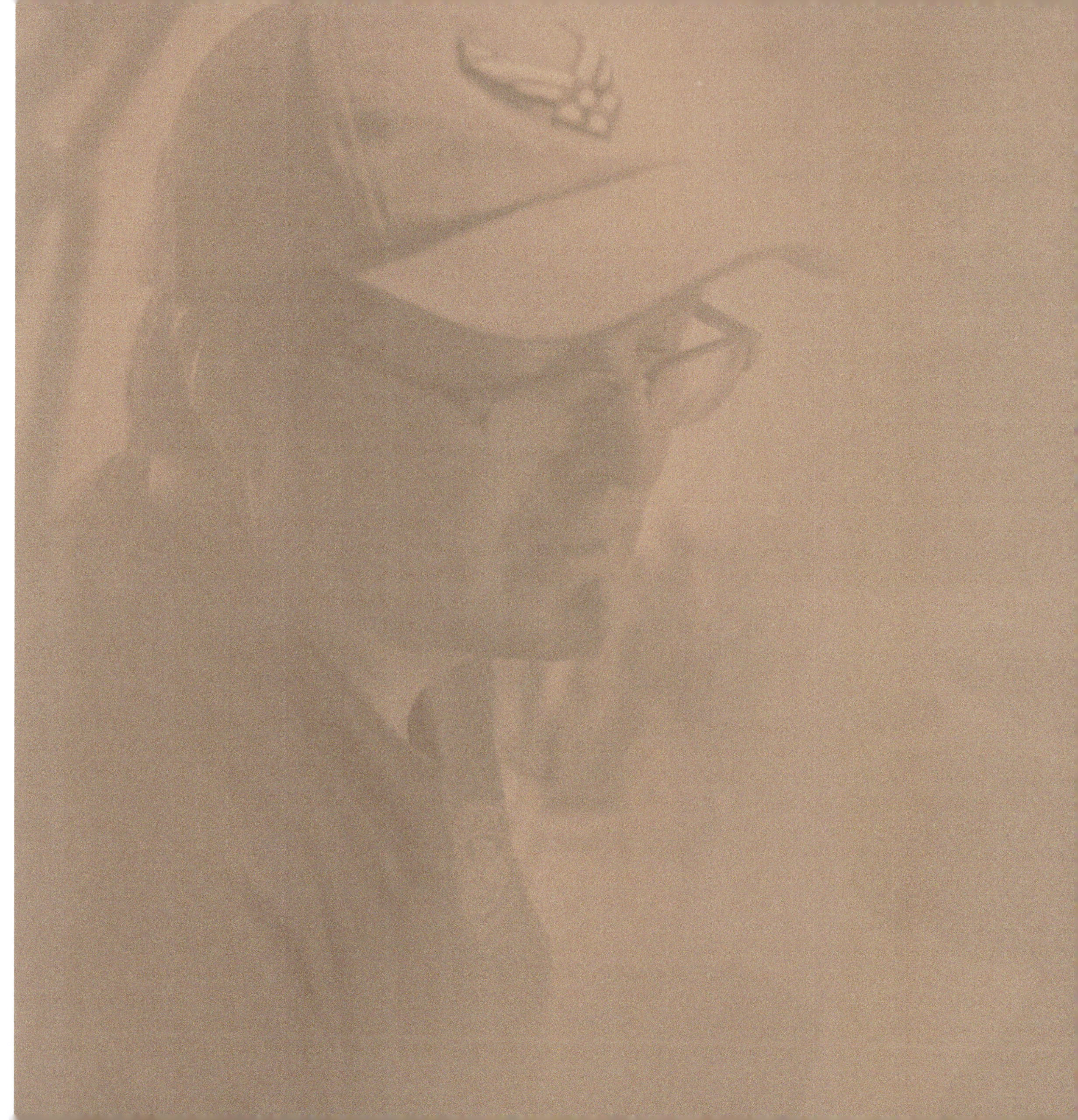

www.ingramcontent.com/pod-product-compliance
Lightning Source LLC
Chambersburg PA
CBHW041032050726
47599CB00018B/1933